THE OAKWOOD PRESS

Great Northern Railway and East Coast Joint Stock Carriages from 1905

by
Michael Harris

THE OAKWOOD PRESS

British Library Cataloguing in Publication Data
A Record for this book is available from the British Library
ISBN 0 85361 477 6

Typeset by Oakwood Graphics.

Printed by Henry Ling Ltd, The Dorset Press, Dorchester.

To the memory of my good friend,
John Parke (1916 - 1994), gentleman,
transport historian and journalist

Rear Cover: The extraordinary armorial device adopted by the Great Northern Railway, produced as a transfer, and used as George Dow recorded in *Railway Heraldry* (David & Charles, 1973) to a limited extent only on carriage bodysides between 1894 and 1910. The transfer was the largest made by the manufacturer, Tearnes, for any British railway company and measured 20¾ in. wide by 27 in. high. The inclusion of an approved achievement such as that of the City of London in the design apparently got the GNR into trouble with the College of Arms. At any rate, the transfer does not seem to be have been applied after 1905. For an example of its application, see the photograph of gangwayed composite No. 2977 (*Plate 8*). *George Dow Collection*

Published by
The Oakwood Press
P.O. Box 122, Headington, Oxford OX3 8LU.

Contents

Foreword

Pre-Grouping carriages? They must be *out of the ark* - I can't see why they should be of interest to *anyone*! Be ready to be surprised, for the multitude of interesting carriages produced for the Great Northern Railway (GNR) , Great Northern/North Eastern Joint Stock (ECJS) and the East Coast Joint Stock were long-lived.

You might well have seen them, once you appreciate that the last of these veterans departed from BR service during the late 1960s and that, if you are a railway modeller, there would be nothing to stop you running a class '40' ('English Electric Type 4') at the head of a rake of stock including either vestibuled former GNR stock in BR blood and custard livery, or a BR maroon-liveried former GNR catering vehicle. It is certainly possible that a 'Western' class diesel-hydraulic might have worked an excursion train which featured a cafeteria car converted from a just pre-1914 GNR restaurant car! The two principal East Coast royal saloons lasted even longer, into the 1970s.

But there was nothing to compare with the original condition of the GNR and ECJS carriages, in their splendid varnished teak panels and elaborate lining-out and coats-of-arms. What splendid models they would make!

Nowadays, it is possible to see former GNR carriages in preservation, such as Rick Edmondson's handsomely restored GNR saloon No. 807, or indeed the former royal saloons, Nos. 395 and 396; perhaps one day someone might find the money to return one of these to its original varnished teak finish. Legend at Doncaster Works has it that a mummified bird was found inside the log of cedar selected for the interior panelling of the smoke-room of the King's saloon.

The attempt has been made to include details of carriage workings and to identify from photographs a number of the carriages marshalled in trains during their heyday or later. Equally, there are many photographs reproduced of the carriages in their last days, or, more sadly, awaiting the call to the scrapyard. It gives some clue both to their staying power and the fact that World War II delayed the replacement of so many over-age carriages. While we as enthusiasts might have enjoyed riding in a carriage in which ghostly travellers might have read in newspapers of the assassination of Archduke Franz Ferdinand, the holiday traveller *en route* for 'Skeggie' in 1955 was less impressed.

Acknowledgements of sources are given at the end of the text, but for all those who helped, thank you. To those who are reading this book, thank you, your interest is appreciated!

Ottershaw,
Surrey
June 1995

MICHAEL HARRIS

Chapter One

'Polished Like A Baronial Dining Table . . .'

Few *aficionados* can see one of the beautifully restored former East Coast carriages now in the National Collection at York without being reminded of one of Hamilton Ellis's typically memorable descriptions of the railway past. In his book *Four Main Lines* (1950), he evoked the atmosphere of Kings Cross station before Grouping. He talked of the stately sleeping cars with their teak sides 'polished like a baronial dining-table, embellished with proud coats of arms and the mystic legend E.C.J.S.' Commenting on the aspects of Great Northern carriage design under Gresley, Ellis gave due credit to the introduction of elliptical-roofed carriages and to articulation. He observed that under Gresley a solid severity was a characteristic of the new GNR and ECJS stock so much so that the carriages built in 1914 for the 'Flying Scotsman' were of 'Cromwellian Plainness.'

Such evocations are rare in railway writing, particularly as the atmosphere of the steam age, even its last days, is outside the memory of anyone under 40 years of age. But there was a romanticism attached to the old railways and to the locomotives and rolling stock that served them. This book is certainly concerned with the work of one notable railway engineer, Herbert Nigel Gresley, best-known perhaps for his locomotives, but a pioneer in that often neglected field of carriage design. From 1905-23, Gresley established so much that was not only basic to the mechanical engineering of the London & North Eastern Railway, but to British railways generally. As far as carriages are concerned, the result was to be seen in the distinguished vehicles turned out to his designs - and principles - for the Great Northern Railway, East Coast Joint Stock, Great Northern/North Eastern Joint Stock and the Cheshire Lines Committee.

Before we get carried away by the carriages themselves, what exactly were they built for? If we talk of East Coast Joint Stock or Great Northern expresses, or milk traffic, even, just what was involved in operating the train services of three human generations away?

When Gresley stock was being added steadily to the GNR and ECJS fleets, eighty years ago, the basic train service north from Kings Cross was remarkably sparse. By day, the principal trains to Edinburgh were at 10 am - the 'Flying Scotsman' - and 2.20 pm - the 'Afternoon Scotsman', with corresponding return workings at the same times, except during the summer - 1st July - 30th September or thereabouts - when they were duplicated or triplicated. There was also the 'unbalanced' 7.45 am from Edinburgh which conveyed GN/NE Joint catering (and other) vehicles from Newcastle. During the summer, there would be a 9.50 am to Edinburgh and 10.15 am from Edinburgh; these were the relief workings to the 'Flying Scotsman' and were timed similarly, as indeed were the 11.20 am down and 10.25 am up seasonal trains. Other summer 'expresses' included the 10.35 am Kings Cross - Edinburgh and 2.30 pm ex-Edinburgh, but these were easily timed, taking 10¼ hr each way for the 393 miles. While the basic service was between London and Edinburgh, the '10 o'clocks', as the railway managers tended to describe them, featured through carriages to/from Glasgow Queen St, Perth and Aberdeen. All of these trains included dining cars. During the so-called 'Grouse Fortnight', any or all of these trains might spawn reliefs in the days before 12th August.

Similarly, the overnight sleeping car expresses had a number of through sleeping and other carriages. Only the first-class offered sleeping berths, third-class passengers travelling sitting-up. What was called a composite sleeping-car had first-class sleeping berths and third-class compartments with seating. In October 1909, at one of their joint meetings, the East and West Coast companies were unanimous that 'the undesirability of running third-class sleeping cars is still maintained', having first apparently discussed the subject in 1906.

Be that as it may, in winter the down East Coast sleeping car services were restricted to the 8 pm down to Aberdeen and 11.30 pm to Glasgow/Perth/ Aberdeen, with up corresponding trains. There was also an 8.45 pm to Edinburgh and Glasgow without sleeping cars in winter, and without a corresponding southbound train. In summer, the picture changed considerably and details for the summer of 1914 are given in Chapter 4.

With the formation in 1905 of the Great Northern/North Eastern Joint Stock, a Kings Cross - Newcastle service was offered, the principal trains being the 8 am from Newcastle and the 5.30 pm down. In time, Joint Stock carriages were added to the 10.28 am from Newcastle which originated as the 7.45 am from Edinburgh and this included ECJS vehicles to Kings Cross. The GN/NE overnight trains were the 11.45 pm Kings Cross - Newcastle and 11.20 pm return; in summer, both trains also conveyed ECJS sleeping cars to Scottish stations. There were other joint GNR/NER trains, operated with each company's own stock. In summer, there were holiday restaurant car trains at 11.25 am from Kings Cross to Scarborough and 1.20 pm to Scarborough, Whitby and West Hartlepool; in both cases the times quoted are for 1914. The latter train was alternately made up of GNR and NER stock. In the case of both trains there were corresponding up workings.

So far it is clear that the summer train services were greatly expanded as compared with the winter timetable.

Less affected by the seasonal imbalance was the GNR's West Riding service. The principal trains were the 7.15 am, 10.10 am, 1.30 pm and 5.45 pm Kings Cross - Leeds. Of these, the 10.10 am was prestigious but the 1.30 pm was the fastest. The notable up workings included the 7.50 am from Leeds, into Kings Cross by 11.30 am; the 1.37 pm ex-Bradford (through carriages from Huddersfield) with the longest non-stop run on the GNR, and the 5.30 pm from Leeds (with through carriages from Halifax). The 5.45 pm down conveyed through carriages to Bradford, Halifax and Hull. There was also the 4 pm down which was formed of non-vestibuled stock in GNR days and comprised through carriages to Bradford, Sheffield and Grimsby. From 1910-2, there had been the pair of 'Bradford Specials' booked non-stop between Kings Cross and Doncaster, put on in response to a competitive Midland Railway service. While they ran, the 2-2-2 or 4-2-2 often at their head contrasted piquantly with the trains' latest Gresley vestibuled stock which included a composite dining-car.

While the Anglo-Scottish and Leeds/West Riding tended to attract more attention, the GNR also operated a service of main line fast/semi-fast trains to Doncaster and beyond. There was the 1.40 pm down which ran to Doncaster, then proceeded to Harrogate via Knottingley and Church Fenton, and the 3.25 pm down which was without catering vehicles but conveyed through carriages for Newcastle, Accrington and Harrogate via Knottingley. The southbound counterparts of these trains included the 9.40 am Ripon/10.10 am Harrogate - Kings Cross; the 12.25 pm to Kings Cross from York via Knottingley; and the 4.10 pm York - Kings Cross semi-fast, the last-mentioned taking just under 4½ hours for its journey. One important night train for postal traffic was the 9.50 pm from York which reached London at 3.10 am the next morning. The 3 am Kings Cross - York and Leeds was primarily a newspaper train but was described in Bradshaw as a 'Special Express', an epithet usually reserved for a crack working such as the 1.37 pm Bradford - Kings Cross.

The GNR service between Kings Cross, Sheffield and Manchester is of particular interest in the story of Gresley carriages, given the significance of the Sheffield Stock of 1906. The GNR had speedily responded to the GCR's brilliant 1905 service of some 10 daily expresses each way between London, Sheffield and Manchester by the fast trains mentioned in Chapter 5, but by 1907 additional intermediate stops had been inserted which dimmed the appeal of the GNR's flyers somewhat. Yet the four-coach 3.20 pm Manchester - Kings Cross survived as a reminder of GNR enterprise even if, by 1914, the Hull portion of the 6.5 pm down was more important than the section for Sheffield and Manchester which was detached at Retford. There was also a semi-fast 12.30 pm Kings Cross - Sheffield whose restaurant car was worked on empty to Manchester for the 3.20 pm up to London.

The Cambridge service of 1914 was nothing like as good as in LNER interwar days, with the usual best timings being some 80 minutes for the 58-mile journey. Indeed, the Cambridge service suffered particularly from cut-backs during World War 1 to the extent that there were just three down and five up trains by 1922. Fastest timing in 1913 was by the 5 pm down which split into three trains at Hitchin, fast for Cambridge in 75 minutes; for Stamford; and, lastly, all-stations to Cambridge. There was also the 3 pm down from Kings Cross which divided at Hitchin into a section non-stop for Cambridge, the rear carriages going forward to Peterborough and then on a protracted trip to South Lynn and Cromer.

During summer peak Saturdays just before 1914 there might be 15-20 special and relief trains on the main line, but special trains were fairly numerous at other times, too. Some of these had dining cars and first-class accommodation and were run to race meetings or for liner sailings from Hull, Immingham or Tyne Dock. Special workings included trains formed of ECJS vehicles such as the regular summer Saturday-only Kings Cross - Edinburgh and return 'guaranteed' trains operated for the Polytechnic Touring Association as part of an eight-day railway touring holiday on lines north of Edinburgh. At the height of the summer, nearly all carriages were hard at work. A census carried out of the ECJS in July/August 1913 showed that only seven out of 364 vehicles were not 'fully employed'.

There were also the astoundingly cheap excursion trains to East Coast resorts such as Skegness: on August Bank Holiday, 1913 no less than eight specials departed Kings Cross for this resort during just 1½ hours. The trains on this occasion comprised four-wheeled suburban stock, Gresley non-vestibuled articulated suburban twins, as well as vestibuled carriages. Suburban and six-wheeled stock was also worked on guaranteed excursion trains over the 187-mile route from Kings Cross to Yarmouth Beach via Peterborough and the Midland & Great Northern Joint line.

Made up into 11-coach sets (a few were 12-coach), the four-wheeled suburban stock still dominated the London area services until the arrival of the new and rebuilt articulated quad-arts during the early 1920s. Services were operated on the main line as far as Hatfield, to Cuffley, High Barnet, Alexandra Palace and on the branch connection between Finchley and Edgware. The GNR engines and stock providing services on these lines were supplemented by North London Railway trains from Broad Street, similarly with the three classes of accommodation provided on the GNR set trains.

Finally, there was the considerable milk traffic on the GNR, for which a number of high-roofed vans were built before 1923. This movement of milk in ten-gallon churns developed once the GNR had gained access from Derby Friargate to stations serving Staffordshire dairy farms, by way of Burton-on-Trent and the line to Stafford Common. From the early 1880s, two express milk trains were run to Finsbury Park nightly, one from Stafford Common, the other from Egginton Junction, routed via Derby, Nottingham Victoria and Grantham. In addition, main line stations and some in Lincolnshire generated loaded milk vans, normally conveyed on passenger or parcels trains to London. Some loaded vans were forwarded via Kings Cross main station to form early morning milk trains to London suburban stations.

Chapter Two

Perspectives to the Design of GNR and ECJS Carriages

It was 1857 before the first Doncaster-built carriages were put into traffic by the GNR although Doncaster had been established in 1853 as the main works for locomotive and rolling stock construction and repair. The locomotive superintendent had direct control of carriage and wagon design policy until the late 1870s although, in all honesty, the basic principles were effectively controlled by the abilities of the foremen and chargehands on the workshop floor. During these years the GNR had built its first bogie vehicles in 1874/5, the three-centre round roof had been adopted as standard from 1876 and, in 1879, the company had inaugurated the first British restaurant car by virtue of sponsoring the Pullman car (supplied by the Pullman company) that entered service between Kings Cross and Leeds in that year.

Increasing pressures on the locomotive superintendent led to the design and construction of rolling stock being devolved as from 1877 to E. F. Howlden who had been appointed carriage and wagon superintendent. Doncaster adopted the Smith vacuum brake in 1879 and, in 1883, Howlden was responsible for the building of the first British side-corridor carriage - ECJS first-class No 87. Next came the introduction of the Gould centre-coupler and gangway during 1889, the introduction of centre-gangway sleeping cars having been agreed with the NER in 1893. From the early 1890s, steam heating was being fitted and there were 209 GNR carriages so equipped by 1895. Steel was used for underframes from *c.* 1902 and, from 1900, equipments comprising belt-driven dynamos and the double batteries for electric lighting were being installed in carriages.

GNR carriage design was not of a high calibre until the mid/late 1890s and compared unfavourably with some other companies. Perhaps its reputation suffered unduly from the strictures of the admirable E.L. Ahrons who, in his article on the GNR in the *Locomotive and Train Working in the Latter Part of the Nineteenth Century* series, expressed 'deep thankfulness that the six-wheeled coaches . . . are only infrequently seen on the main line . . . they were the hardest-riding coaches in the country. So much so that I frequently suspect them of having octagonal wheels.' When it was decided by the GNR during 1888 to build a royal saloon for the use of the Prince of Wales, Stirling was adamant that it could not be built at Doncaster. Poor in quality or not, the GNR's stock of carriages was certainly inadequate numerically. In May 1894, F. P. Cockshott, the superintendent of the line, reported to the General Manager, Henry Oakley that Patrick Stirling had said that 'the stock of carriages is insufficient . . . should be at least 100 carriages added to stock.' Such was the shortage that down trains from Kings Cross had to be formed of carriages arriving on immediately preceding up workings. Some 100 years later, such expediency would be regarded as essential practice for the economic working of InterCity trains!

Patrick Stirling had idiosyncratic ideas regarding the design of locomotives and rolling stock alike. 'I must however enter a strong protest against the bogie

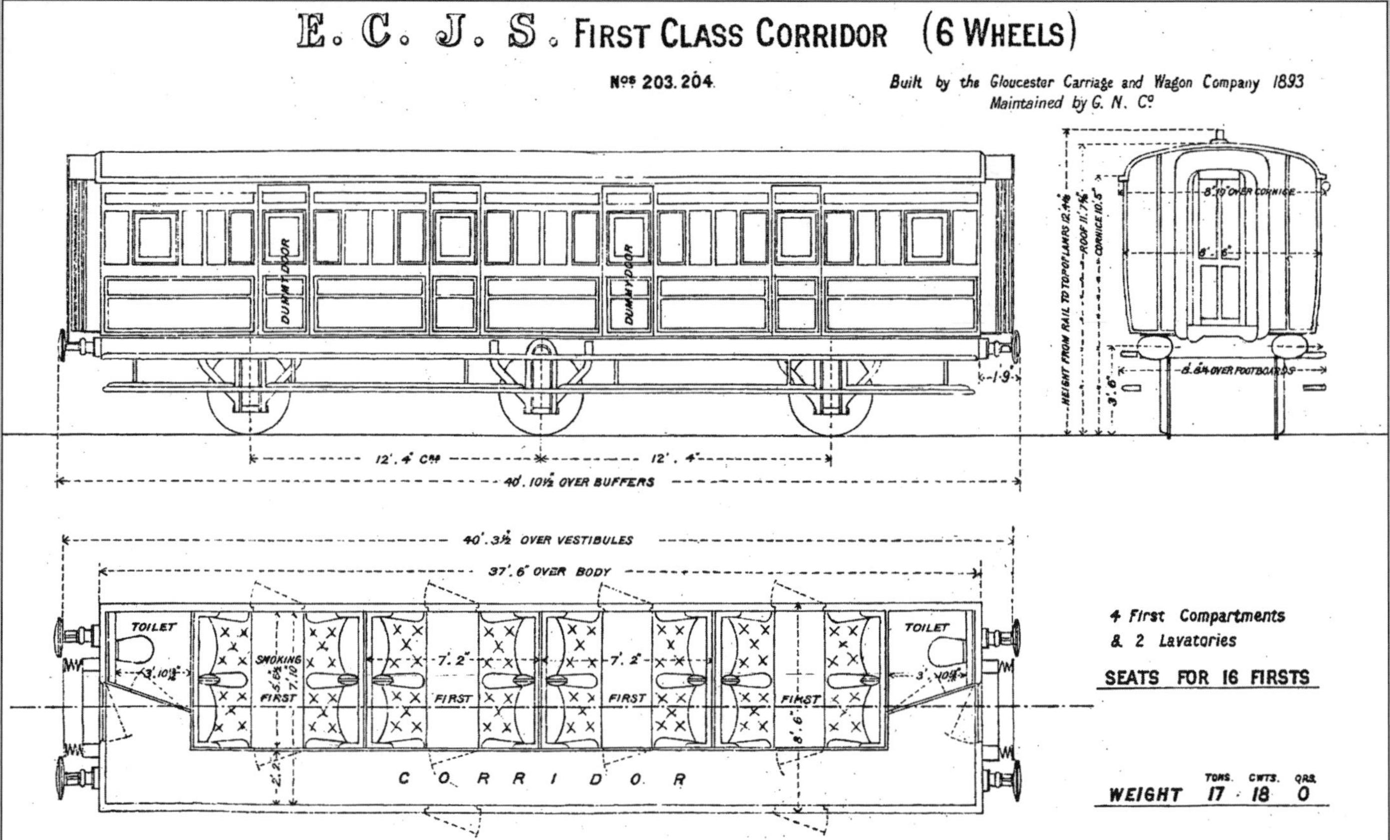

ECJS corridor firsts, built by Gloucester C&W Co., 1893, to EC Dia. 61. These were marshalled in the four sets which included contractor-built bogie dining cars. To all intents and purposes, these were traditional Stirling/Howlden carriages. The Gould-type gangway connection shown is erroneous as these vehicles had side-gangways.

principle', he commented, when writing to Oakley in January 1893 regarding Worsdell's sketches for a new ECJS sleeping car. The rigid eight-wheeler vehicle was preferable to Stirling who considered that the maintenance costs of bogies themselves were unacceptable, as was the rate of wear of wheel flanges. His enthusiasm for the rigid eight-wheeler was at the time shared by no less than the London & North Western Railway. But the North Eastern Railway would not accept rigid eight-wheeled sleeping cars. It was hardly a vote of confidence when Oakley reported to the GNR Board that, in considering the renewal of four East Coast Joint Stock sleeping cars, 'Most modern GN carriages (he was referring to sleeping cars built for the ECJS) are not up to modern standards - there is no provision for an attendant and no heating.' Doncaster was producing six-wheeled stock with the three-centre roof for the ECJS as late as the end of the 1880s, even into the early 1890s. The nine six-wheeled composite sleeping carriages of 1889-92 with four berths arranged in parallel pairs were 39 ft 9½ in. over buffers and weighed just over 15½ tons. These were clearly inferior alongside the GWR 'bay-window' sleeping cars of 1890.

Oakley had agreed with George Stegmann Gibb, General Manager of the NER, that the Doncaster-built six-wheeled sleeping cars should be renewed as soon as possible and that the gangways of the replacements should be designed for the through movement of attendants between two or three cars. In any event, the initiative was to pass to the NER and, until 1922, all ECJS sleeping cars would be built at York to that company's designs. Even the dining cars built at Doncaster in 1894 for the afternoon 'Scotsman' paid some debt to the designs of David Bain, the NER carriage superintendent.

Stirling was carried along in the tide of changing policies on rolling stock, whatever his personal preferences may have been. By July 1895, at a meeting regarding East Coast Joint operations presided over by Gibb, he presented proposals prepared by Howlden for twelve-wheeled corridor stock, all three trains of which were delivered for East Coast service the following summer. Ironically, Stirling's death in late 1895 meant that he was not to see the finished article.

New brooms had indeed swept clean. Change was first effected with the first ECJS vestibuled sets built in 1893 by Lancaster Carriage and Wagon Company, Oldbury Carriage Co. and other contractors, and maintained by York. These sets included 46 ft bogie dining cars, indeed the first ECJS bogie stock, but the rest of the vehicles, all gas-lit, were six-wheeled. The bogie vehicles ran on 8 ft wheelbase bogies, soon after adopted by Doncaster for GNR use. The example of the ECJS stock probably resulted in the building at Doncaster during the late 1890s of bogie carriages for the GNR, similar in general outline and with three-centre roofs.

When it was decided in 1895 to build new rolling stock for the '10 o'clocks', the meeting of East Coast managers held on 20th June, 1895, and chaired by Oakley, came up with specifications that stood comparison with any others in Britain. These were for carriages with: six-wheeled bogies; with bodies 'about' 60 ft long but not exceeding 65 ft; clipper-built and with clerestories; corridor connections throughout the train; centre vestibules and sliding doors to the compartments. More exceptionally, it was decided that exterior doors should

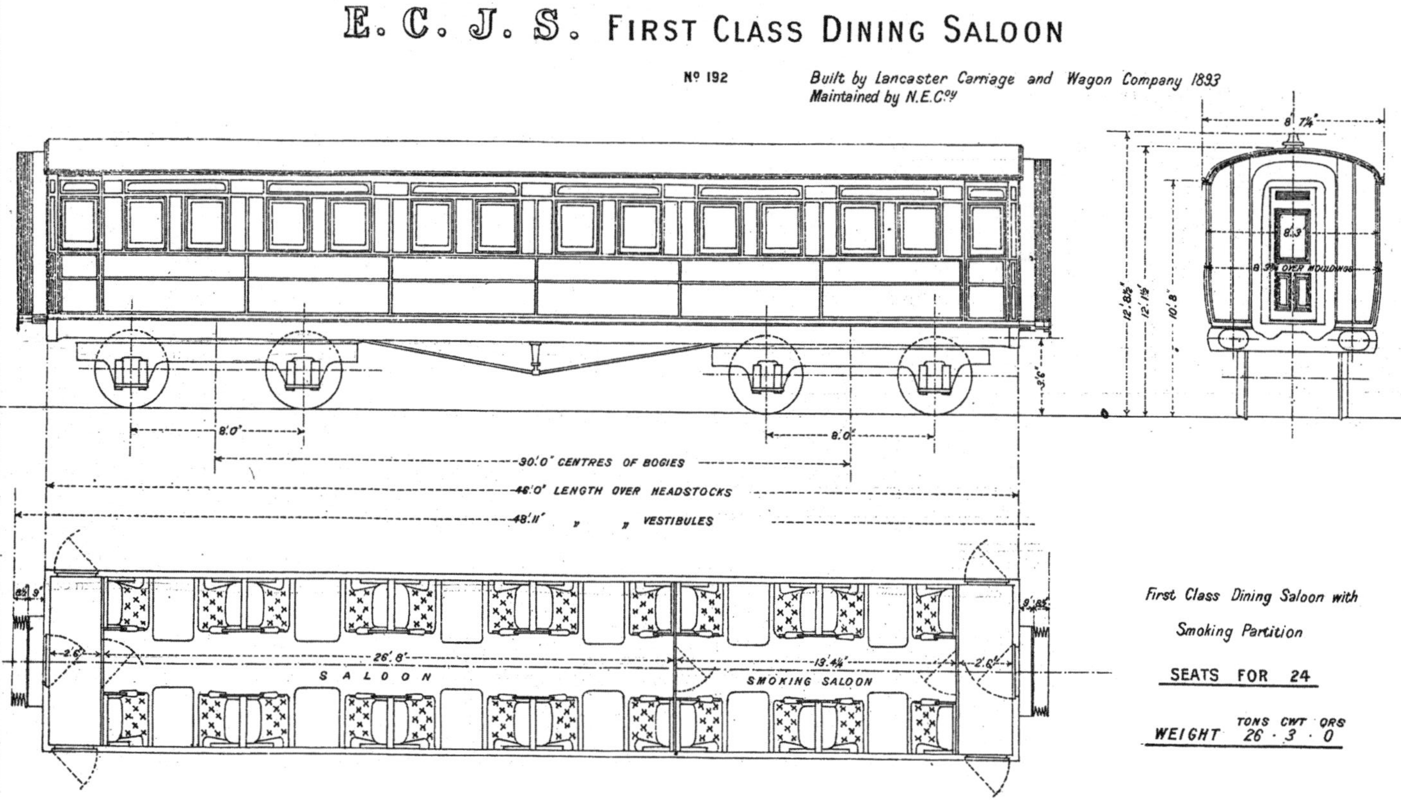

E. C. J. S. FIRST CLASS DINING SALOON

Nº 192

Built by Lancaster Carriage and Wagon Company 1893
Maintained by N.E.Cºy

8' 7¼"
8' 3"
8' 3¾" OVER MOULDINGS
12' 8½"
12' 1½"
10' 8"
3' 6"
8' 0"
8' 0"
30' 0" CENTRES OF BOGIES
46' 0" LENGTH OVER HEADSTOCKS
48' 11" " " VESTIBULES
2' 6"
26' 8"
SALOON
13' 4½"
SMOKING SALOON
2' 6"

First Class Dining Saloon with Smoking Partition

SEATS FOR 24

WEIGHT TONS 26 · CWT 3 · QRS 0

ECJS first-class dining car, built 1893 to EC Dia. 60; almost identical to Dia. 59 but the saloons were of differing lengths.

be at the ends only and not to compartments. Meetings held by the East Coast managers in July 1895 took matters further and Howlden prepared something like three sets of drawings before satisfaction was reached, in the course of which it was agreed that body side doors should be provided to compartments and not only at the end vestibules. On 22nd August, 1895, Oakley told Stirling that the 'Chairman has authorised me to instruct you to get on with the stock at once', Stirling having informed his General Manager that the GN would build all three trains of the new carriages in time for the summer 1896 service.

The press run of the new stock took place on 29th June, 1896, with two new GNR dining cars for the Leeds service attached to provide lunch. The return run was with two of the new NER-designed and built transverse sleeping cars added to the formation. The day marked an impressive step forward in the progress of the East Coast services. The new stock had Gould gangway connections and Gould automatic couplers. The new GNR Leeds third-class restaurant cars and the new ECJS sets entered regular service on 1st July, 1896, the first of the York-built transverse-berth sleeping cars having been at work since 10th December, 1895.

If the East Coast's standards had been revolutionised, then so had Doncaster's. Perhaps there is a danger of maligning Stirling because the failure until then to introduce modern rolling stock should not be taken in isolation. The GNR had no rail in use heavier than 85 lb/yard in 1895 and the St Neots accident of that year, caused by the fracture of a faulty rail, led to the Directors deciding to renew the two fast tracks of the main line with 92 lb/yard rail. This was to accommodate the operation of faster and heavier trains. The need for these was appreciated by the GNR Directors as a result of the decision of the Midland to provide third-class as well as first-class dining cars on the London - Leeds expresses. Competition between the companies led to a reduction in passenger fares - and increased patronage. With the steadily increasing weight of passenger trains - and to operate heavier freight trainloads - more powerful locomotives were required than the Stirling designs that were so successful on light, fast workings.

These developments ushered in the 1900/1 stock for the Leeds service: all twelve-wheelers of 62 - 65 ft in length, with Gould couplers, Pullman gangways and with all third-class accommodation in open saloons. H. A. Ivatt had led a party of other railways' officials to the United States in the spring of 1899. If this study-tour was to have its effects on GNR locomotive design, the same was true for carriage practice, with confirmation of the decisions to adopt Pullman gangways, buckeye couplers and the like. A total of 79 generically very similar vehicles to the GNR's Leeds stock appeared for the ECJS services in 1902/3, built at Doncaster, York and Cowlairs. The basic design was produced by Howlden and, from this time, the appearance of the carriages was altered by extending the quarterlights up to the cant-rail. The York vehicles, generally the restaurant cars and sleeping cars, featured larger windows, producing a more harmonious and modern appearance.

ECJS requirements for general service were met by clerestory twelve-wheeled vehicles to these general specifications turned out by Doncaster up until 1905. The very last examples were 64 ft 2½ in. body composite diners Nos. 196/7 and

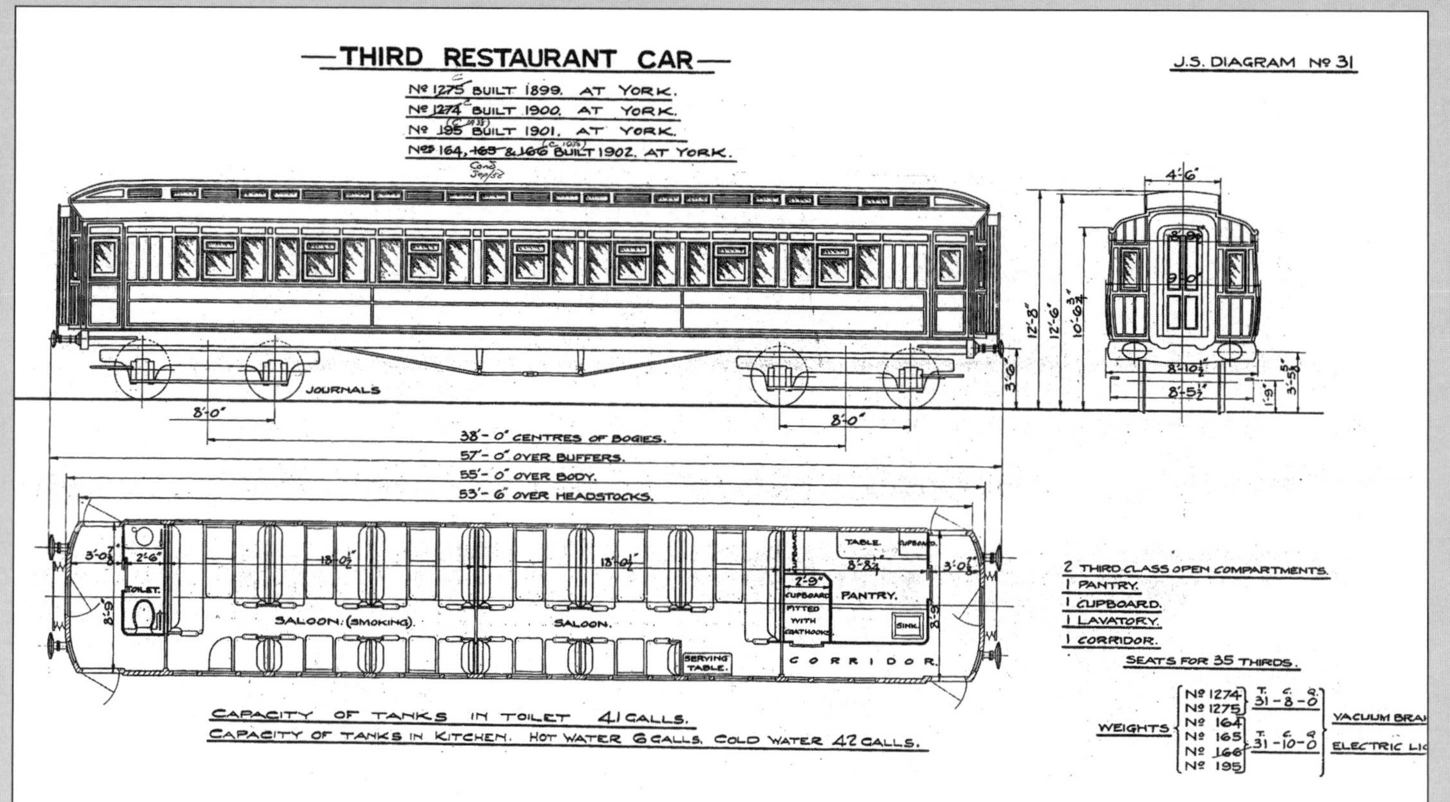

ECJS open third to EC Dia. 31, exemplifying one of the clipper-built vehicles of ECJS stock with a 55 ft body. A photograph of No. 68J of this type and Diagram appears as Plate 24. In this 1920s Diagram, these open thirds are described as Third Dining Cars as early LNER policy was to re-designate such cars, previously plain 'open thirds'. The pattern of vehicle was what the LNER later called Pantry Third and they were intended to be marshalled next to a first-class dining car with kitchen, in order to supplement the latter's facilities.

352/3 and 65 ft 4¼ in. long composite brake No. 23. Yet York was once more moving ahead as stock built by the NER in 1904 for the ECJS comprised day and sleeping vehicles with elliptical roofs and flat, matchboarded bodysides.

Indeed, despite their imposing appearance, the twelve-wheeled 'turn of century' clerestory stock built for the GNR and ECJS was soon outdated. They were not mechanically efficient, the result of their underframes and headstocks being wooden and of the inadequate bracing and trussing. Nor was their size commodious for passengers, the lavatories being particularly cramped. For its 65 ft length and 36 tons weight, the five-compartment brake composite No. 23 of 1905 seated only 26 passengers in none too spacious seating.

Gresley writing to Raven in February 1919 characterised these twelve-wheelers as: 'expensive to maintain, very heavy and out of date'. He was, he said, very much in favour of scrapping all but the dining and sleeping cars and drew attention to their small lavatories and excessive luggage space in relation to the passengers carried. Yet, during 1918-20, a number were reconditioned, modernised internally and mounted on four-wheeled bogies.

Returning to the 1900s, E.F. Howlden retired at the end of 1904. He had begun his railway service at Doncaster in 1853. His replacement was Herbert Nigel Gresley. Not long after his appointment in March 1905 as carriage and wagon superintendent, Gresley must have decided on a radical change to the GNR's carriage design. His prototype was a corridor composite No. 2977 (*see Chapter 5*) which featured the elliptical roof, electric lighting and the combination of side-corridor and saloon accommodation found in a number of GNR Gresley vehicles. It appears likely that it was originally to be built with a clerestory roof.

A major building programme for ECJS stock was in prospect and at a meeting in York of the East Coast partners on 28th March, 1905 it was agreed that the GNR would prepare plans of the 10 vestibuled thirds and 12 bogie vans to be built while the NER's contribution was the design and building of six sleeping cars. The NBR's Cowlairs Works would build six of the vans. All vehicles would be electrically-lit. In a subsequent meeting in Edinburgh on 28th July, 1905, details were concluded and the building programme was expanded to include additional thirds and brake thirds in replacement of earlier vehicles.

The East Coast companies had decided to adopt the elliptical roof for their new carriages, the general outline of which was not to be in doubt. Minute 910 of the Edinburgh meeting recorded that the GNR's representative 'would not agree to vehicles with matchboard sides, or elliptical roofs, unless constructed with sloping ends as present East Coast clerestory stock.' Before matters proceeded, there had to be confirmation that elliptical roofed stock would meet the loading gauge of each of the East Coast companies. During July and September 1905, special gauging clearance runs were conducted between Kings Cross, Edinburgh and Aberdeen, and to Mallaig.

These gauging runs preceded the meeting of the East Coast General Managers at York on 10th November, 1905, when various matters connected with the building of ECJS vehicles were considered and, to quote, 'it was agreed to adopt elliptical roofs curved downwards at the end, and curved side panels as a standard pattern for the future.' This was essentially a description of the

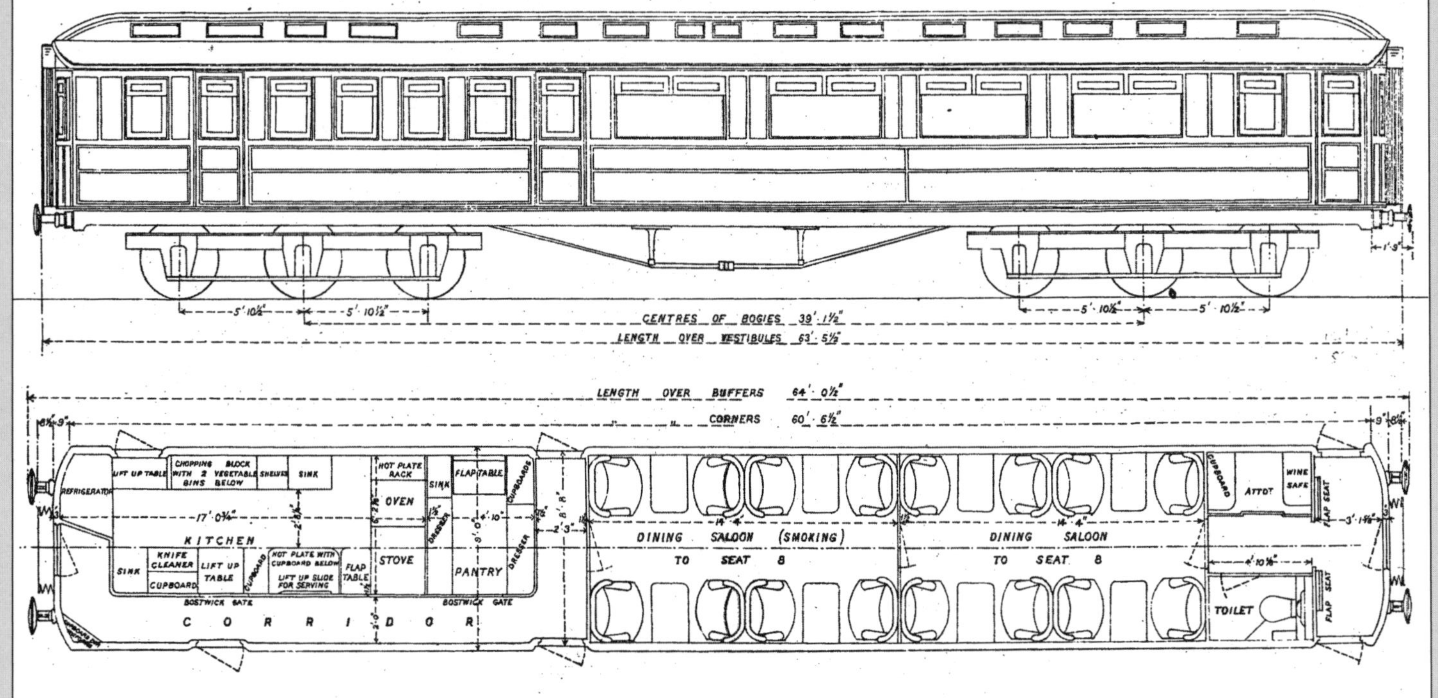

ECJS first-class dining car on EC Dia. 77, built by Doncaster in 1902. This shows the type after fitting with large windows, a process which began in 1911.

GNR Gresley carriage which had now made its appearance.

The scene was being set for the evolution of the Gresley elliptical roofed carriage that was to be a feature of the East Coast main line for half a century or more. The standard was established by the Sheffield Stock sets of 1906, in terms of exterior design and a simplicity of interior finish. Both changes indicated the particular contributions to carriage design that would be made by Gresley.

Over the next ten years, the Gresley carriage matured in design. Two important decisions had been reached in 1905. The Traffic Committee recommended that all new dining and sleeping cars should be fitted with electric lighting and, towards the end of the year, its members advocated that all new GNR carriages should be electrically-lit. Subsequently, the GNR backtracked somewhat following the production of more effective - and cheaper - incandescent gas lighting and, for a period from 1910, there was a reversion to gas lighting.

Yet, as indicated in Chapter 5, the vestibuled carriages built at Doncaster for GNR service from 1907 onwards were almost restlessly varied, in general specification and dimensions. But the passenger managers and operating staffs were the arbiters in such matters and the specific requirements of individual trains or services receiving new carriages were more important in their eyes than standardisation. The Sheffield stock had given Gresley an opportunity for an impressive debut, the GNR having decided to tackle head-on the competition offered by the Great Central - not forgetting the Midland either - for London - Sheffield and Manchester traffic that Kings Cross had latterly neglected. The three new trains comprising the Sheffield stock were constructed on capital account as an addition to existing stock.

But external appearances and interior finish were far from the last words on carriage design and Gresley was an innovator in mechanical engineering. There was the Gresley development of the Spencer-Moulton compound-bolster bogie which was used for GNR and ECJS stock from 1908 and effectively standardised soon after World War 1. The Gresley/Spencer-Moulton collaboration covered other aspects of carriage design, including suspension and buffing gear. One of the engineer's most characteristic contributions to carriage design was articulation whose adoption originated from passengers' complaints regarding the rough riding of six-wheeled stock on express trains. The prototype conversion of ECJS stock dated from January 1907 and its success led to the GNR Board's approval in the July of that year of the conversion of 40 GNR six-wheelers into what at the time were called 'double-coaches'. These were for use on intermediate expresses and some Yorkshire and Nottinghamshire services. A GNR memo from Grinling noted that: 'The question of converting East Coast coaches will have to be discussed with the North Eastern and North British companies'.

If inevitably associated with the teak-bodied carriage, Gresley nonetheless had contemplated the building of an all-steel carriage for the GNR as early as 1914. By that date, users of all-steel construction included the Paris-Orleans Railway, the Prussian State Railway, the Central London Railway and a number of railroads in the United States. Immediately preceding World War I there were no major innovations at Doncaster either in carriage practice or design.

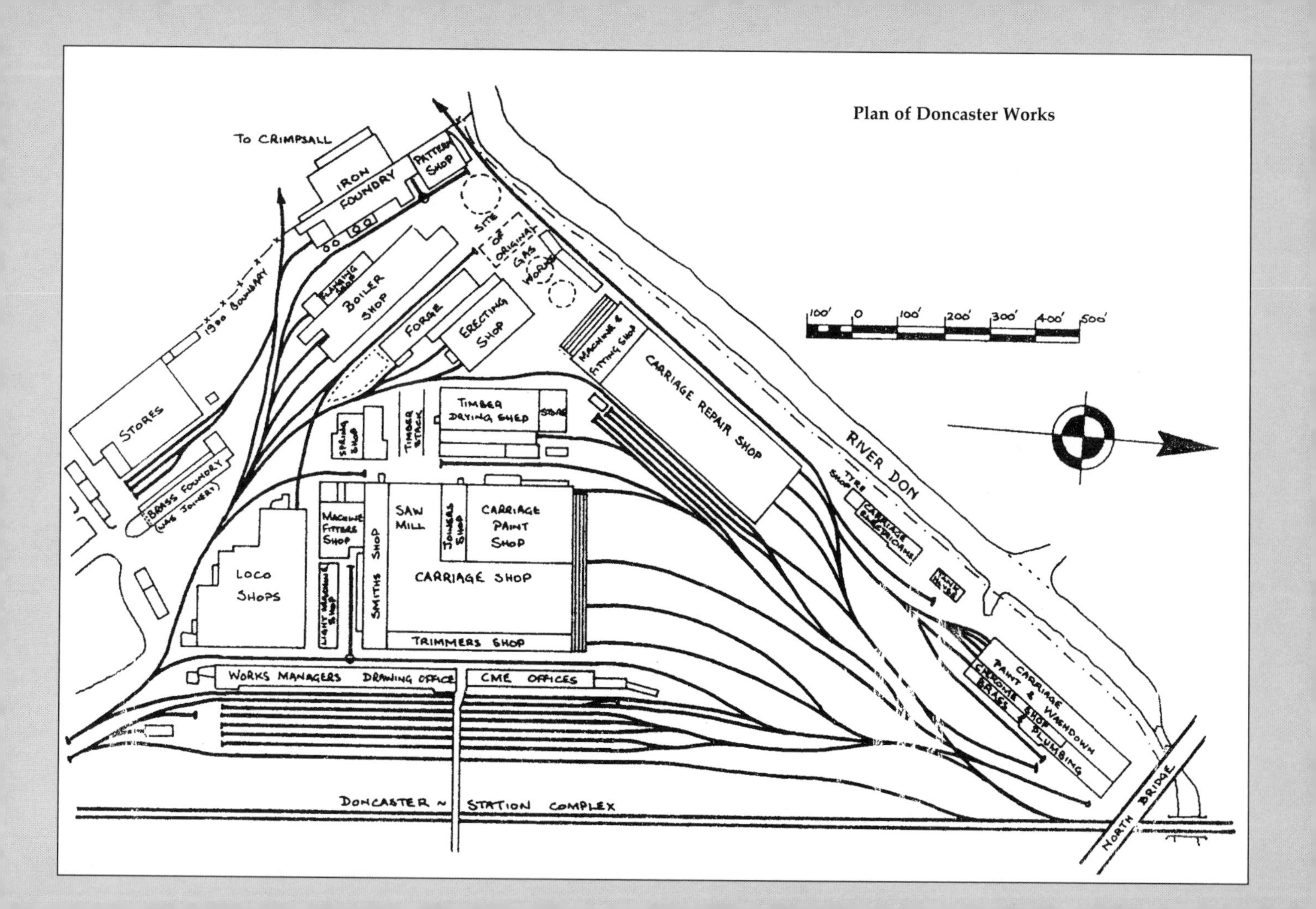

Plan of Doncaster Works

More of interest was to come after 1920, coincident with O.V.S. Bulleid's appointment as assistant carriage and wagon superintendent, and particularly notable were the Leeds quintuplet set and the twin-articulated sleeping cars for the ECJS.

At the end of 1913 Gresley had charge of the following passenger stock, not including carriage trucks and horseboxes:

GNR stock	Vestibuled bogie and non-bogie	406	
	Non-vestibuled bogie	344	
	Non-vestibuled non-bogie	2,269	
	Rail motors	6	Total: 3,025
ECJS stock maintained by Doncaster	All types	213	
GN/NE stock maintained by Doncaster	All types	17	
	Total carriages maintained by Doncaster		3,255

Of the above carriages maintained at Doncaster Works in 1912/3, some 300 were electrically-lit and 2,900 gas-lit.

Doncaster Works and Carriages

The main carriage building shop at Doncaster Works was opened as a separate entity in 1889 and the wagon works was moved to Carr in 1890. The West carriage shop was brought into use in 1897 with alterations made in 1901 and 1913 when the installation of 20-ton overhead cranes was completed. By 1913, the carriage building and repair facilities had been grouped in three areas. The offices were in the long building adjacent to the station, the trimming shop being a continuation of the offices. Immediately behind the offices, adjacent to and north of the locomotive shops, was the sawmill 384 ft long and 132 ft wide. To the west of this shop lay the log-yard and timber drying sheds. The carriage building shop, part of the same block of buildings, was 300 ft long and 199 ft wide and had 12 roads; a 60ft traverser had been installed in 1906. Here the bodywork was constructed and lifted on to underframes which had been fabricated in the locomotive shops. The paint shop, a continuation of this same block, was 264 ft long and 180 ft wide and could stable 44 carriages on its twelve roads.

Alongside the River Don lay the West carriage shop, 593 ft long and 182 ft wide. This dealt with carriage repairs and was grouped into woodworking and lifting areas. In all, 24 bogie carriages and 48 six-wheelers could be accommodated. Finally, at the extreme north of the works, was the North carriage shed, 380 ft long and 110 ft wide with eight roads. Varnishing and light running repairs were handled there in addition to carriage washing facilities.

Until the early 1960s the East Coast royal train was stabled in this shed.

The layout of Doncaster Works was reasonably modern and compact and, by 1913, its workshops had been equipped with all-electric machines. Nevertheless, the carriage works' facilities were primarily those of a woodworking factory, relying on the locomotive works and outside contractors for steel forgings and sections. By 1913, the 'Plant' as a whole covered 200 acres and employed 4,600 people. At maximum capacity, 100 carriages could be constructed annually and 3,000 given various categories of repair, not that maximum capacity was reached in the years before Grouping. Specimen figures for 1912 are as follows:

New Stock

GNR and GN/NE stock	42 Capital Stock, 16 Ordinary renewals - includes carriage trucks

Repaired Stock

	Elliptical/Clerestory Roofed	*Ordinary*
Retrimmed	22	146
Revarnished	68	353
Touched-up	27	21
Lifted	266	949

Light repairs - 742 carriages both categories

The influence of the East Coast Joint Stock and the way it was worked

Essentially seen as a way of protecting the interests of the East Coast companies in northern Scotland, the creation of the East Coast Joint Stock in 1860 marked, as Grinling said in his history of the GNR, 'the definite admission of the Great Northern as London partner in the East Coast alliance.' By the same token, the ECJS's emergence signified the effective demise of the 'alternative East Coast route' via Derby and Normanton.

It had been the GNR's suggestion that a special stock of carriages should be provided for through workings between Kings Cross and Edinburgh (and beyond) and that these should be the common property of the GNR, NER and NBR. The scheme was drawn up by the GNR in June 1860, the principle being that stock for the Anglo-Scottish services would be paid for in proportion by the GNR, NER and NBR. Each company's share was estimated in proportion to the mileage covered on its metals by through Scottish trains. For the number of vehicles required for the first services in 1861, each railway paid a share of the total cost of that stock: the GNR 47.75 per cent, NER 37.75 per cent and the NBR 14.5 per cent. In 1880, the proportions changed to GNR 40 per cent, NER 35 per cent and NBR 25 per cent.

There was no separate ECJS capital account, and each company managed its share in its own way. For instance, the GNR capital account had a portion allotted to East Coast Joint Stock and when new vehicles were built the GNR (after 1880) contributed 40 per cent of the cost and debited its capital account with that amount. When vehicles were withdrawn from the ECJS fleet, or otherwise disposed of, the GNR took 40 per cent of the total or its equivalent and transferred the value of this 40 per cent to the GNR carriage account. However, the ECJS vehicles stood in the respective companies' account at their original cost and no charge was made for their depreciation.

The East Coast companies - the GNR, NER and NBR - discussed and reviewed matters of mutual interest in different forums. There was the East Coast Conference which dealt with matters such as traffic levels and timekeeping of through trains. There was an East Coast Directors' Committee, and an East Coast Joint Committee, the latter being extremely high-powered in membership but not very productive. The real work was done at meetings of the East Coast companies' traffic superintendents who also met with the locomotive superintendents. Policy was formulated by the General Managers of the East Coast companies who then sought the approval of their respective Boards for their recommendations. The Great North of Scotland Railway was conspicuously absent from the discussions. When the East Coast companies were considering the construction of ECJS fish vans in 1911, the GNoS effectively vetoed further action by making it clear that they would not use any but their own stock!

Until 1893, all ECJS carriages were built by the GNR at Doncaster but the Lancaster Railway Carriage and Wagon Company constructed the sets that entered service on the 'Flying Scotsman' in that year and, from then, vehicles were built by Doncaster, the NER's York carriage works and, to a much lesser extent, by the North British Railway's Cowlairs Works.

The evolution of a common style of twelve-wheeled carriages in the mid/late 1890s has been referred to already and their construction continued until Gresley's appointment to the GNR. These vehicles were followed by an experimental period in carriage design on both the GNR and NER, both companies having taken a close look at what was happening in the United States. Not least, this led to the austere, straight-sided ECJS carriages built at York. The subsequent adoption by the East Coast companies of the Gresley-pattern of elliptical-roofed carriage has been mentioned above.

The companies' participation in the provision of stock for the ECJS led to the adoption of the design innovations in carriages for their internal services such as the elliptical roof, buckeye couplings, steel underframes, electric lighting and steam heating.

There were some misgivings about the adoption of the centre coupler and Pullman gangway for the ECJS. William Whitelaw for the NBR said at the October 1910 meeting of the EC Joint Committee that: 'it caused considerable difficulties in working and annoyance to passengers' (on grounds of noise, vibration and when vehicles were being shunted to couple up). The difficulties in working referred to the inability of connecting the Pullman and British Standard gangways. In pursuing the point, the EC General Managers asked the mechanical engineers and traffic superintendents of the EC companies to produce a full report and whether they would recommend that the buckeye and Pullman gangways should be continued 'as the permanent East Coast pattern.' They reported by April 1911 and, although agreeing that the centre couplings were noisy, upheld the case for the centre coupler and Pullman gangway and recommended minor changes in design of both fittings to alleviate some of the complaints. They also proposed the use of an adaptor to allow Pullman gangways to couple to the BS type.

The requirements of the ECJS served to test the design staff and carriage-builders at the respective drawing offices and works. Even so, the ECJS vehicles were regarded by the owning companies as a cut above what was acceptable for internal services. Possibly, their enhanced status was a way of ensuring that some of their passenger comforts did not have the effect of rendering the internal services' stock obsolescent.

The Doncaster and York works were each responsible for the maintenance of an allocation of ECJS vehicles and this policy continued with East Coast stock built to LNER design. It was agreed in May 1913 that Cowlairs should cease to be involved with the maintenance of ECJS vehicles. For the stock built after 1905, at the outbreak of World War I York was responsible for the following ECJS vehicles:

The two composites to Dia. 3A; seven bogie brakes to Dia. 39B; the two thirds to Dia. 16; six thirds built 1906 on Dia. 34 and 19 on this Diagram built 1907; the sleeping-car on Dia 63; the three sleeper composites on Dia. 69; the four sleeping-cars on Dia. 70A; the one sleeping-car on Dia. 74; the three kitchen cars on Dia. 80A and the Queen's saloon.

Doncaster's apportionment of post-1905 ECJS vehicles at the same date was as follows:

The four composites on Dia. 2A; the two composites on Dia. 2B; the six Cowlairs-built bogie brakes on Dia. 35; the royal train brake No 82 on Dia. 35; six bogie brakes on Dia. 39, five on Dia. 39A and six on Dia. 39B; the clerestory six-wheeler No 23 (q.v.) on Dia. 44, built 1905; the one brake composite on Dia. 47A; the eight brake thirds on Dia. 49 and the two on Dia. 49A; two firsts on Dia. 58; the four thirds on Dia. 17, the four on Dia. 18 and the sixteen on Dia. 22; the two third-class dining cars on Dia. 29A; the two first-class dining cars on Dia. 75A and the King's saloon.

During the winter months, when train loadings were lighter, all ECJS sleeping cars were in turn examined at York works which was responsible for their maintenance and they were usually thoroughly cleaned and lifted. Those requiring a general overhaul were dealt with at the same time. In due course, this routine was followed for the vehicles making up the principal day trains. On the GNR, ECJS vehicles were cleaned at Hornsey, except the 10 o'clock stock which was dealt with at Finsbury Park.

A outline of NER carriage stock until 1922

The NER's principal C&W establishment was at York carriage works, set up in 1880 on a site between Leeman Road and Poppleton Road and adjacent to the latter. The main design offices and chief mechanical engineer's headquarters were situated at Gateshead until 1910 and were then transferred to Darlington.

York's maximum capacity for new construction was given in 1908 as 200 bogie vehicles annually, but in the years before World War I production never exceeded 80 - 90 carriages. In the heyday of British railways here was an instance of renewal programmes being slowed down, at a time when the book life of a carriage was taken as 28 years. Most of those built in this period at York lasted considerably longer. The York Works wages staff comprised 1,578 persons in December 1913, of whom 230 were engaged on new construction, the rest on repairs.

As to the extent of the NER's carriage fleet, by 1908 this was as follows:

	Bogie stock	*Four/six-wheeled stock*	*Total*
Ordinary train sets	1,391	Nil	1,391
Excursion stock, spares, float carriages	183	2,365	2,548

Having set the scene as far as the building works and the size of the NER's own carriage fleet are concerned, it is appropriate to turn to the NER's carriage design history. In the 1890s David Bain was the carriage and wagon superintendent. The standard NER carriage of the 1880s was a six-wheeled vehicle, but by 1895 clerestory bogie stock was produced in 45 ft and 52 ft lengths, together with 49 ft low-roof carriages. We have already seen how, in the mid/late 1890s, NER-built carriages for the ECJS were ahead of GNR practice and the Lancaster-built dining cars in the 1893 '10 o'clocks' are said to have been credited to Wilson Worsdell, the NER locomotive superintendent. He was certainly responsible for the five handsome clerestoried sleeping cars with transverse berths built at York in 1895/6. The 23 carriages built at York for the afternoon Scotsman sets in 1902 were to Howlden's designs.

With an eye on American practice, the stock built by the NER for the Tyneside electrification in 1903 had teak matchboarded lower body panels and slab sides. Elliptical roofed carriages with the straight sides and matchboard panelling were produced by York as the NER contribution to the new ECJS sets turned out for the summer 1905 timetable and also in the shape of dining cars constructed for the GN/NE train set later that year. In addition, there were three ECJS sleeping cars to the same general appearance. Though the corridors were wide, the compartments were somewhat cramped. The matchboarding was difficult to keep clean, and although no more expensive than large body panels lacked their strength.

The result of the adoption of the GNR Gresley outline for ECJS stock seems to have influenced the appearance of the NER's carriages for its internal services. Some attractive sets were produced at York for the Newcastle - Liverpool, Hull - Liverpool and Leeds - Glasgow services. These vehicles were of 53 ft 6 in. body length - 65 ft for the restaurant cars - and had electric lighting and British Standard gangways. If the earlier straight-sided carriages had appeared angular by comparison with the GNR's elliptical-roofed designs, the later NER stock had a 'softer' and sometimes more graceful look than some of the

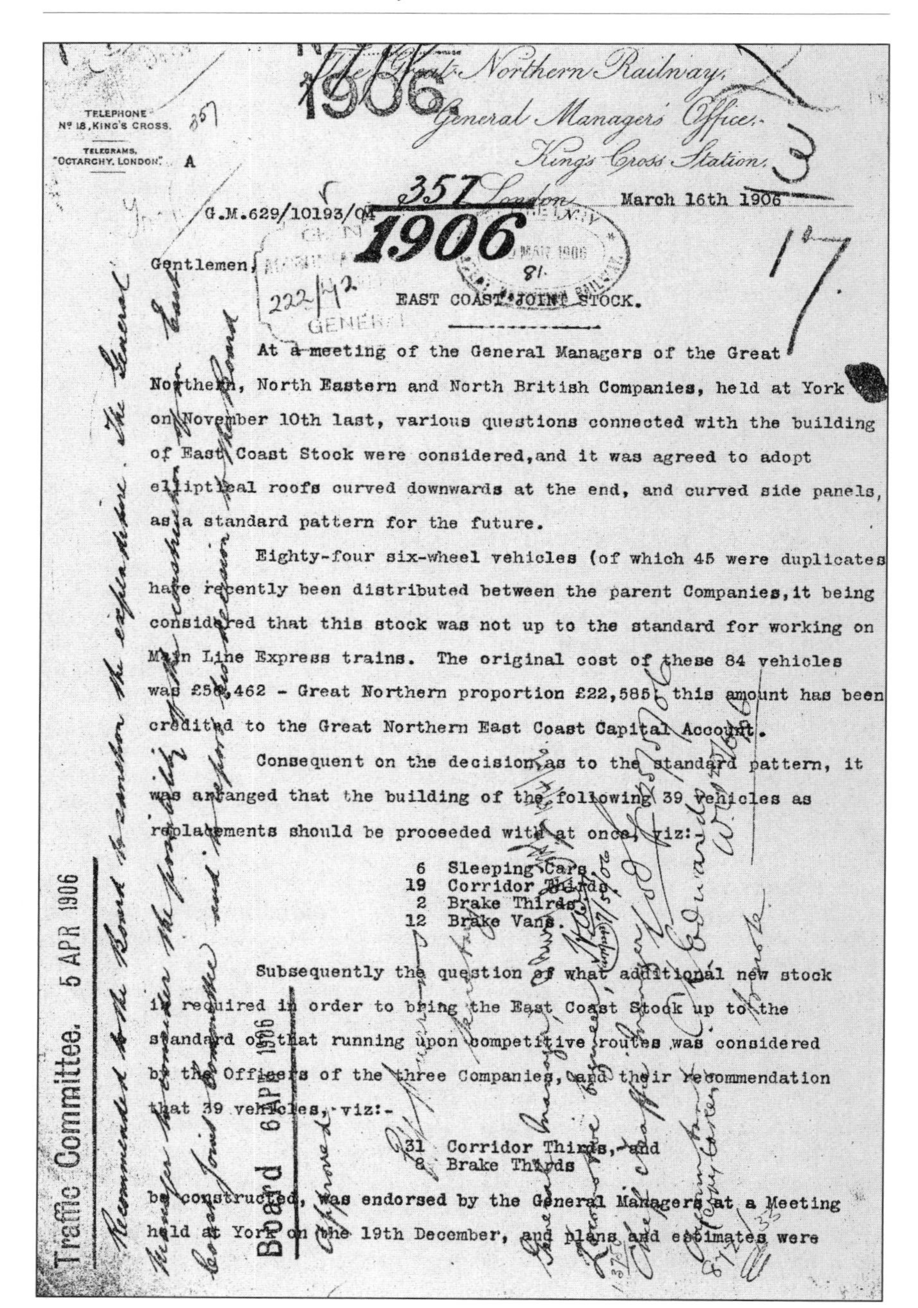

TELEPHONE
Nº 18, KING'S CROSS.

TELEGRAMS,
"OCTARCHY, LONDON."

A

The Great Northern Railway,
General Managers' Office,
King's Cross Station,
London

G.M.629/10193/04 March 16th 1906

Gentlemen,

EAST COAST JOINT STOCK.

At a meeting of the General Managers of the Great Northern, North Eastern and North British Companies, held at York on November 10th last, various questions connected with the building of East Coast Stock were considered, and it was agreed to adopt elliptical roofs curved downwards at the end, and curved side panels, as a standard pattern for the future.

Eighty-four six-wheel vehicles (of which 45 were duplicates) have recently been distributed between the parent Companies, it being considered that this stock was not up to the standard for working on Main Line Express trains. The original cost of these 84 vehicles was £56,462 - Great Northern proportion £22,585; this amount has been credited to the Great Northern East Coast Capital Account.

Consequent on the decision as to the standard pattern, it was arranged that the building of the following 39 vehicles as replacements should be proceeded with at once, viz:-

6 Sleeping Cars.
19 Corridor Thirds.
2 Brake Thirds.
12 Brake Vans.

Subsequently the question of what additional new stock is required in order to bring the East Coast Stock up to the standard of that running upon competitive routes was considered by the Officers of the three Companies, and their recommendation that 39 vehicles, viz:-

31 Corridor Thirds, and
8 Brake Thirds

be constructed, was endorsed by the General Managers at a Meeting held at York on the 19th December, and plans and estimates were

Traffic Committee. 5 APR 1906

Board 6 APR 1906

Statement A.

NEW EAST COAST JOINT STOCK.

G.M. Minute.	Stock authorised.	Estimated cost per vehicle. £	By whom to be built.
1905 194 May 30th	6 Sleeping Cars	2,300	North Eastern
	10 Corridor Thirds	1,750	8 Great Northern 2 North Eastern
	12 Bogie Vans	1,125	6 Great Northern 6 North British
209 Nov. 10th	9 Corridor Thirds	1,750	4 Great Northern 5 North Eastern
	2 Brake Thirds	1,660	Great Northern
228 Dec. 19th	31 Corridor Thirds	1,750	Not yet settled.
	8 Brake Thirds	1,660	

Summary

6 Sleeping Cars	@ £2,300 each	-	£ 13,800
50 Corridor Thirds	@ £1,750 "	-	£ 87,500
10 Brake Thirds	@ £1,660 "	-	£ 16,600
12 Bogie Vans	@ £1,125 "	-	£ 13,500
78	Total		£ 131,400

Great Northern proportion	40%	-	£52,560
North Eastern "	35%	-	£45,990
North British "	25%	-	£32,850

General Manager's Office,
Great Northern Railway,
KING'S CROSS.
Feb. 14th 1906.

Documents from the GNR files relating to the major re-equipment of the ECJS in 1906. The letter and statement were under the signature of Oliver Bury, General Manager to the GNR Traffic Committee and are dated 16th March, 1906. *Public Record Office*

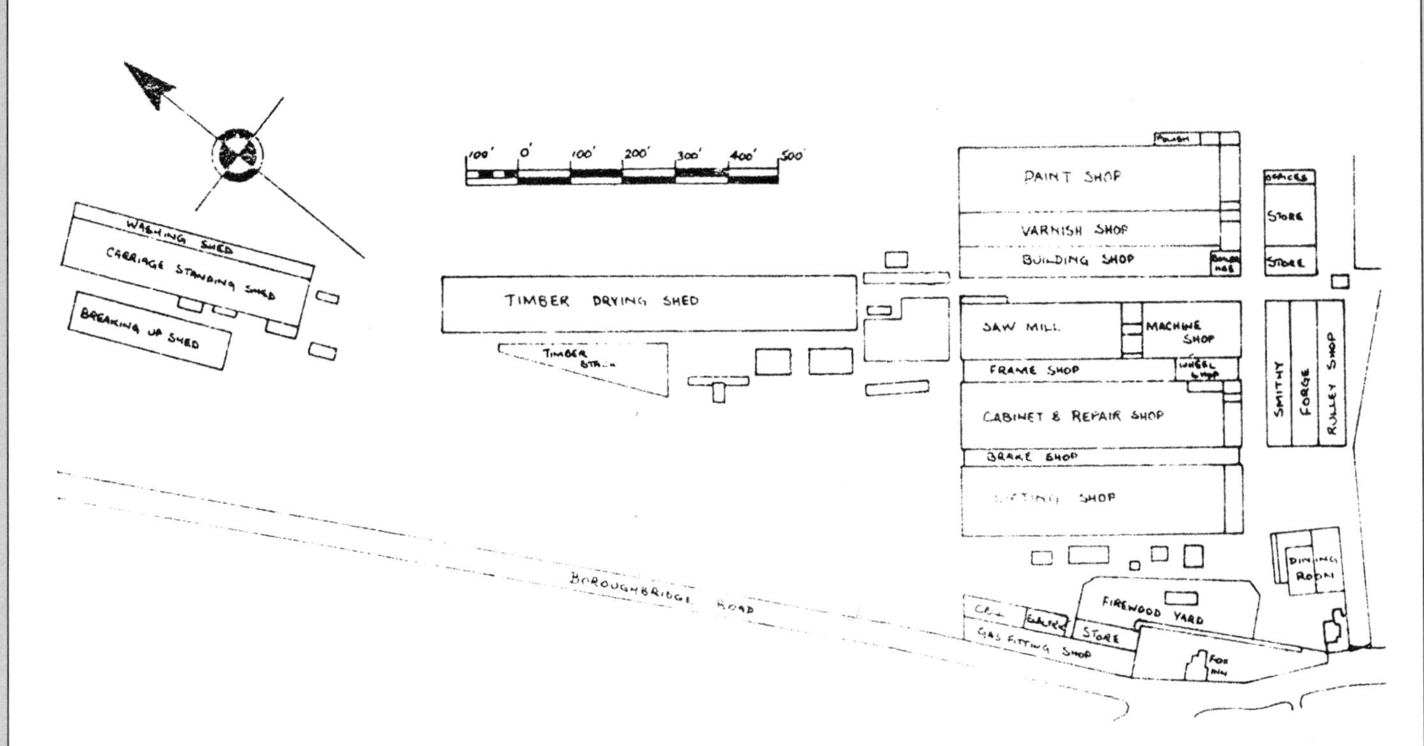

Layout of York Carriage Works 1922

Doncaster-built carriages, the consequence of their roofs having a more rounded profile and the radiussed corners to the bodyside mouldings and windows.

To the author, J.D. Twinberrow, the NER's chief carriage & wagon draughtsman at Gateshead Works from 1905 - 10, is an unsung contributor to British carriage design and practice. He tried without success to obtain support for building ECJS stock with doors at the end vestibules only, but in August 1906 was told by Vincent Raven, the chief mechanical engineer, that 'the Traffic people will not agree not to put doors in the compartments of corridor carriages.' Twinberrow had cogently argued in a letter to Raven dated May 1905 that the elimination of side-doors - excepting, of course, those entering directly upon the vestibules - would allow the body sides to be better constructed with longer wooden members. To quote Twinberrow, the result would be, 'reduced weight and cost, increased stiffness and greater security against collapse in accidents. There would also be a considerable gain to appearance owing to the sides and arrangement of the lights being unbroken by the side doors'. Twinberrow was correct, if ahead of his times, as far as British railways were concerned. Raven's reply - after no less than 15 months! - effectively illustrates the constraints placed on the engineers by the traffic departments.

From the NER's point of view, the similarity of York-built ECJS stock with the Doncaster product was dictated by the effective domination of the East Coast policy by the GNR and its carriage design practices. In 1906, when writing to Raven, Twinberrow saw the position as follows: 'The Joint Committee and others appear to evince a preference for GNR recommendations; it is advisable to place NER recommendations on record, for reference when the course of time shall establish their superior soundness'.

The matter of the differences between the practices of the two railways was gone into quite thoroughly, not least because the NER-built vehicles for the ECJS were both costlier and heavier than those constructed at Doncaster. A comparison was made of corridor thirds built for the ECJS by both Doncaster and York in 1907, given that the latter's product weighed 66 cwt more than the GNR build. Mr Twinberrow suggested that the differences were due to the York finish being 'better inside and out - and longer-lasting'. Raven's investigation showed that the 66 cwt excess was, among other things, down to the provision by the NER of more packing in the ceilings and body spaces, greater use of panel blocking in the York-built stock, more plate cells to the batteries and larger water tanks. Some 18 cwt of the excess was down to the brake gear and bogie type used by York.

There was also the different external appearance of ECJS stock built by the two works. Writing to Raven in January 1906, Twinberrow was to say: 'I do not like the GN plan of building main line carriages with single pillars between the large lights. I consider double pillars and a small panel a much better mechanical job, and free from a certain vulgarity in appearance.'

But Doncaster practice in carriage design was virtually an imposition on the NER when it came to ECJS and GN/NE Joint Stock built in the 1906-10 period. In April 1907, Mr Pick, the carriage and wagon works manager at York, informed Twinberrow that he had 'definite instructions that all GN/NE and ECJ stock to be built exactly to GN style in future'. That had followed discussions during December 1906 between the GNR and NER regarding the building of additional GN/NE Joint stock. Most of the comparisons between the Doncaster and York practices were resolved in favour of the former's preferences.

Yet this was not to be the final word. In 1911, a detailed comparative statement was drawn up by Messrs Pick and Twinberrow in response to an instruction from their General Manager. This set out their recommendations on preferred - and cheapest - future practice in practically every aspect of ECJS carriage design. They were admirably impartial in their report and a number of changes were made which owed nothing to either Doncaster's or York's practices, such as the design of the underframe and brake gear. The application of the Pick/Twinberrow recommendations to the specification of corridor thirds built at York during 1912 saw a reduction in price per vehicle by something like £150, to £1,740.

In 1906, the 53 ft 6 in. body stock built at York for the ECJS was the first to have the timber content in the underframes restricted to the headstocks. The next year, an all-steel underframe was introduced as this allowed easier incorporation of the buckeye couplers while the headstock itself was consequently much stronger. Among the standard types of NER carriages built in the 1910s were the ubiquitous 49 ft elliptical roofed compartment thirds with gas lighting; the 52 ft lavatory composites of the same general outline; and 53 ft 6 in. body corridor firsts and thirds with electric lighting. All these types ran on 8 ft wheelbase pressed-steel bogies. Their external appearance was characterised by wide-radiussed body mouldings and rounded corners to the windows. They looked neat and modern and indeed were built to much the same features up to, and after, Grouping. It reflected well on the NER that all scheduled trains were normally worked by bogie stock, although of the total less than 10 per cent of the company's bogie carriages were vestibuled. Perhaps the most interesting York-built carriages of the period were the three all-steel kitchen cars designed by Raven for the 1914 'Flying Scotsman' sets and described in Chapter 4.

Standard LNER Gresley carriage designs were put into production soon after Grouping and the NER's contribution to the new company's practices was very limited. For various reasons there was construction of some NER designs for other Areas within the LNER until 1925/6.

Chapter Three

Gresley GNR and ECJS Carriages - Construction, Liveries and Interiors

Underframes and running gear etc.

In GNR days, most large steel components were purchased from contractors. Underframe sections came from the Steel Co. of Scotland, carriage wheels (3 ft 7 in. diameter) from Cravens, Sheffield while Leeds Forge supplied the bogies. Gresley's proposal for an all-steel carriage in 1914 would have employed steel framing from Leeds Forge and, unless construction of steel carriages at Doncaster was to have been on a major scale, on price alone steel could not have compared with teak.

The move to all-steel underframes at Doncaster in 1905 marked a fundamental change in policy by Gresley. Carriage tare weights were increasing beyond the ability of wooden underframes to carry the bodies and the wooden underframe was technically inferior to steel. Steel channels for longitudinal members and bulb angles for solebars were used in the fabrication of the all-steel underframe and this was done in the 'Plant' locomotive shops. The latter-day Howlden underframes had begun to incorporate steel components but iron truss-rods and wooden solebars were still employed. To reduce noise and vibration, india-rubber cushions were used between floors and underframes; these were introduced with the King's Saloon in 1908 and then in the series of London area suburban stock from 1911.

Buckeye couplers had been used for vestibuled stock since 1896 and were standard for all East Coast stock. Non-vestibuled GNR carriages were screw-coupled.

The adoption of all-steel underframes was combined with other contemporary improvements in the design of carriages to produce a considerably safer vehicle. That became clear in the behaviour of some modern ECJS vehicles in an accident which occurred soon after Grouping. Inquiring into the collision at Retford on 13th February, 1923, in which an up sleeping-car train ploughed into an up goods, the Inspecting Officer of the Board of Trade, Col. J.W. Pringle, made the following observations regarding the leading three post-1905 ECJS vehicles of the express: brake composite No. 347 which took the force of the impact; third No. 31 and twin-sleeping car Nos. 181/181A.

> But there can be no doubt that in three particular directions the construction of the passenger stock on the express train helped to resist any tendency, under severe compression, for the coaches to override or run wild - these are the central buffer (buckeye) coupling, the strength of the coupling bars and the powerful springing of the vestibule gangways . . . The vestibule (Pullman type) connection, extending from the floor level to the roof, with springs in compression, itself acts as a buffer and helps to distribute the violent effects of the collision.

One of the few subsequent destructive accidents to involve Gresley or ECJS stock was at Castlecary in December 1937, as mentioned in Chapter 4. Three of the vehicles taking the brunt of the collision between the two trains were ECJS thirds dating from 1906/7. Two of these were carriages built at York with wooden headstocks and, interestingly enough, although telescoping did not really occur in the accepted sense with any but three vehicles involved in this accident, two of these were the old East Coast thirds with composite underframes.

The 'bowstring' type of underframe used on the King's Saloon was built at York to a NER design and also chosen at the time for various dining cars and sleeping cars for NER and ECJS fleets. Later these underframes were replaced on the ECJS sleeping cars.

Works' plates were fitted to underframes of GNR and ECJS vehicles. Doncaster used a particularly ornate pattern, also applied to the carriages the works built for the Cheshire Lines Committee.

For GNR articulated stock, the underframes were not substantially modified although the adjoining headstocks were stiffened by channel sections. To these, centre castings and brackets were fixed which served as topside friction blocks for the bogies.

Bogies

From 1896, a conventional cast-steel framed four-wheel bogie was employed for the majority of GNR carriages. The six-wheel type on dining cars was of 11 ft 9 in wheelbase; some of these later had the centre wheelset removed and became single-bolster four-wheel bogies. In 1914, a heavy duty version of the 8 ft bogie was produced. This had 9½ by 4⅜ in. journals and was employed for the articulation bogies of twins, triplets, quads and quintuplets converted from Howlden non-bogie stock, as well as for suburban articulated carriages and for re-bogied luggage and milk vans whose payload was accordingly increased. For the first batches of GNR 61 ft 6 in. stock - mostly firsts or composites - a 10 ft wheelbase bogie with outside solebars was used. In due course, the majority of post-1905 GNR and ECJS elliptical-roofed carriages had their 8 ft bogies replaced by the compound-bolster 8 ft 6 in. wheelbase type.

This compound-bolster bogie of 8 ft 6 in. wheelbase was developed by Gresley during 1908, in conjunction with Spencer, Moulton & Co and working from their prototypes; the principle of a compound bolster was covered by a patent (No. 26060) in Alexander Spencer's name, this having been accepted by the Patent Office in 1907. A number of GCR carriages were also mounted on bogies to this manufacturer's design. In place of one bolster and one swing-beam, the Gresley/Spencer, Moulton development had a compound, duplex bolster. With this, the main bolster carrying the vehicle was not supported on the bogie frame but on a second compound bolster located on either side of the first and similarly free-swinging. A third bolster carrying the bogie pivot had swing beams suspended from the bogie frame. The outside solebars of these bogies made them instantly distinguishable but was neither helpful for inspection nor maintenance. A pressed-steel main frame was used. A simplified version of the compound bolster arrangement was patented in 1915 by Alex Spencer of Spencer, Moulton.

These bogies were of two main types. The 'light' type, with 8 in. by 4 in. journals, appeared first about 1910 but did not become standard until 1911/2. It was designed to carry a maximum of 12 - 12½ tons on the bogie pivot. The 'heavy' type was designed for vehicles with a tare weight exceeding 35 tons, the maximum load that could be carried on the pivot being 18 tons. This had 10 in. by 5 in. journals, first appeared in 1914 and was used for articulated stock. Both heavy and light types were adopted as standard by the LNER.

GNR bogie types 1914 - 21

Wheelbase	*Journals*	*Doncaster DO drawing No.*	
8 ft 6 in.	8 in x 4 in.	1367N	Light-type, drawing dated 13th August 1914. To carry 12 - 12½ tons max load.
10 ft	9½ in. x 4⅜ in.	2108N	Outside solebars, drawing dated 18th August, 1914.
8 ft	9½ in. x 4⅜ in.	1776N	Heavy-type, drawing dated 3rd October, 1914.
11 ft 9 in.	8 in. x 4 in. or 9½ in. x 4⅜ in.	3262N	Six wheels. Drawing dated 27th August, 1920.
11 ft 9 in.	9½ in. x 4⅜ in.	3263N	Six-wheeled bogie converted to four wheels. Drawing dated 27th August, 1920.
8 ft 6 in.	10 in. x 5 in.	3378N	Compound-bolster type. Heavy-type bogie. Drawing dated 13th July, 1921.

Braking

The GNR used the vacuum brake while the NER and NBR were Westinghouse (air) brake lines. A number of GNR vehicles were dual-fitted for through working. In pre-Grouping days there were isolated instances of NER locomotives working to London on specials of air-braked stock of their own company.

East Coast Joint Stock was dual-fitted but, in 1911, the East Coast authorities decided to adopt the vacuum brake as standard. By May 1911, the Boards of the GNR and NER had agreed to the decision and were prepared to institute vacuum-only working almost at once, but the NBR was more cautious. Before long, that company confirmed that the necessary vehicles in its own fleet had been fitted with vacuum braking and, as from 1st November, 1912, all East Coast trains formed of ECJS vehicles ran with vacuum braking. Naturally, some ECJS vehicles would be required to run in air-braked trains beyond the East Coast main line and so, in December 1912, it was decided that 82 ECJS vehicles, including sleeping cars and the King's and Queen's saloons, would remain dual-fitted. This was to allow them to work over the GNoS and the Caledonian and on local NER/NBR services. Some vehicles in the ECJS fleet retained dual vacuum/air fittings until the early 1930s.

Body construction

A standard Gresley pre-1914 elliptical roofed carriage had a body with the framing constructed of teak and pine sections and varnished and polished teak body panelling. As described in Chapter 2, there were some differences as between Doncaster and York practices, as summarised below:

Items	*GNR Doncaster c. 1910*	*York for ECJS c. 1907*	*NER York c. 1910*	*ECJS standard as agreed by GNR and NER 1911*
Crossbars	Teak	(Teak	Oak	Oak
Body pillars	Teak	(and	Oak	Oak with teak waist rails
Cant-rails	Pitch-pine	(oak	Teak	Pitch-pine
Roof-sticks	Iron channels	(Ash (+ steel angles	Steel angles	Iron channels
Roof boards	Pine	Pine	Pine	Pine

The GNR had the most liberal loading gauge of the Eastern group of companies and yet the majority of its vehicles were built to a width of 8 ft 6 in. over the panels, as were those for the ECJS. But a number of special vehicles including the dining cars were of 9 ft width and the Leeds quintuplet set of 1921 was built to the full extent of the GNR's loading gauge. Bogie vestibuled brakes for both GNR and ECJS service were of 8 ft width while non-vestibuled brakes were to a 8 ft 3 in. dimension.

The overall length over the end panels was not a rigidly-standardised dimension. Much of the GNR and ECJS general service stock was 58 ft 6 in. long, but some GNR excursion stock carriages were only 52 ft 6 in. in length and the earliest GN/NE Joint stock was only 53 ft 6 in. long. The familiar 61 ft 6 in. length vehicle on a 60 ft underframe was restricted chiefly to those GNR brake composites, composites and firsts built after 1910 and mounted on compound-bolster bogies, as well as a few ECJS carriages. Non-vestibuled GNR semi-fast stock was 58 ft 1½ in. over end panels while the stock built at Doncaster for the Cheshire Lines Committee was only 51 ft 1½ in. over the ends. From 1911, plates giving the vehicle's tare weight began to appear on the body ends rather than on the solebars of ECJS vehicles.

Differences in the roof-end outline between York and Doncaster-built ECJS carriages were attributable to constructional features. With the Doncaster roof the curve was formed by a twist on end roof boarding near the eaves while on the York vehicles the curve began from the arch rail at the end of the last compartments. There was also a difference in curve area and height. In each case, the shape of the roof was a true semi-ellipse with the axis - at the level of the bottom of the cant-rail - 2 ft 5½ in. below the highest point of the roof curve. In the York product this last dimension was 3 ft 5½ in.

Plate 1: Epitomising the pre-Grouping Great Northern scene, 'C1' Atlantic No. 1442 passes Greenwood box, north of New Barnet, with the down 5.45 pm Leeds/Bradford express, *c*. 1919. This was the company's 'Royal' engine and the GNR crest was displayed on the rear splashers.
Rail Archive Stephenson

Plate 2: GNR composite dining car No. 3040 (Dia. 60, built Doncaster, 1906). This was one of the vehicles comprising the Sheffield Stock, the lightweight nature of the trains on this service necessitating restricted dining accommodation. The destination board reads 'London (Kings +) Sheffield Manchester Central'. This shows well the distinctive style of lettering and numerals introduced from this time. Photograph dated July 1906. *National Railway Museum*

Plate 3: Ex-Great Central Railway 'B4' 4-6-0 No. 6103 nearing New Southgate with an up excursion from Leeds, *c*. 1928-30. Such traffic was extensive: midweek throughout the year there were regular trains from the West Riding, returning from Kings Cross at midnight. No. 6103's train comprises a fair mixture of GNR clerestory vehicles, but the leading carriage is a Gresley semi-open brake third of Diagrams 284 or 285. *Rail Archive Stephenson*

Plate 4: The driver of 'C1' Atlantic No. 4401 checks slipping as the 1.40 pm to Leeds and Harrogate departs from Kings Cross in February 1925. The Harrogate portion ran via Knottingley and Church Fenton. Leading the formation is an articulated twin composite of Dia. 218CC. *Rail Archive Stephenson*

Plate 5: The move to modern bogie stock for the ECJS came with the dining cars built by contractors and formed into four new trains built in 1893. This is first-class dining car No. 191. A somewhat untidy appearance is presented by what seem to be blank telegraph forms placed below the luggage racks. East Coast antimacassars would be complemented by silver plate and glassware with East Coast or ECJS designations. These vehicles were regarded by the East Coast managers as 'out of date' by 1909 and were distributed to the constituent companies the next year. *National Railway Museum*

Plate 6: GNR Howlden open third No. 2916 built in 1898, and photographed in October 1900 after conversion to a semi-open, having been in traffic for a couple of years. Note the GNR monogram on the four doors: the intervening quarterlights flanking droplights were 'dummy' doors. *National Railway Museum*

Plate 7: The twelve-wheeled clerestory stock was built for the ECJS from 1896 to 60 ft-plus lengths, but 55 ft eight-wheeled vehicles were built at York and Doncaster in the 1898 - 1903 period, such as third No. 13 (York 1898). This was a sister vehicle to the preserved No. 12 and is seen here outshopped as 41810, after transfer to GN Section stock in November 1925. On older vehicles, when the teak panels darkened they were sometimes bleached by the use of oxalic acid, and this may have been the case with this 25-year old vehicle. *National Railway Museum*

Plate 8: The pioneer elliptical-roofed carriage built at Doncaster: No. 2977 (GN Dia. 101, built 1905). The photograph is dated December 1905 and shows this vehicle, with minimal lavatories. No. 2977 displays various Howlden features, such as the roof ventilators, and carries the Howlden era livery with the GNR coat-of-arms (not quite) amidships. This contained the emblems of England and Scotland, and of no less than twelve towns and cities.
National Railway Museum

Plate 9: The distinguished appearance of the interior of GNR first-class dining-car No. 3250 (GN Dia. 75, built 1912). However, the arrangement of oval tables was to prove unpopular, probably with the catering staff, and so the interior was altered. These original furnishings are described in Chapter 5. *National Railway Museum*

Plate 10: The construction of one of the ECJS all-steel kitchen cars (Dia. 80A, 1914) at York Works. The body framing was of rolled angles, channels and T-sections, secured by knees and gusset-plates to the underframe and cant-rails. The steel panelling was secured by countersunk riveting. *National Railway Museum*

Plates 11/12: A comparison of two designs of composites built for the two East Coast 'Flying Scotsman' sets of 1914 reveals some of the differences in their practices, despite the decision to standardise: (*above*) is the Doncaster-built locker composite No. 77 (EC Dia. 2B, and much later LNER 42515) and (*below*), the York-built composite No. 78 (EC Dia. 3A, and much later LNER 7819). Note the glass-louvred ventilators to the corridor windows of No. 78 and 8 ft wheelbase pressed-steel bogies, changed in 1925 to those of compound-bolster design, whereas No. 77 has the 10 ft wheelbase outside solebar type favoured by Doncaster at the time. There are also differences in the underframe trussing. Whereas No. 77 has a full-point after the number and 'East Coast', No. 78 is lettered 'E. C. J. S.'; the destination board reads LONDON KING'S + & EDINBURGH. In fact, Nos. 78/9 worked to/from Glasgow. Photograph of No. 78 dated May 1914. *National Railway Museum*

Plate 13: GNR 1904-built third brake No. 1267 (Dia. 253, then 254) was withdrawn in 1940 but appropriated for service use and is seen here as mobile workshop DE 960915 at Stratford, in August 1957. This is one of the twelve-wheelers modernised by the GNR after World War II, with improved interior, reconditioned underframe and with the six-wheel bogies converted to four wheels, as per drawing 3263N. *R.M. Casserley*

Plate 14: ECJS 58 ft 6 in. third No. 24 (EC Dia. 34, built York 1906, and much later LNER No. 31049). Photograph dated November 1906. This attractive view shows the body end windows, as well as the grained and varnished wooden headstock and steel solebars. Dia. 34 is illustrated both by the usual ECJS Diagram Book drawing and by the set of drawings accompanying an article appearing in the *Railway Engineer* of December 1907. *National Railway Museum*

Plate 15: To commemorate the centenary of King's Cross station in October 1952, ECJS third No. 12 (EC Dia. 14, built York, 1898 and LNER No. 41805 from 1925) was restored to very nearly its original exterior condition and fortunately has survived for posterity. This photograph is of interest for showing detail of the lining-out and transfers. No. 12 was not restored again until 1985 when its total refurbishment for public display cost some £100,000. Until the turn of the century, the rounds of the roofs of ECJS vehicles were grained so that the whole side-view of the carriage appeared to be in teak finish.. *C.R.L. Coles*

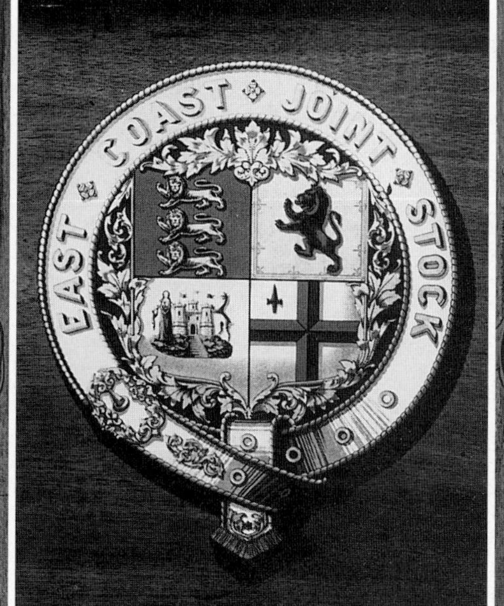

Plates 16/18: The 'crowning glories' of the external finish of ECJS carriages - the coats of arms, rightly described by George Dow as constituting 'an heraldic extravaganza': (a) Viewed broadside, at the left end of the carriage body was a version of the arms of England, the emblem transfer measuring $21\frac{3}{4}$ in. wide by 26 in. high. (b) At the right-hand end was a version of the Scottish coat of arms, the emblem transfer measuring $22\frac{1}{4}$ in. wide by $26\frac{1}{4}$ in. high. The transfers were chiefly tinted gilt, red, buff and pale greyish-green.

Both George Dow Collection

Plate 17: The circlet carried on the lower side body panels of ECJS vehicles. Most of the non-passenger carrying stock did not carry the large coats-of-arms. The shield features the quartered coats-of-arms of England, Scotland, Edinburgh and London. This was the transfer on the side of ECJS No. 12, as restored in 1952.

C.R.L. Coles

Plates 19/20: The finish of, and livery carried by two ECJS carriages: (*Above*) Third No. 73 (EC Dia. 22, built Doncaster, 1906, and much later LNER No. 31081); (*Below*) Third-class dining saloon No. 192 (EC Dia. 29A and much later LNER No. 3925), from one of the 1914 'Flying Scotsman' sets. Note the appearance of the running number on each door, also the spacing-out of the lettering and coats-of-arms. Compound-bolster bogies under No. 192.

National Railway Museum

Plates 21/22: A comparison of the lettering of GNR carriages before, and after Gresley. (*above*) Howlden non-vestibuled brake third No. 2589, built Doncaster, 1897. Modest serifed lettering and numerals (appearing once each side) and GNR without full-points, with GNR monogram on the doors. (*below*) Semi-open third No. 51 (Dia. 219, built 1908). The Gresley era brought the use of prominent serifed and extended lettering and numerals. Running number appears twice each side, and with full-point. G. N. R. repeated each side. Photograph dated November 1908.

National Railway Museum

Plate 23/24: Detail shots of ECJS vehicles: (*above*) Brake third No. 391 (EC Dia. 49, built Doncaster, 1908), and of interest for showing an ECJS vehicle in 'work-worn' livery after Grouping. Full-point after '391'; (*below*) Open third No. 68J (EC Dia. 15, built York, 1902) is typical of the clipper-built ECJS vehicles and is seen here in 1925 when it had been fairly recently varnished and lettered LNER, and 68J. The engine is ex-North British 'D32' 4-4-0 No. 9886, at Craigentinny, and presumably it is going to work the 'Fife Coast Express' which will include 68J. Control instructions were that: 'East Coast vehicles are provided for working on the main line between London, York, Newcastle, Edinburgh and beyond. They must NOT be used on other sections of the line except on direct instructions from the District Superintendent.'

Rail Archive Stephenson

Plate 25: The interior of GNR open third No. 1710 (Dia. 248A, built 1911). These had gas lighting. Although the interior is neat, there are a surprising number (ten) of framed photographs of scenic spots in view; fiddly panelling and mouldings, and framed advertising panels for GNR hotels. There were sliding ventilators to the windows, but half-drop windows were fitted to most of the Dia. 248A carriages during 1915-7. *National Railway Museum*

Plate 26: Compartment partition of GNR third No. 4745 (Dia. 248D, built 1913), as seen in 1956. There is passenger control of the steam heating: On - Off - Medium. The upholstery is the LNER 'rabbit's ear' plush, in bluish and brown tones. *R.M. Casserley*

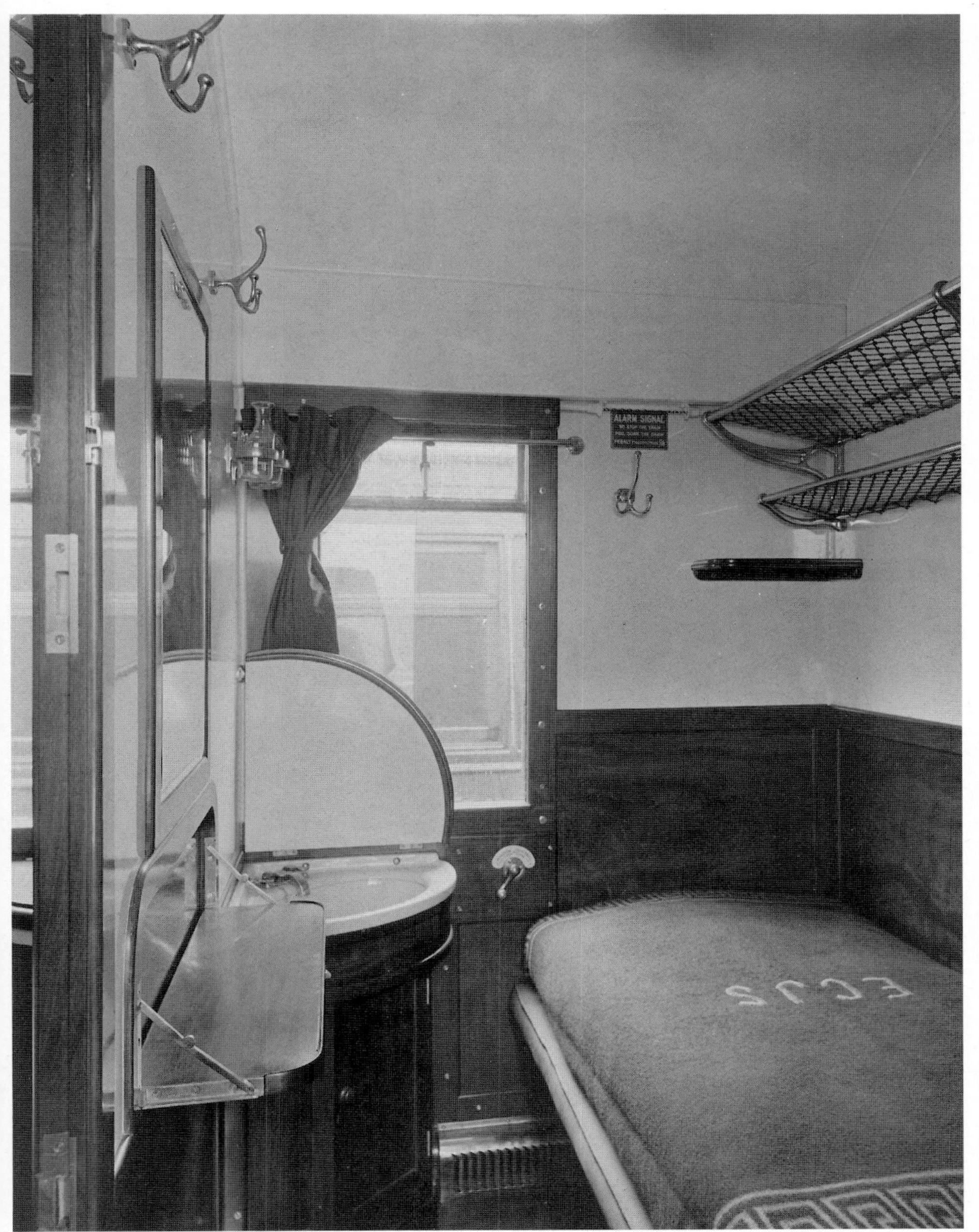

Plate 27: The interior of a sleeping berth of twin articulated cars Nos. 181/181A (EC Dia. 68, built Doncaster, 1922). Note that this berth and the adjoining one could be opened up to create a double-room. This shows the simplicity of the finish - white enamel and polished woodwork, also the winding handle for the window - see Chapter 4. *Author's Collection*

Plate 28: Semi-open first No. 121, in original condition (EC Dia. 57, built York, 1905, much later was LNER No. 4150). The two vehicles on this Diagram later became full-firsts.

National Railway Museum

Plate 29: ECJS No. 92, rebuilt as a full-first, and photographed in its twilight as 4149, at Skegness in April 1954, by which time it seems to have been in departmental use although in LNER varnished teak, or teak paint livery. Withdrawn in May 1951. *R.M. Casserley*

Plate 30: Compartment side of 53 ft 6 in. third No 33, in original condition (EC Dia. 17, built Doncaster, 1906, much later was LNER No. 52033). Note that one lavatory is located between the fifth and sixth compartments. Photograph dated July 1906. *National Railway Museum*

Plate 31: Corridor side of 53 ft 6 in. locker third No. 35, in original condition (EC Dia. 18, built Doncaster, 1906, much later was LNER No. 61798). Photograph dated July 1906. The locker compartment is at the right-hand end and was retained after transfer to the GE Section. All vehicles to Diagrams 17/18 had lost their 8 ft wheelbase bogies for the compound-bolster type by the late 1920s. *National Railway Museum*

Plate 32: Corridor side of 58 ft 6 in. third No. 29, in original condition (EC Dia. 16, built York, 1906, much later was LNER No. 22142). Note that one lavatory is located between the fifth and sixth compartments. *National Railway Museum*

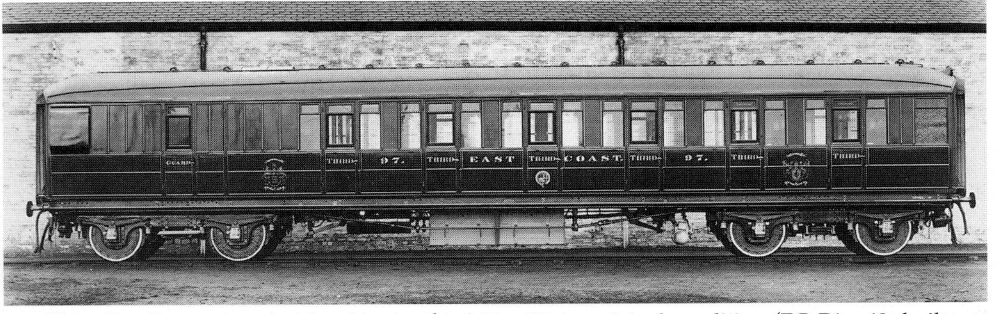

Plate 33: Compartment side of brake third No. 97, in original condition (EC Dia. 49, built Doncaster, 1908, much later was LNER No. 52092). This vehicle was later rebuilt with less passenger seating for the 1914 'Flying Scotsman' sets. The lighting of this March 1909 photograph clearly shows up the Mansell wheels. *National Railway Museum*

Plate 34: Corridor side of brake third No. 388 (EC Dia. 49A, built Doncaster, 1908, much later was LNER No. 62650). This shows its appearance as converted to three compartments in 1914; photograph from the June of that year, one month before the 'Flying Scotsman' sets entered traffic. No. 62650 went to the GE Section in 1934, as a result of a complicated set of moves arising from the disbandment of the Midland & North British Joint Stock. *National Railway Museum*

Plate 35: Compartment side of brake third No. 394, as SC 3937 E (EC Dia. 49, built Doncaster, 1908). By the date of this photograph, July 1957, the vehicle was running on compound-bolster bogies and painted in BR carmine and cream livery. *R.M. Casserley*

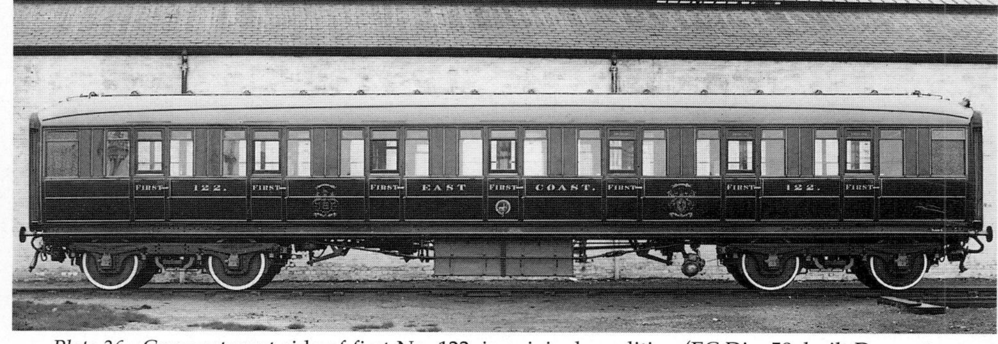

Plate 36: Compartment side of first No. 122, in original condition (EC Dia. 58, built Doncaster, 1908, much later was LNER No. 4194). Photograph dated August 1908.

National Railway Museum

Livery and external finish

As a general rule, all GNR and ECJS stock built at Doncaster had varnished and polished teak body panelling which was not painted in any way. From the earliest days of carriage-building at Doncaster this had been adopted as the standard finish and it was then used for ECJS vehicles. The painting and varnishing work on a GNR vestibule composite carriage was as follows *c.* 1911:

Steel underframe:
Clean and paint four coats of 'teak colour'. One coat of varnish applied to exterior. Interior, bogies and brake gear two coats of 'teak colour'.

Body exterior:
One coat of gold size; six coats of preparing varnish; four coats of body varnish. Pick out in size, gild and fine line. Size and varnish top and droplights. GNR stock had the lining out on the mouldings in gold, edged with blue.

Roof:
Four coats of white lead paint. Up to 1911/2 a red oxide paint had been used.

In the 1890s, the mouldings on the exterior of ECJS compartment stock had been picked out in white, then gilded, fine-lined in blue and varnished. The roof was painted white. A painting specification dated 1893 for one of the contractor-built sleeping cars notes that the mouldings were to be picked out in cream, then gilded, fine-lined in red and varnished. But by 1914 or so, practice seems to have changed, the mouldings being painted lemon-chrome, gilded with gold-leaf and fine-lined in vermilion. While the roofs of ECJS carriages built at or maintained by York Works before World War I tended to be painted slate-grey, those carriages which were the responsibility of Doncaster had their roofs painted white.

The crowning glories of ECJS carriages from the mid-1890s were the handsome coats-of-arms and circlets. The coats-of-arms were in two versions, surrounded with much mantling. The English device included a shield with three lions passant guardant, below which was the motto, *Honi Soit Qui Mal Y Pense*, and above the mantling the motto, *Dieu et Mon Droit*. The Scottish device featured the lion rampant on the shield and the two mottoes from the Royal Arms of Scotland, *In defense* above (rather than the correct *In defens*), and *Nemo me impune lacessit* below. Whether the East Coast companies had the right to display components of the Scottish royal coats-of-arms is another matter!

The circlet, lettered 'East Coast Joint Stock', enclosed a shield with the quartered devices of England and Scotland and the arms of the cities of Edinburgh and London. The circlet usually appeared once, sometimes twice, on the centre panels of each side of the carriage. The coats-of-arms were displayed at the end of each side of the carriage, the Scottish arms on the left-hand, as seen from the side elevation, the English on the right-hand end. Bogie brake vans - and some other vehicles - were adorned with circlets only. While composite No 180, outshopped by York in September 1921, was photographed by York Works with full coats-of-arms, the works' photograph of twin-sleeping car No 181/181A completed at Doncaster the following year shows it to have the circlets only.

Gold lettering and numbering transfers were used with heavy herringbone-style shading to the left and below in blue and white for GNR stock, red/pink for GN/NE Joint Stock and green for ECJS stock. The lettering style was of serifed characters, elongated after 1906. GNR carriages carried the legend 'Great Northern' or 'G.N.R.' with the running number to the left and right, with full stops after the legends and running numbers. 'First' and 'Third' were shown in full on the body side doors until 1906, thereafter '1st' and '3rd'. Carriage numbers were repeated inside the doors on the garnish rails.

On ECJS carriages from the 1900s, the York-built examples tended to have the designation 'E.C.J.S.' and those from Doncaster, 'EAST COAST.', not forgetting the final full-point! 'DINING SALOON.' and 'SLEEPING CARRIAGE.' appeared as appropriate. The running number usually appeared twice on Doncaster-maintained stock and once each side on the York vehicles. Once again, Doncaster could not resist a final full-point! As always, there were exceptions and at one stage Doncaster had a penchant for putting the running number on all the passenger doors of dining cars: in some cases, it appeared three times each side.

There was no doubt that the varnished teak finish of the ECJS (and GNR carriages) was expensive but it was upheld by the East Coast authorities. At their September 1909 meeting, the East Coast superintendents took what was otherwise a rare opportunity to review the question of the specification for the ECJS vehicles and their minute serves to stand as an authoritative statement on the subject:

> Minute 1289. The question of building East Coast stock at a less cost than in the past was fully considered. Carriage Department representatives said that a small reduction could be achieved by substituting oak for teak and painting vehicles instead of varnishing the exterior of vehicles, and it was agreed that such a radical alteration in a distinctive feature of East Cost stock could not be recommended.

Carriage interiors

Seating layouts

The usual arrangement for GNR and ECJS vestibuled stock was for two-a-side seating in the first-class compartments, and three-a-side in the third-class. A limited number of GNR brake composites and composites, together with the 1921 quintuplet set, were arranged with four-a-side seating in the third-class and three-a-side in the firsts.

Non-vestibuled GNR stock for semi-fast services sat four-a-side in the first-class and five-a-side in the third-class. The twin-arts for suburban service sat five-a-side in the first-class and six-a-side in both second and third-class. The non-vestibuled carriages built for the CLC sat five-a-side, except where there was access to a lavatory.

Lighting and heating

From the turn of the century, Doncaster had adopted Stone's double-battery lighting system as standard for most ECJS and some GNR vehicles. The GNR decided on the use of electric lighting in dining and sleeping cars from 1905, with a gradual extension to other new stock; but there was a reversion to gas-lighting for vestibuled carriages from *c.* 1910 while non-vestibuled stock, including suburban articulated sets, was built with gas-lighting after 1913. The proportions of gas and electrically-lit stock maintained by Doncaster in 1912 were as follows:

Stock	*Electrically-lit*		*Gas-lit*	
	Stone's	*Maxim*	*Incandescent*	*Ordinary*
GNR	158	40	2,264	546
ECJS	82	-	78	41
GN/NE Joint	34	-	2	-

Usual arrangements for electric lights in the compartments were as follows: GNR vestibule stock *c.* 1906 - first-class, four lamps on the compartment partitions and two bulbs in the ceiling; third-class, two ceiling mounted lamps only. From 1911, the ECJS standard was: first-class, four lamps on the partitions and three in the ceiling; third-class, three ceiling lamps.

Until 1906, the GNR heated its trains by means of the steam-storage system. In March 1905 the carriage and wagon superintendent was asked to investigate heating systems. As a result, in January 1906 comparative trials were held between the GNR system and the more effective low-pressure system, as adopted by the NER which used steam from the locomotive. The 1906 Sheffield stock was probably the first to be fitted as new with the low-pressure system which was also adopted for ECJS vehicles. The GNR did not have steam heating for the water supplies in the lavatories, something that gave rise to complaint in later LNER days, by which time it was not thought worth altering ex-GNR vestibuled vehicles. The York-built ECJS vehicles from 1907 had steam heating of water for the lavatory washbasins, with controlling valves by which the cold water from the roof tank was heated by the carriage steam supply before reaching the basin.

Interior decor - GNR and ECJS carriages

Great Northern Railway

Type	*Interior woodwork*		*Upholstery*		*Fittings*
	First-class	*Third-class*	*First-class*	*Third-class*	
Vestibuled stock 1906 - 10	Mahogany, sycamore	Teak	Tapestry, usually green	Crimson and black pile	Steel net brackets
Artic suburban stock	Teak, sycamore	Teak	Patterned blue cloth	As above	Aluminium
	+Mahogany		+Brown and gold		+Brass

Type	*Interior woodwork*		*Upholstery*		*Fittings*
	First-class	*Third-class*	*First-class*	*Third-class*	
Vestibuled stock *c.* 1920	Mahogany / white enamel	Teak	Green tapestry	Red and black rep	

The GNR circlet appeared on GNR leather upholstery, door - straps etc.

Notes: With the woodwork, the second entry refers to the inlay or contrasting finish.
+ Second-class - this had brass fittings.

East Coast Joint Stock

Type	*Interior woodwork*		*Upholstery*		*Fittings*
	First-class	*Third-class*	*First-class*	*Third-class*	
1907	Dark teak	Teak, /light oak	Blue cloth* Green Morocco leather**	Crimson and black pile	First-class - brass Third-class-bronze

Dark-coloured Lincrusta was used for the lower panels in the corridors.

From 1911, dining cars were trimmed in green Blenheim tapestry.

In January 1914, the EC authorities approved both a standard colour scheme and the materials to be used in ECJS carriages, the intention being that these should feature in the new 'Flying Scotsman' sets then being constructed. The new standards were as follows:

Type	*Interior woodwork*		*Upholstery*		*Fittings*
	First-class	*Third-class*	*First-class*	*Third-class*	
1914 Standard	Dark teak /sycamore above waist-rail	Teak, light oak below, sycamore above waist rail	Blue cloth* Green Morocco leather**	As above	First-class - brass Third-class-bronze
			First-class dining car: Green Blenheim tapestry* Green Morocco leather** Crimson pile carpeting		
			Third-class dining car: Crimson and black velvet pile		

Notes: With the woodwork, the second entry refers to the inlay or contrasting finish.
* Non-smoking accommodation. ** Smoking accommodation.

Corridors were finished in dark, polished teak offset by sycamore in the first-class and, in the third-class teak framing, with light oak and sycamore panelling. There were flush-closing armrests in first-class and rugs in the compartments. Hot and cold water was provided in lavatories and passengers had control of steam heating.

In 1913, it was decided by the EC General Managers that the lavatories of ECJS carriages should be 'brought up to date'. The standard lavatory agreed to in November 1913 had a flooring of black and white tiles, walls covered in a patented white finish, and a millboard ceiling. The new lavatories featured in the vehicles built for, or chosen to run in, the 'Flying Scotsman' sets of 1914. Earlier vehicles in general service were brought up to standard.

ECJS carriages had various additional passenger comforts, as compared to the individual companies' stock, such as leather mats covering the footplates over the gangways, and fibre mats flush with the floor in the vestibules of sleeping cars. From 1913, the standard rugs provided in first-class compartments were in wine-red and black colours, with the letters 'ECJS' in old-gold script while sleeping car berths had green and yellow rugs embellished with the ECJS monogram. Spring blinds were fitted to ECJS carriages from 1914. Train attendants on the premier East Coast trains were each custodians of three hassocks which were supplied to passengers on request. Cushions were provided in the first-class, and were introduced with the full firsts built in 1922.

The following drawings were prepared by the *Railway Engineer* and accompanied an article in its December 1907 issue which featured the 25 ECJS third- class carriages to EC Dia. 34, built at York in 1906/7: Nos. 24, 69 - 72, 207, 356 - 374.

End elevation. Note the large end lights.

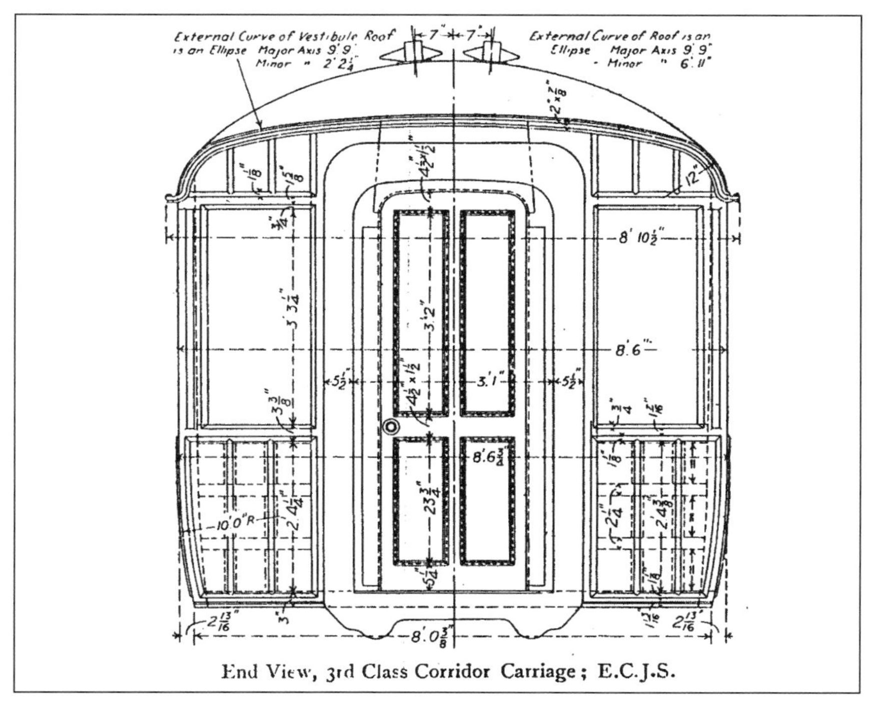

End View, 3rd Class Corridor Carriage; E.C.J.S.

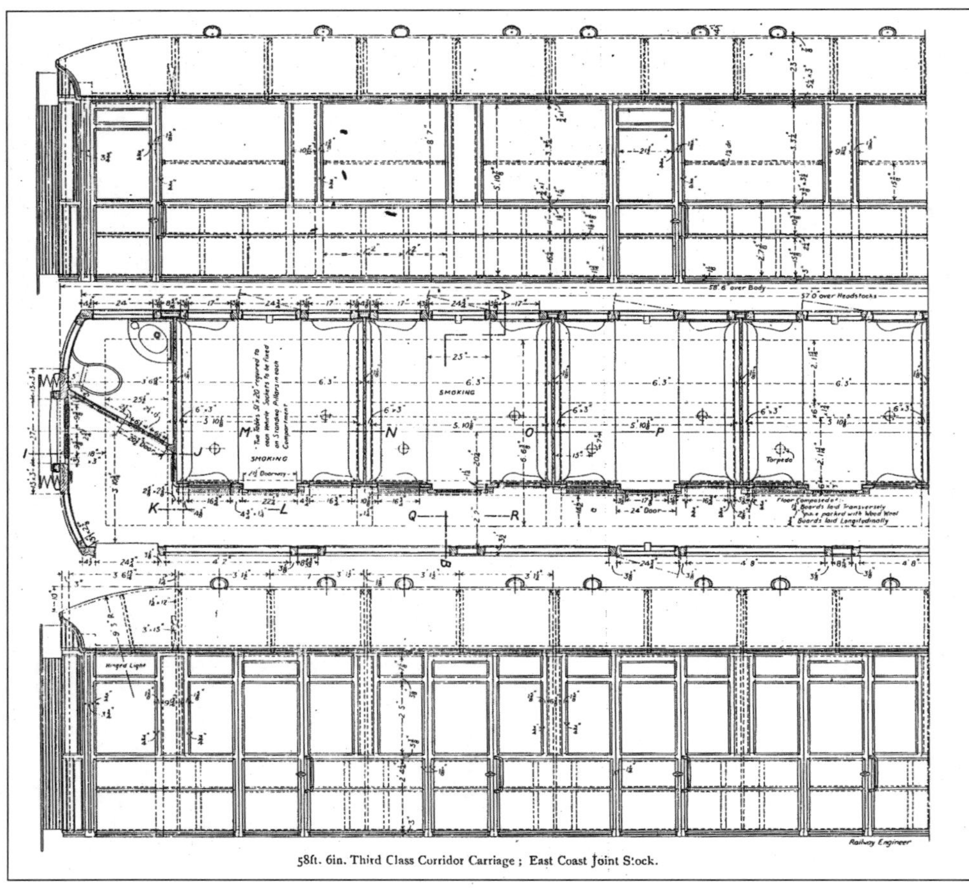

58ft. 6in. Third Class Corridor Carriage ; East Coast Joint Stock.

Side elevation - corridor side - the York design had a door entering into the limited space of the corridor, in front of the lavatory; plan; side elevation - compartment side.

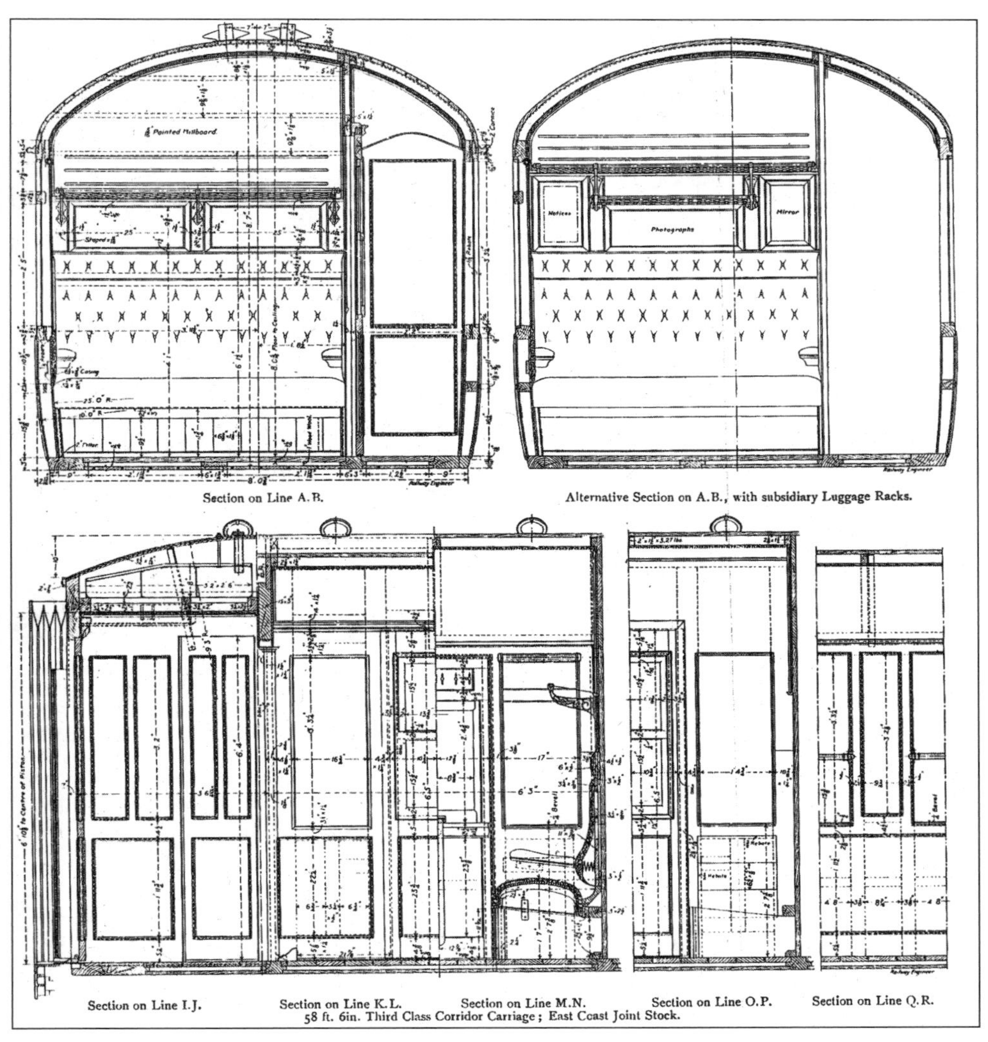

Section on Line A.B. — Alternative Section on A.B., with subsidiary Luggage Racks.

Section on Line I.J. — Section on Line K.L. — Section on Line M.N. — Section on Line O.P. — Section on Line Q.R.

58 ft. 6in. Third Class Corridor Carriage; East Coast Joint Stock.

Cross-section of the compartments, two carriages to Dia. 34 had subsidiary racks for walking-sticks and umbrellas; sections showing panelling on corridor side of the lavatory, each side of the compartment, and panelling to corridor.

Underframe: the headstocks, longitudinals and diagonals in the end bays were of oak.

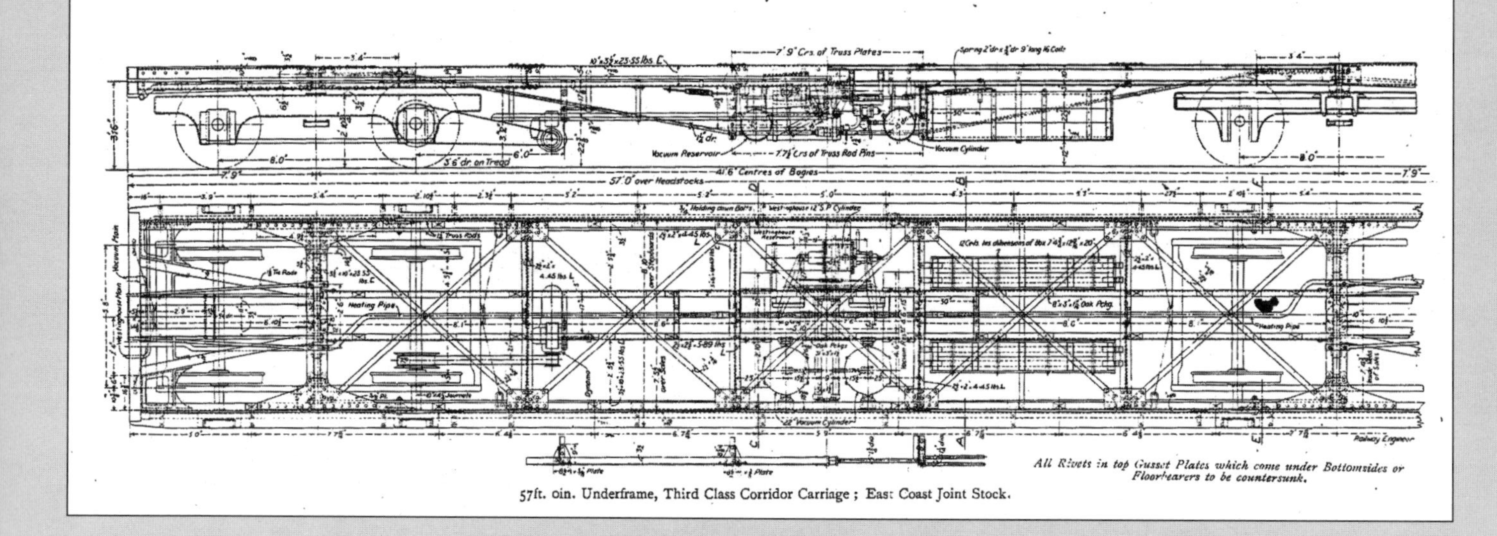

57ft. 0in. Underframe, Third Class Corridor Carriage; East Coast Joint Stock.

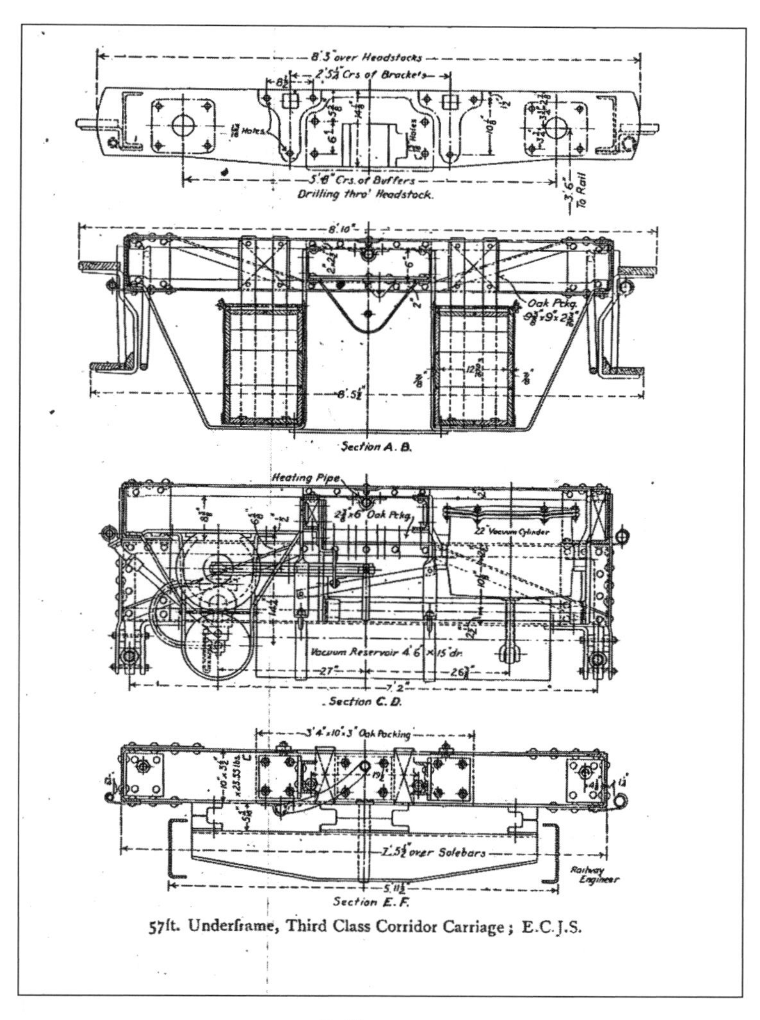

57ft. Underframe, Third Class Corridor Carriage; E.C.J.S.

Buffing gear.

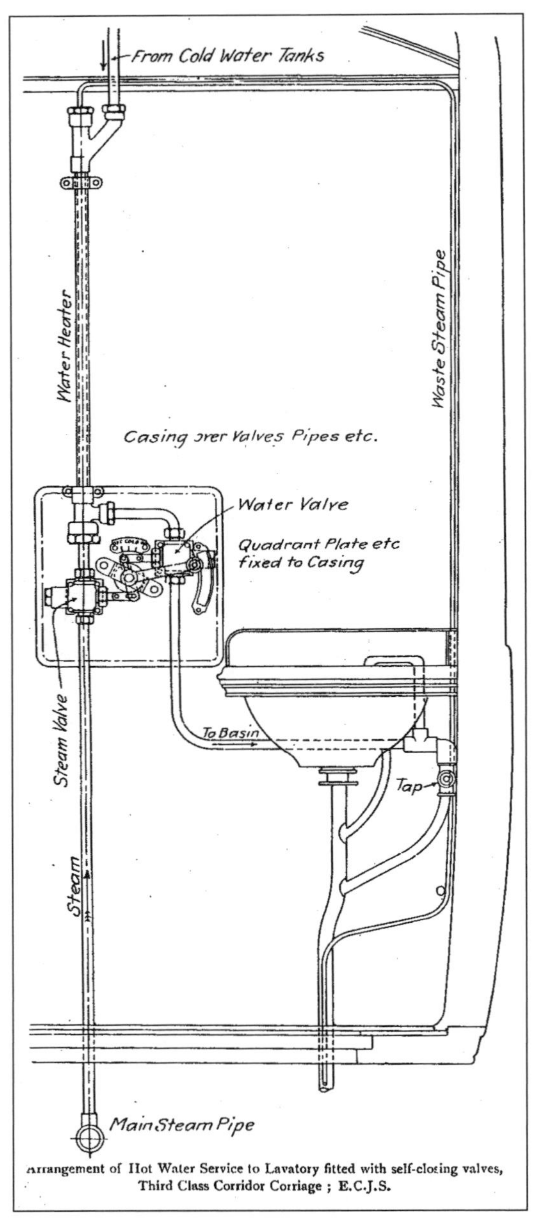

Arrangement of Hot Water Service to Lavatory fitted with self-closing valves, Third Class Corridor Corriage ; E.C.J.S.

Water and steam supplies to the lavatory.

Chapter Four

East Coast Joint Stock and Great Northern/North Eastern Joint Stock

East Coast Joint Stock 1905 - 1923

In Chapter 2, there was mention of the resolution adopted at the meeting in York of East Coast General Managers on 10th November, 1905, namely that the standard pattern for the ECJS in the future was essentially what was to become recognised as the Gresley carriage, with elliptical roof curved downwards at the ends and with curved panels to the bodysides. In some ways, this was rather strange as it would appear that there was no such vehicle in being at the time! What was effectively the prototype was the GNR corridor composite No. 2977, completed at Doncaster a month after the meeting had been held at York. Even more remarkably, the new design was to be applied to all 78 ECJS carriages, the construction of which was confirmed by the East Coast General Managers at another meeting held at York, in December 1905. It can only be seen as a striking vote of confidence in H.N. Gresley, the 29-year old carriage and wagon superintendent of the GNR.

The York-built straight-sided vehicles - 1905

There was another design of elliptical-roofed carriage available to the East Coast managers: the straight-sided, match-boarded NER product and, moreover, these were just being turned out by York at about the time of the November 1905 meeting. There were four 65 ft 6 in. twelve-wheeled composite brakes, closely followed by two 53 ft 6 in semi-open firsts and three 55 ft composite sleeping cars. Their construction was approved in 1904, and their building overlapped the production at Doncaster of the last clerestory-roofed stock for the ECJS. The three sleeping cars displaced to the duplicate list the first ECJS bogie sleeping cars dating from 1894.

Approved	*Quantity*	*Type*	*Builder*	*Built*	*ECJS Nos.*
Mar. 1904	4	Brake composite	YK	Oct. 1905	80/1, 142/3
Mar. 1904	2	Semi-open first	YK	Dec. 1905	92/121
Mar. 1904	3	Composite sleeping car	YK	Dec. 1905	90, 106/87

Writing to Wilson Worsdell, chief mechanical engineer of the North Eastern Railway, on 25th October, 1904, Chairman Sir G.S. Gibb said that York Works should proceed with the construction of the four brake composites so that they would be ready for the following summer's traffic and, to quote, 'They should of course be built with elliptical roofs and matchboard sides, the same as the other stock mentioned in my letter to you'. This letter was dated 20th October, 1904 and referred to the other coaches comprising the order. Of these, Worsdell noted that they were 'to be teak finished and varnished'.

The firsts were intended to be used with an adjoining dining car and, apart

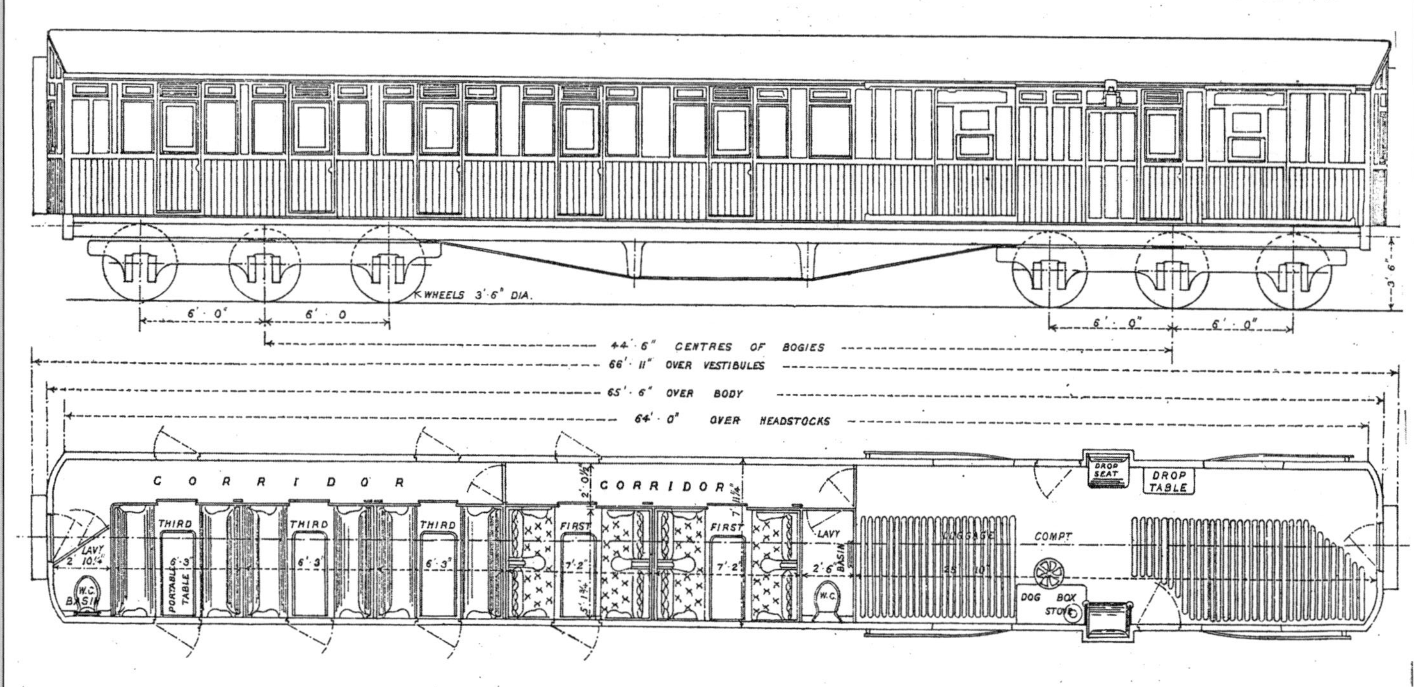

ECJS brake composite on EC Dia. 45, built by York in 1905.

from tables being laid up in the open section, the official diagram noted that the compartments would seat 16 when tables were provided in the compartments. By 1910, the semi-open firsts - and the 1903, York-built clerestories to the same layout - were being reported as generating complaints from passengers who, presumably, resented travelling in the draughty open sections and preferred compartments. It took until May 1913 for the East Coast managers to agree to the conversion of the semi-open firsts which at one stage looked like being downgraded to third-class. At last, Nos. 92/121 were rebuilt as side-corridor firsts at York in 1914.

Whatever their original duties, by 1914 the brake composites and, naturally enough, the contemporary sleeping cars were to be found on the overnight trains. The sleeping composites generally worked as the Glasgow car on the 11.30 pm from Kings Cross, and 9.35 pm from Glasgow. Sleeping car No. 187 was converted to a full (first-class) sleeping car, being chosen in preference to the intended No. 231, and as modified was returned to traffic by July 1921. In 1925, Nos. 190, 1106/87 all received 8 ft 6 in. compound-bolster bogies.

In April 1929, the monthly meeting of the LNER's Superintendents and Passenger Managers reviewed the remaining gas-lit vehicles in East Coast stock and decided that Nos. 192 and 1121 should be transferred to the Areas. This meant that the East Coast fleet only comprised electrically-lit carriages once the two firsts had been sent to the GN section during 1931. The three sleeping cars had been condemned by the end of 1933, No. 190 becoming a Touring Camping Coach for a short while until passing to service use.

In September 1934, the decision was taken to replace the remaining straight-sided carriages in EC stock. The Superintendents' and Passenger Managers' Committee commented: 'There are eight straight-sided vehicles still in East Coast stock. In view of their age and appearance and as they are maintained at York, it is recommended that. . . . all eight vehicles are transferred to the North Eastern Area.' Four of the vehicles referred to were from the former GN/NE Joint fleet, the others being former ECJS brake composites Nos. 180/1 and 1142/3 which went to the North Eastern Area in late 1936, excepting No. 1143 which was condemned in March 1937 while still in EC stock. In the summer timetable of 1935, not long before their transfer was effected, one of the brake composites (Nos. 180 etc.) was diagrammed for the North Berwick portion in each of the two sets used for the 10.35 pm Kings Cross - Edinburgh and its balancing working.

The major renewal programme of 1905

The ECJS renewal programme had been discussed as early as October 1904 and, in its final form comprising the 78 carriages costing £131,400, it was concluded in December 1905. The list was made up as follows:

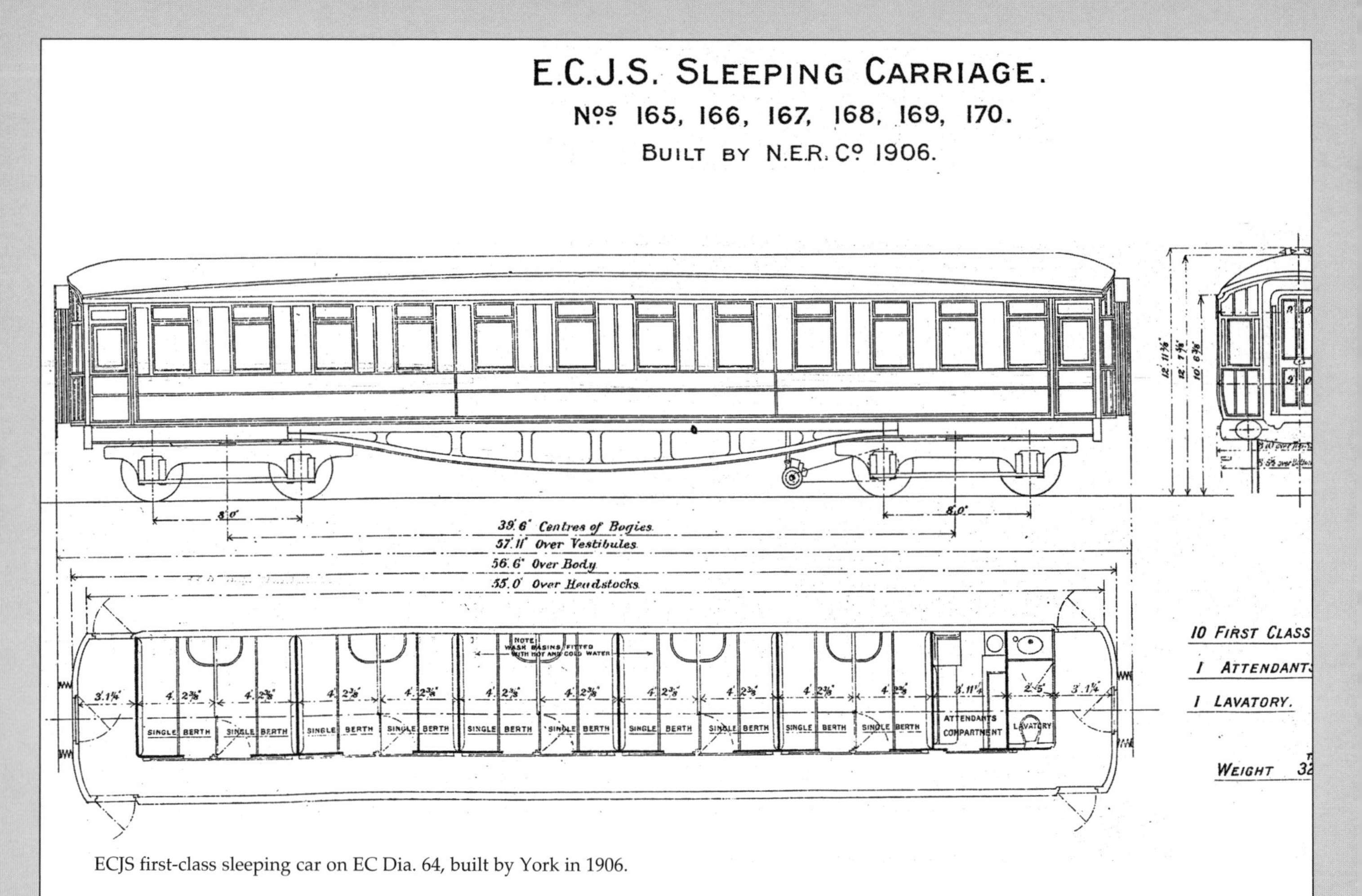

ECJS first-class sleeping car on EC Dia. 64, built by York in 1906.

Approved	*Quantity*	*Type*	*Builder*	*Built*	*ECJS Nos.*
30/5/05	6	First-class sleeping car	YK	late 1906	165 - 70
	10	Corridor third (42 seats)	DR	1906	30 - 33
		Locker third (36 seats)	DR	1906	34 - 37
		Corridor third (42 seats)	YK	late 1906	27/29
	12	Bogie brake van	DR	1906	126 - 8/30-2
			CW	1906	19, 133 - 7
10/11/05	9	Corridor third	DR	}	Not built
			YK	}	
	2	Corridor brake third	DR	1908	97/8
19/12/05	31	Corridor third	DR	1907	73 - 5, 96, 375 - 86
			YK	1906	24, 69 - 72, 207
				1906/7	356 - 74
	8	Corridor brake third	DR	1909	387 - 94

CW - Cowlairs; DR - Doncaster; YK - York

There were differences in construction and outline as between the York and Doncaster-built carriages, for reasons noted earlier in this Chapter, but they were all of the same general appearance, with large corridor-side windows, square quarterlights and panels, compartment- side doors and windows in the body ends. The bodies were to a 8 ft 6 in. width, except for the sleepers - 9 ft - and the full brakes - 8 ft - and the length over the ends varied from 53 ft 6 in. for the earlier thirds to 58 ft 6 in. for the series ordered in December 1905. One of the thirds had a different interior finish, with green figured rep upholstery and the distinction of reproductions of water-colour sketches in place of the framed photographs used in the other carriages in this series.

All these carriages were electrically-lit and initially dual-braked, the air equipment being removed from the those still so fitted by the early 1930s. They ran on 8 ft wheelbase bogies. The first vehicles to appear were the full brakes. No. 126, usually recognised as the first to be built, was outshopped from Doncaster in March 1906.

These carriages remained at work on East Coast trains until at least the late 1920s when transfers to the LNER Areas and sections began. None was left in East Coast stock by the late 1930s when in any case they were becoming fairly elderly.

No less than three of these old ECJS corridor third carriages, by then allocated to the Southern Scottish Area, were involved in the destructive Castlecary accident of 10th December, 1937 when the 4.3 pm Edinburgh - Glasgow collided at speed with the 2 pm Dundee - Glasgow. They were Nos. 72 (as LNER No. 31061), 357 (as LNER No. 31083) and 383 (as LNER No. 31090). Nos. 31083/90 were destroyed but the strength of the buckeye couplers and Pullman gangways were instrumental in preventing worse injury than might have occurred in this awful collision. Another accident victim was locker third No. 35, by then No. 61798, which was badly damaged in the Sleaford derailment of 15th February, 1937.

As built, the sleeping cars were mounted on the bowstring girder underframes used by York, not least for the East Coast royal saloons. This

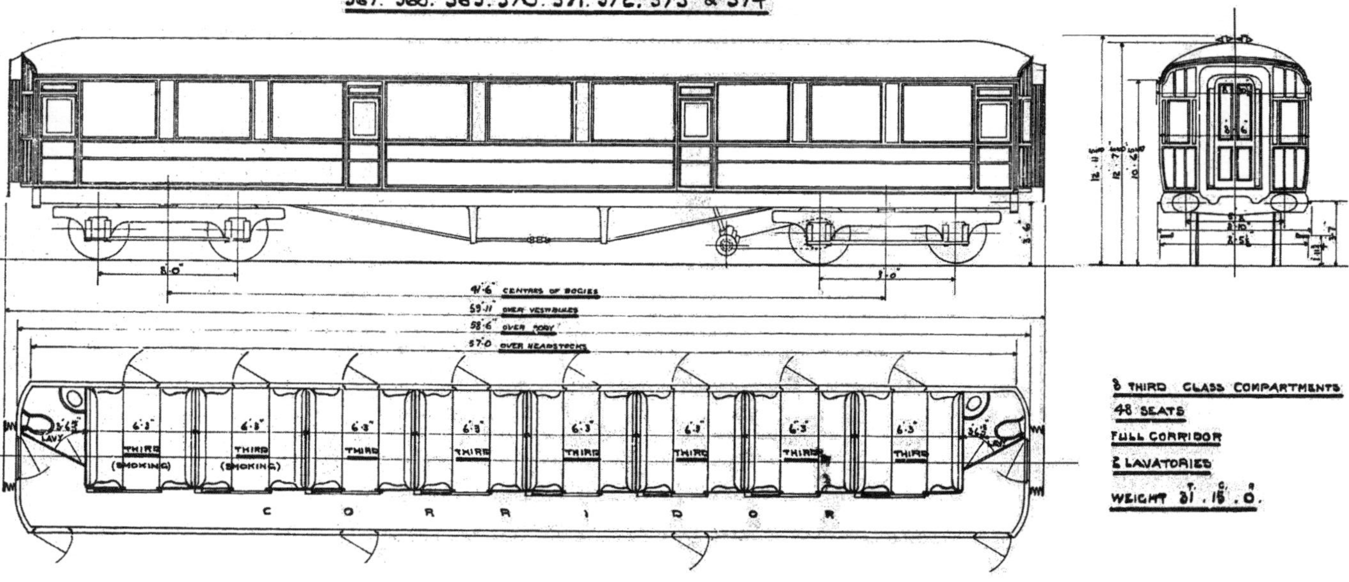

ECJS third on EC Dia. 34, built by York in 1906/7. This is the outline Diagram Book drawing - compare this with the *Railway Engineer* drawings obtained from general arrangement drawings and reproduced in Chapter 3. *National Railway Museum*

design was to Darlington drawing No. 6487 of 1907. For reason unknown, these underframes were replaced in 1924/5, Darlington preparing a new design, Drawing reference No. 11954 of 1923, for a 55 ft underframe of conventional construction. At the same time that the new underframes were fitted, Nos. 165 - 70 received compound-bolster 8 ft 6 in. bogies and were converted from dual. braking to vacuum only. Yet the batch was withdrawn as soon as 1931/2, after the arrival of new LNER first-class cars.

Although intended for the summer Fort William service, before 1914 Nos. 165 - 70 were used for the Aberdeen car working in the 8 pm down and 11.15 pm ex - Edinburgh and for the Dundee car in the 11.30 pm down and 10.50 pm ex - Edinburgh.

Sleeping cars 1907 - 1910

Two sleeping cars were built at York during 1907 in replacement of those of the same numbers, lost in the derailment of the 8.45 pm down sleeping car express at Grantham on 19th September, 1906. One was a full first-class, ten-berth car, No. 120, while No. 231 was a sleeper composite, with six first-class berths and two third-class compartments. Both followed the outline of the 1906 first-class sleeping cars described above, and had the bowstring girder underframes.

No. 120 was fitted with electric fans in 1911 and, in August 1923, its bowstring underframe was replaced by one of the conventional pattern obtained from ECJS van No. 6. This lasted only until September 1924 when it, too, was replaced, by one to Drawing No. 11954; this second change must have had a strange effect on the body! At the same time, No. 120 lost its unpopular folding washbasins for a pedestal type.

Soon after its construction, the composite sleeper No. 231 was fitted with Stone's 'new system of ventilating and heating' which no doubt owed something to the installation in the royal saloons. It was reported to be satisfactory, in March 1909. In 1920, it was intended to convert No. 231 car to a full ten-berth sleeping car but, because of its pressure ventilation equipment, it was passed over in favour of 1905 car, No. 187. No. 231, like the other cars with the bowstring underframes, was mounted on a new 55 ft frame, and given compound-bolster bogies in July 1924. At the same time, electric water heating was fitted, to allow patrons to have heated water outside of the steam heating 'season' - and the folding washbasins were replaced. In modified condition, and retaining its pressure ventilation system, No. 231 were effectively a prototype for the new LNER cars of the early 1930s.

Four sleeper composite cars were built at York in 1910 to the same general specification as Nos. 231; these were Nos. 146/8/50/1. Their construction was proposed in September 1909 when it was agreed that they should be similar to No. 231 but not to be fitted with Stone's pressure ventilation; this cost £130 extra per vehicle, or some 6 per cent of the building cost.

Nos. 146/8/50/1 were used in 1914/5 for the seasonal Inverness and Fort William workings. In 1920, the East Coast partners agreed to convert five sleeper composite cars to full (first-class) ten-berth cars and Nos. 146/8/50/1 were altered by July 1921, being reclassified as Dia. 63A. The fifth vehicle was

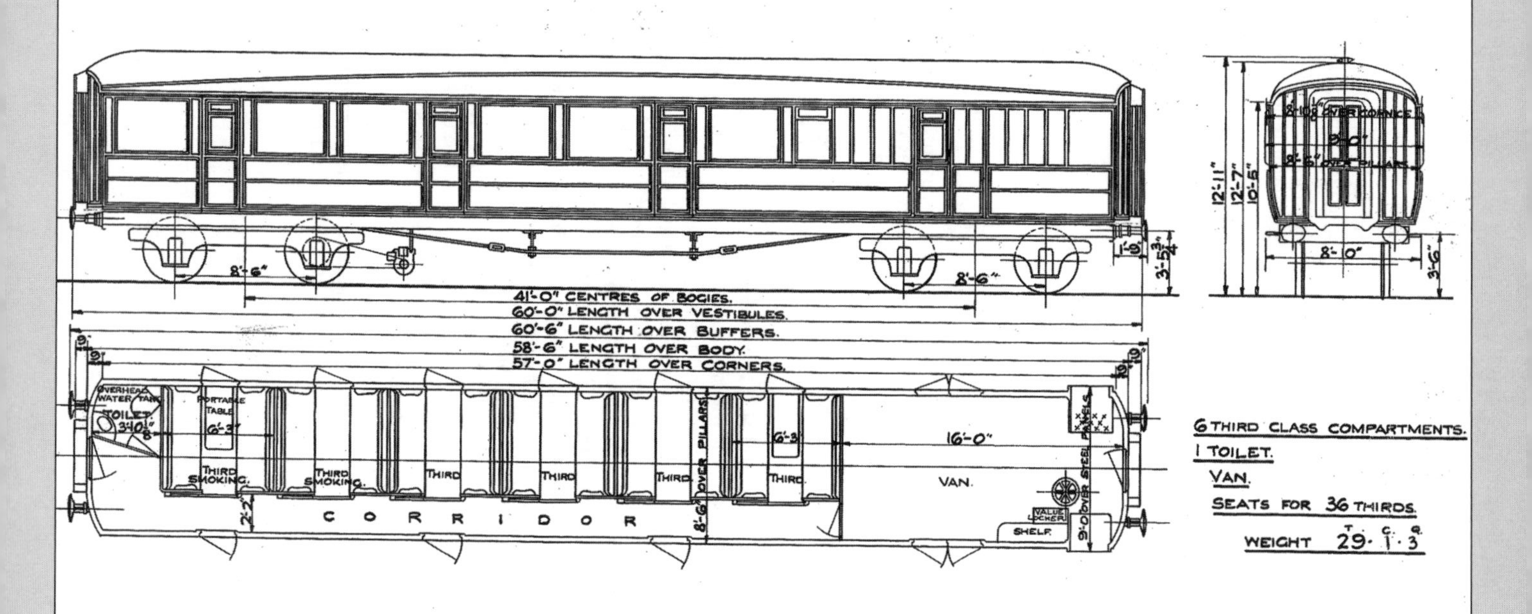

ECJS brake third on EC Dia. 49, built by Doncaster in 1908.

No. 187. Following withdrawal during January 1935 in anticipation of replacement by new cars in the 1935/6 LNER Carriage Building Programme, the underframes of Nos. (1)146/8/51 were used for new bogie brake vans to LNER Dia. 208, this stratagem arising from an accountancy device to save money.

Some of the sleeping cars built from 1906 - 10 were not destined to last their book lives of 28 years, withdrawals beginning in 1931 and being completed by 1937.

Miscellaneous vehicles 1908 - 11

Quantity	*Type*	*Builder*	*Built*	*ECJS Nos.*
2	Corridor first	Doncaster	Aug 1908	122/295
8	Bogie brake van	York	1910	5 - 7
		Doncaster		8 - 10, 26, 129
4	Corridor composite	Doncaster	1911	1 - 4
1	Corridor brake composite	Doncaster	1911	347

In July 1909, the East Coast General Managers reviewed ECJS vehicles considered to be 'out of date', principally 12, six-wheeled composites Nos. 1 - 10 of 1893; on displacement these would be distributed between the constituent companies. In their place was proposed the construction of 'new stock to be built to the latest pattern', comprising eight additional brake vans, 'similar to No. 126' of 1906, and four composites whose construction was deferred until early in 1910. The NBR said that it was not in a position to build any of the new ECJS vehicles which were constructed at Doncaster and York. Later proposals included the sleeper composites mentioned above.

The new stock of 1910/1 comprised standard elliptical-roofed vehicles. Predating the replacements authorised in 1909 were the seven-compartment corridor firsts which by 1914 were used in the afternoon 'Scotsmen'. They were fitted with compound-bolster bogies in 1924/5 and remained in the East Coast fleet until 1935/6. The corridor composites of 1911 were also included from July 1914 in the newly formed 'Flying Scotsman' sets. In 1914/5, there were two of these composites in each of the two sets, working to/from Kings Cross - Edinburgh or Aberdeen. All were fitted with compound-bolster bogies in 1924. In 1935, Nos 11 - 14 (as they had become) were diagrammed to work in the 10.35 pm Kings Cross - Edinburgh and in the 10.45 pm Kings Cross - Newcastle sleeping car trains, and their return workings.

Underframes were exchanged between Van No. 6 and sleeping car No. 120 in August 1923. Van No. 7 was the second vehicle in the formation of the 8 pm Kings Cross - Aberdeen on 14th April, 1914 when this train was involved in the accident at Burntisland. The damage sustained in this collision with a goods train saw the withdrawal of No. 7. Most of this series of vans was transferred to the GE section during 1928, coincident with the allocation of new all-steel bogie brake vans to East Coast stock.

In April 1910, the EC General Managers agreed to build a replacement for the clerestory brake composite No. 347, destroyed by fire in May 1909. The new

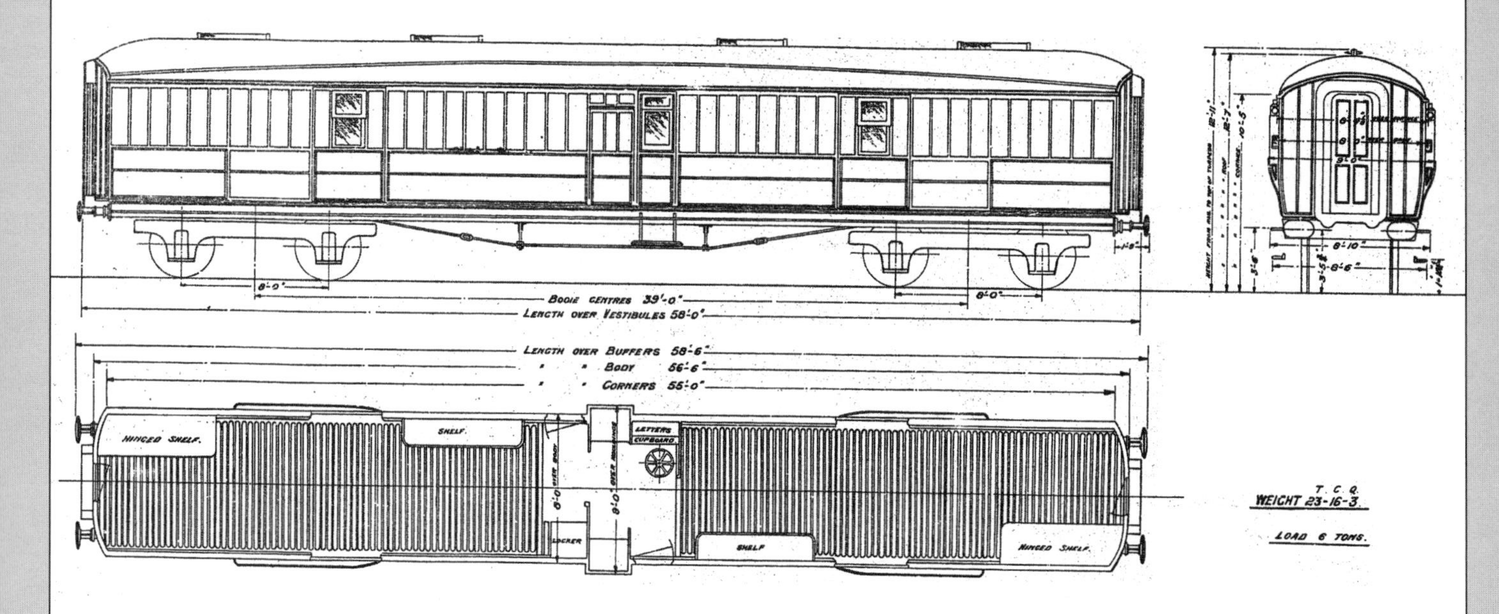

ECJS full-brake on EC Dia. 39A, built by Doncaster in 1910. *National Railway Museum*

No. 347 was also unlucky as it was the leading vehicle in the up Aberdeen sleeping car express involved in the collision at Retford on 13th February, 1923. The carriage was so badly damaged as to be broken up on site.

The 'Flying Scotsman' sets of 1914

As yet, complete sets of elliptical roofed carriages had not been built for use on the 'Flying Scotsman.' In 1910, the East Coast authorities had considered the replacement of the ECJS 1893 contractor-built dining cars and asked that Gresley and Raven should prepare plans for two new sets of carriages for the 'Flying Scotsman'.

Discussions between Gresley and Raven were under way by January 1912, by which time there was agreement on the standard practice to be followed for new ECJS stock whether built at Doncaster or York, to which reference was made in Chapter 2. By April 1912, it was decided that each of the new train sets should include a three-car set of catering vehicles - two dining saloons and a kitchen car - which at that time were indicated as working through to Aberdeen. But it was by no means clear that there would be a uniform set of new carriages and, in April 1913, both men were considering a mixture of clerestory and elliptical-roofed stock for the 'Flying Scotsman' sets. By this time, the traffic superintendents were pointing out that most of the stock in the '10 o'clocks' was 13 - 17 years old and that 'the West Coast is running up to date trains, East Coast trains should be, too . . .'

In the end, it was decided to form two ten-coach sets, only of elliptical-roofed stock, comprising a mixture of new and existing carriages, including 61 ft 6 in. locker composites. These were so called because there was a luggage compartment for passengers' belongings and such vehicles were a feature of East Coast trains. The total seating capacity was for 60 first-class and 222 third-class passengers. The building proposals were agreed by the EC General Managers at their meeting in November 1913 and the construction of 11 new carriages was put in hand, at a cost of £21,350. As part of this programme, two existing brake thirds were to be altered.

The new carriages were as follows:

Type	*Builder*	*ECJS Nos.*	*Details*
Corridor Locker Composite (61 ft 6 in.)	Doncaster	76/7	2½ First compartments, 4 Third compartments + locker
Corridor Composite (58 ft 6 in.)	York	78/9	2½ First compartments, 4½ Third compartments
Restaurant first (58 ft 6 in. by 9 ft)	Doncaster	190/1	Two saloons - seating 12 and 16
Restaurant third (58 ft 6 in. by 9 ft)	Doncaster	192/3	Two saloons - seating 24 and 24
Kitchen car (53 ft 6 in. by 9 ft)	York	211 - 3	all-steel

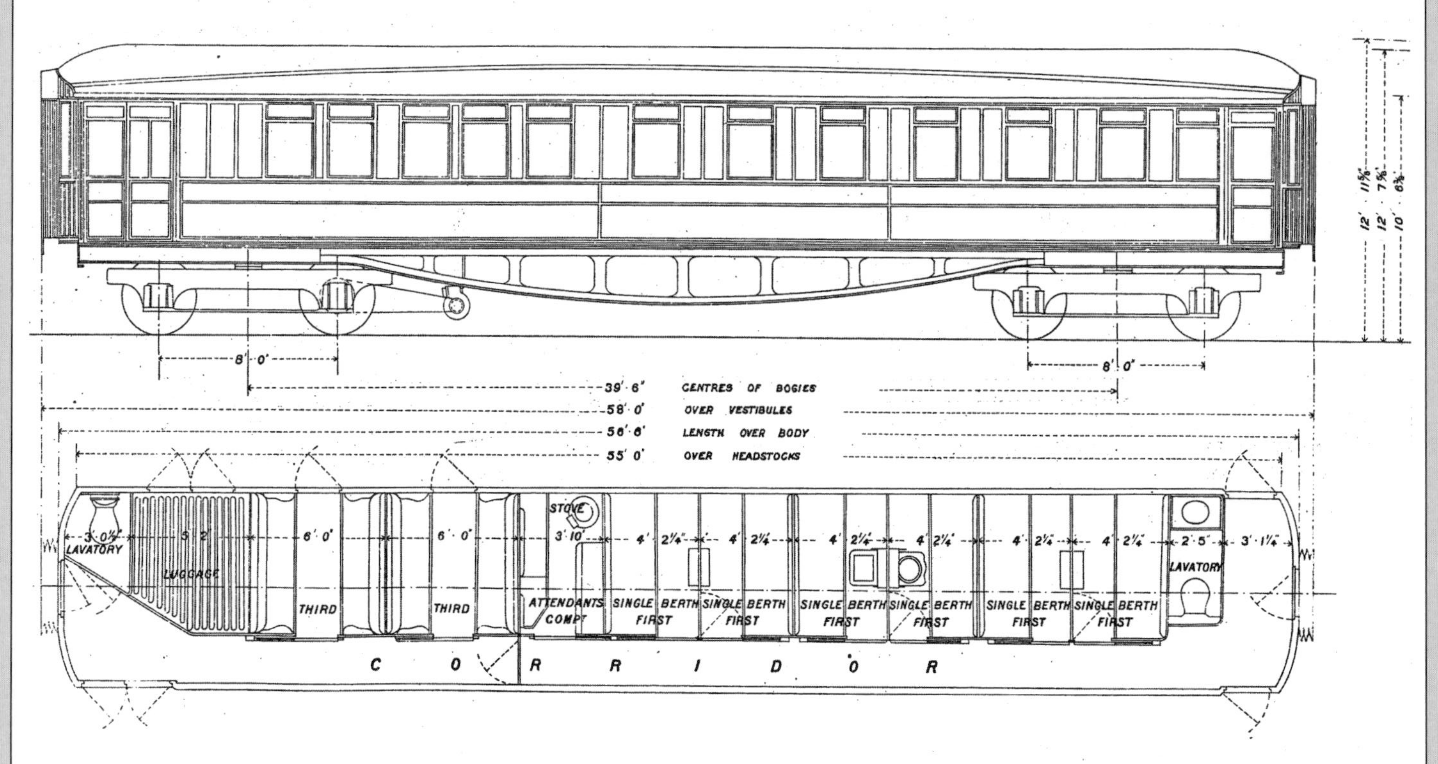

ECJS sleeper composite on EC Dia. 74, built by York in 1907.

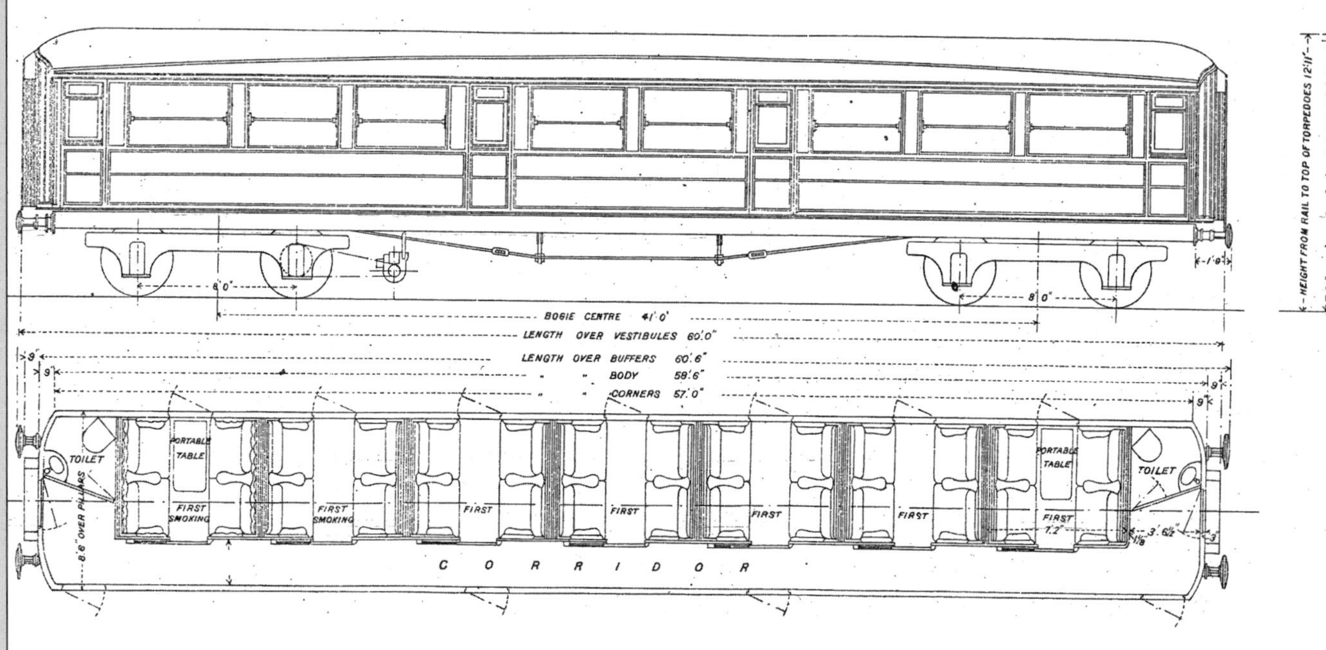

ECJS first on EC Dia. 58, built by Doncaster in 1908.

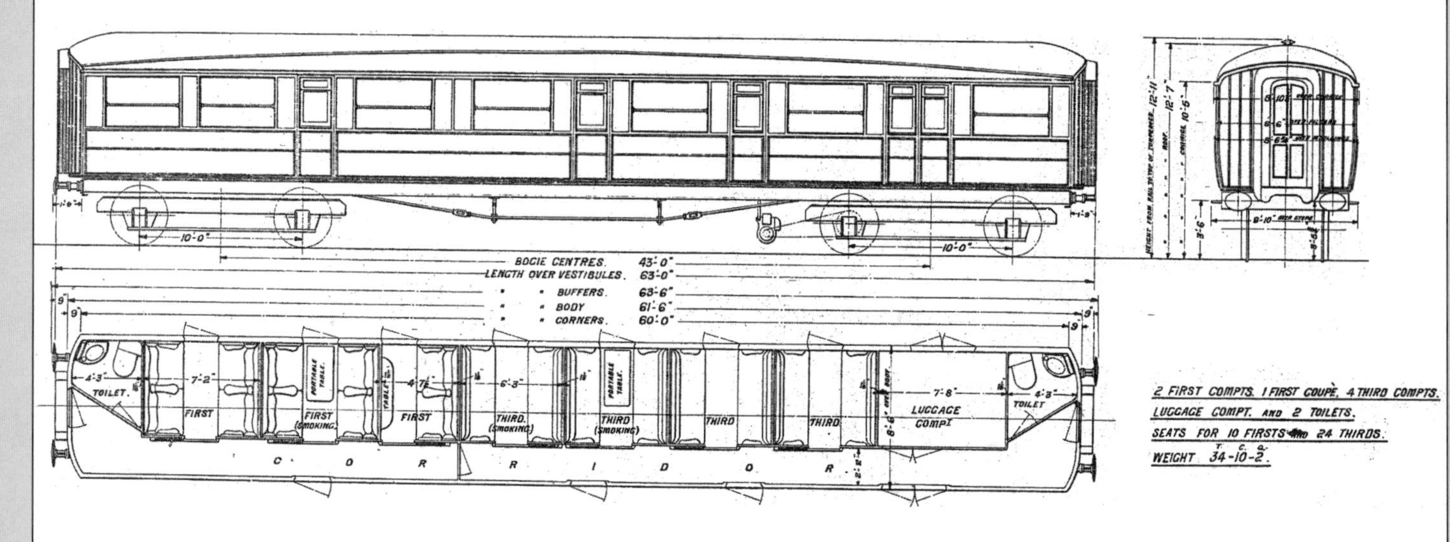

ECJS luggage composite Nos. 76/7 on EC Dia. 2B, built by Doncaster in 1914. The Diagram shows them with their later 1925 numbers as 176/7.
National Railway Museum

The earlier Doncaster-built brake thirds, Nos. 97 and 388, were rebuilt to have a larger van space by the removal of two compartments. The lavatory in each carriage was converted to provide a train attendant's compartment and remained as such until 1928. The train attendant assisted passengers to their seats, as well as plying them with East Coast literature, kept an eye on the cleanliness of the carriage interiors, lighting and heating, replaced light-bulbs and other items as necessary, and reported defects to C&W staffs.

Two of the so-called 'No 1' class of composites, dating from 1911, were included in the new formations, as was a EC Dia. 34 third of 1906/7 in the Aberdeen portion.

The two new types of composites featured glass, louvred ventilators to three of the large corridor windows, the louvred ventilators also appearing in the two types of dining car. While composites Nos. 76/7 had 10 ft wheelbase bogies as built, Nos. 78/9 were fitted with the 8 ft wheelbase version which was exchanged for the compound-bolster type in 1925.

The new and existing stock used to make up the 1914 'Flying Scotsman' featured the standard interior fittings approved by the East Coast General Managers in January 1914 and described in Chapter 3, as well as the new standard lavatories. The dining cars (originally to have been 53 ft 6 in. in length) followed the successful interior schemes introduced with the GN/NE Joint sets and, like them, they were admired by contemporary observers. The firsts had a similar Adam-style of interior decor, but with dark polished teak panelling. The loose chairs upholstered in green tapestry contrasted with the rose-coloured carpet and curtains. The seven electroliers had opal glass bowls. The third-class cars had polished teak panelling with inlaid dado, and iron-framed tip-up seats trimmed in standard red and black pile. This was so that these could be used for ordinary seating when meals were not being served. Net racks were provided.

It seems to have been Raven's influence that prevailed with the choice of vehicles in the sets. Certainly, the separation of the kitchen facilities from the seated accommodation allowed the dining cars to be lighter and eight- rather than twelve-wheeled, as well as providing more space for meal preparation.

The steel kitchen cars were in part a response to public concern at the recent number of train fires. The *Railway Magazine* was to comment: 'steel kitchen cars are quite new to the main lines of railway companies in this country, this being the first instance of their adoption'. Gas cooking was the reason for the all-steel construction. NER official documents commented that 'it is difficult to procure sufficient current for efficient electrical cooking' and they were also gas-lit. The bodies did not follow the lines of the ECJS standard and they were somewhat utilitarian in appearance. The body framing was of steel angles, channels and T - sections, and to this the steel panelling was riveted. The resulting weight of 36 tons was by no means excessive and the cars rode on 8 ft wheelbase bogies. One of the cars was a 'spare'.

The new sets began work on the 'Flying Scotsman' on 1st July, 1914. The catering vehicles remained as three-car units in East Coast Joint Sets Nos. 3/4 sets, as used for the relief 'Flying Scotsman', until the delivery of the second series of LNER triplet restaurant cars in July 1928. With the LNER's 1929/30

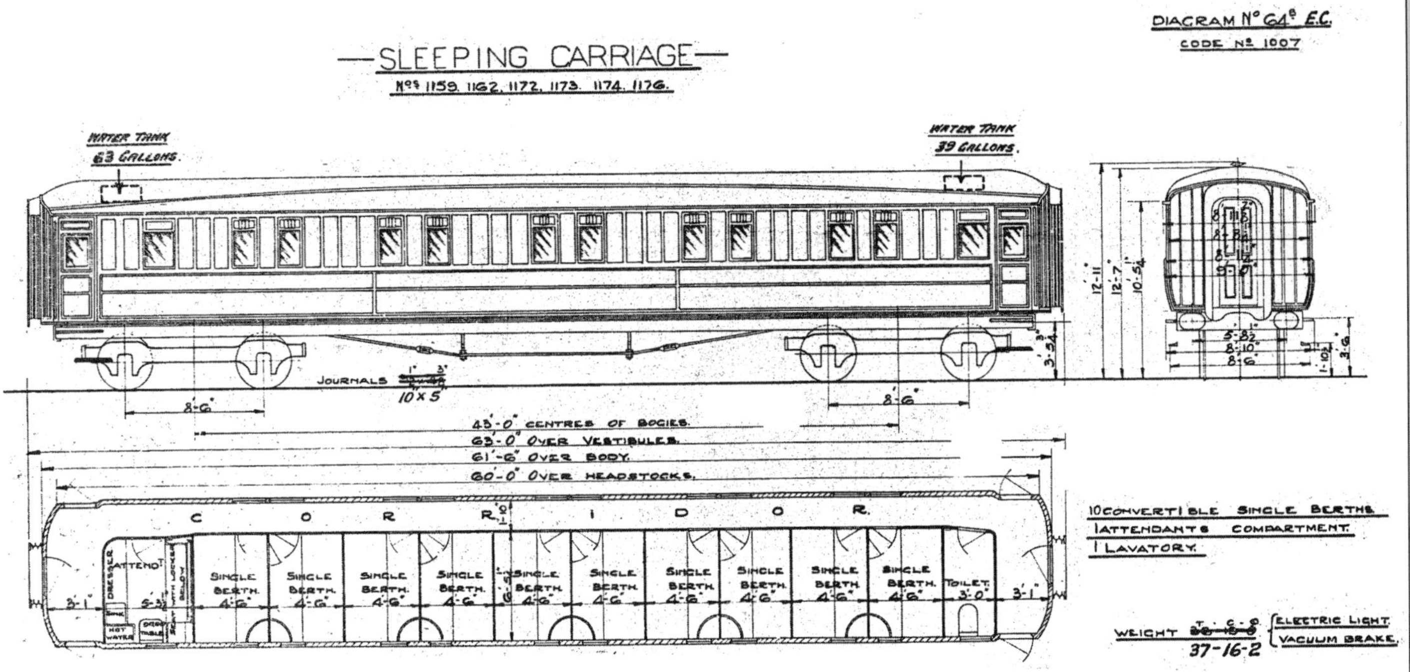

DIAGRAM N° 64B E.C.
CODE N° 1007

SLEEPING CARRIAGE
N°s 1159. 1162. 1172. 1173. 1174. 1176.

WATER TANK 63 GALLONS.
WATER TANK 39 GALLONS.
JOURNALS 10 x 5
8'-6"
43'-0" CENTRES OF BOGIES.
63'-0" OVER VESTIBULES.
61'-6" OVER BODY.
60'-0" OVER HEADSTOCKS.
C O R R I D O R.
ATTEND^T DRESSER SINK HOT WATER DROP TABLE SEAT WITH LOCKER BELOW
SINGLE BERTH. 4'-6"
TOILET. 3'-0"
10 CONVERTIBLE SINGLE BERTHS
1 ATTENDANTS COMPARTMENT.
1 LAVATORY.
WEIGHT 37-16-2
ELECTRIC LIGHT.
VACUUM BRAKE.

ECJS first-class sleeping car on EC Dia. 64B, built by York in 1923. The Diagram shows them with their later 1925 numbers as 1159 etc whereas they appeared first as 159J etc. *National Railway Museum*

Carriage Building Programme, the three kitchen cars were transferred to the Areas, No. 1211 to the GC section and Nos. 1212/3 to the GN. One intention was to rid the East Coast fleet of gas-lit (and gas cooking equipment) stock. Despite this, No. 1212/3 - as 42182/3 - achieved some prominence as a result of their use in the annual 'Northern Belle' train cruises from 1933, one being used in the set, the other held as spare. Nos. 1190/2/3 were transferred from the East Coast allocation in 1935/6, becoming an open first (1190) and thirds respectively.

The contemporary composites were similarly transferred from the East Coast fleet, a meeting in September 1934 of the LNER Superintendents and Passenger Managers noting that composites Nos. 11 - 14 and 176 - 9 were 'not suitable for transfer in their present form and should be converted to third-class and the locker compartments made into ordinary third-class compartments.' On assumption that the alterations would be carried out, the eight carriages were to be transferred to Areas, a process completed by 1937.

The remaining pre-war vehicles

In May 1913, the East Coast General Managers proposed the building of 12 bogie brake vans, similar to those produced by Doncaster in 1910 and on EC Dia. 39A. The intention was that these would reduce the borrowing of GNR vans for East Coast trains at the height of summer. The NBR did not wish to undertake the building of any of the 12 vans whose construction was split evenly between Doncaster and York. They were classified as EC Dia. 39B.

Type	*Builder*	*ECJS Nos.*	*Details*
Bogie brake van	York	44, 158/60/1/4/75	Built 1914
Bogie brake van	Doncaster	152 - 157	Built 1914

Early in 1914, there was discussion of the need for nine new brake composites, principally for use as through carriages between Kings Cross and St Andrews, in view of the current fashion for golfing which had increased traffic to the resort. The proposal was dropped in June 1914 in view of the increased weight of the new 'Flying Scotsman' sets about to go into traffic. The requirement for the nine new brake composites was revived after World War I, but dropped in 1920.

East Coast train formations in 1914/5

Among the most interesting surviving records relating to the working of East Coast Joint Stock are two carriage working books headed 'East Coast Railways Through Working and Instructions for loading luggage etc' for July - September 1914 and October 1914 - June 1915, thus providing examples of winter and summer timetables. Although the latter embraces the early months of World War I, the details of train working are not noticeably changed from pre-war days.

The formations of the principal East Coast trains for that fateful summer of

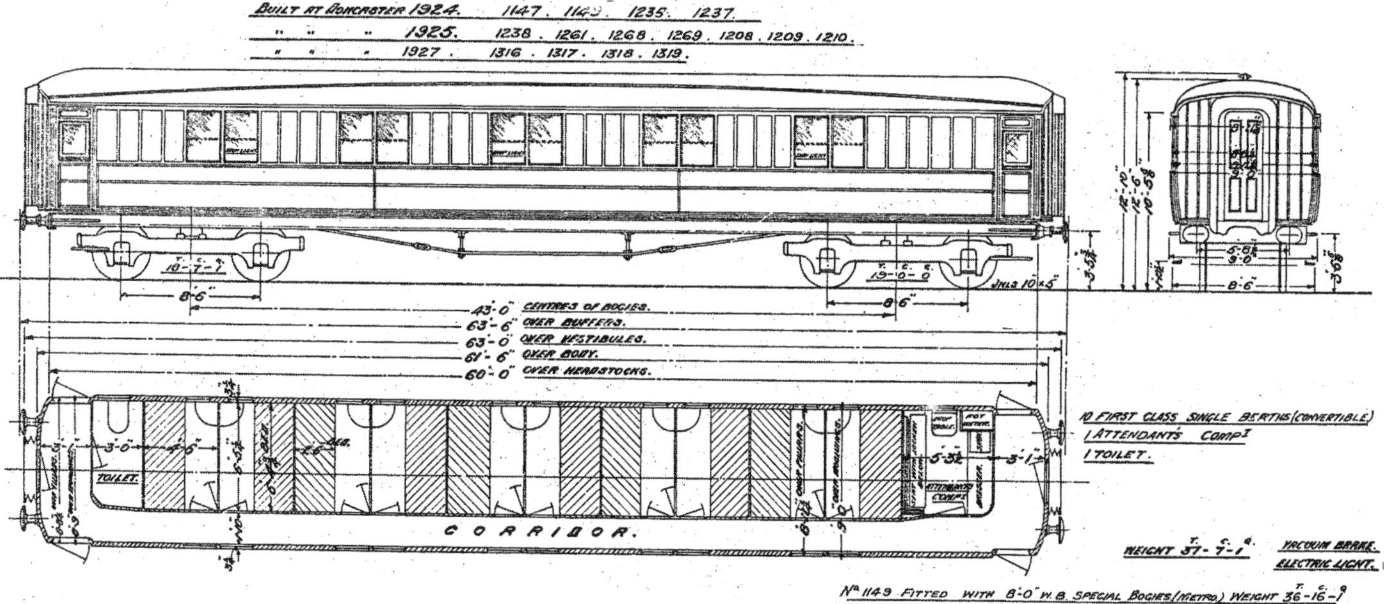

ECJS first-class sleeping car on EC Dia. 64C, built by Doncaster from 1924. These were post-Grouping vehicles, later shown on LNER Diagram 17, but very much to ECJS specification. The 1924 batch originally appeared as 10194 - 7J in the short-lived numbering scheme of the time for LNER standard vehicles. The Diagram shows the corridor side whereas that for 64B shows the berth side.

National Railway Museum

1914 are reproduced in this chapter and are largely self-explanatory, or as noted in the accompanying text. In the winter 1914/5 timetable, the 9.50 am Kings Cross - Edinburgh and 10.15 am Edinburgh - Kings Cross ran during October only. In previous years, it was usual for the relief trains to cease running at the end of September. Despite the number of elliptical-roofed carriages to hand, the afternoon 'Scotsmen' retained a number of clerestory vehicles in their formations. The night expresses required a number of ordinary seated carriages and vans, as well as full brakes.

Post - World War I vehicles

A similar three-compartment brake third to the conversions to EC Dia. 49A for the 'Flying Scotsman' sets was built in 1920 as No. 41, nominally a replacement for a clerestory third of the same number destroyed in the Burntisland collision of 1914. This replacement, as No. 141, was in turn wrecked at Welwyn Garden City on 15th June, 1935 when formed in the second portion of the 10.45 pm Kings Cross - Newcastle.

With the ending of World War I, a modest building programme for the ECJS went ahead, to replace old vehicles that were to be condemned, or sold to the individual companies. It was approved by the GNR Board on 4th June, 1920 so far as the GNR's share of expenditure was concerned and the complete programme comprised:

Type	*Quantity*	*Builder*	*Completed*	*Running Nos.*
Corridor First	6	Doncaster	Dec. 1922	49/60/87/123/196/353
Corridor Third	6	York	Oct. 1921	163/71/7/8/80, 206
Bogie Brake Van	7	York	June 1921	214/8/9/60
		Doncaster	Dec. 1922	128/44/5
Twin - sleeper	1 twin	Doncaster	April 1922	181 + 181A

The ordinary carriages were generally similar to what had gone before, and were of 61 ft 6 in. length, the vans being 56 ft 6 in. Apart from the increased length, the firsts were described as being 'as EC Dia. 58, except that they had flush-closing armrests in the compartments . . .' but they also differed as that the partition to partition dimension was 7 ft 6 in. The thirds were generally similar to EC Dia. 22, built in 1907. Compound-bolster 8 ft 6 in. wheelbase bogies were used for the carriages, except for the thirds and the vans which had the single-bolster 8 ft pattern. The vans were similar to earlier versions of EC Dia. 39, except that the heavy-type bogies allowed their payload to be increased to eight tons.

Compound-bolster bogies were fitted to the thirds during 1924/5 while first No. (1)49 received 8 ft bogies in 1930. The thirds featured glass, louvred ventilators to three of the large corridor windows, in the style of the 1914 'Flying Scotsman' composites. At least two of the firsts - Nos. (1)196 and (1)353 - remained in the pool for the principal East Coast sets until mid - 1935, thereafter being transferred to the LNER Areas; at the same time the thirds were also being dispersed from East Coast stock.

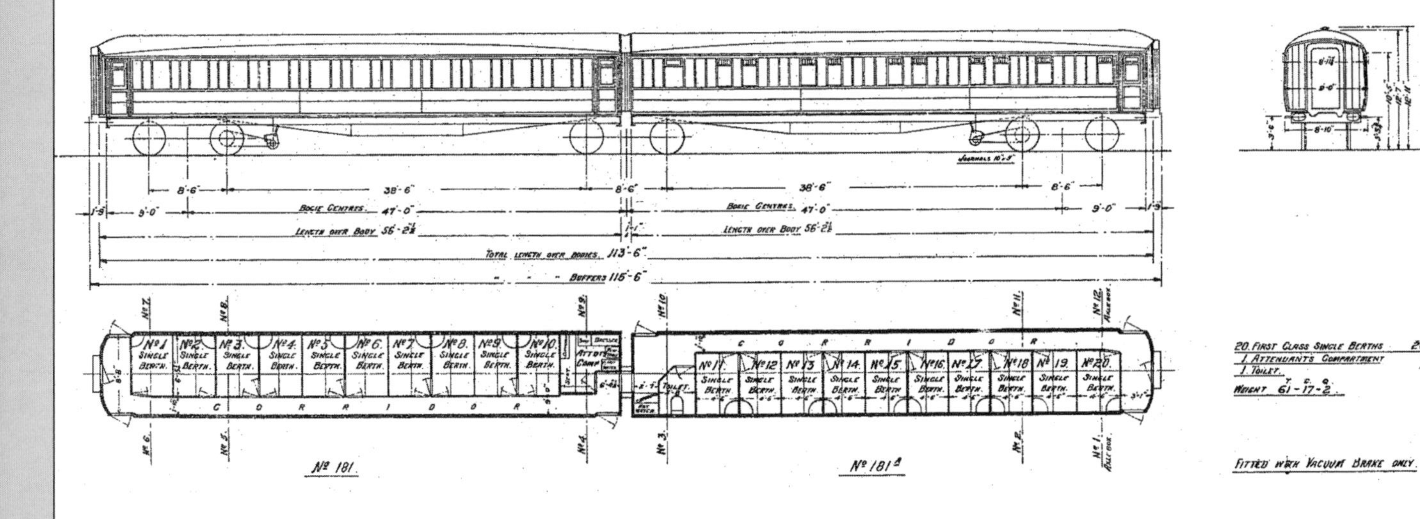

ECJS articulated twin first-class sleeping car on EC Dia. 68, built by Doncaster in 1922.

National Railway Museum

No. (1)49 had been damaged on 10th May, 1926 when the up 'Flying Scotsman' was maliciously derailed between Annitsford and Cramlington during the General Strike. The formation of the train on that date is of some interest:

Type	*Recorded Number*	*Vehicle details*
Brake third	1060	LNER Dia. 40, built 1924
First	149	ECJS Dia. 59, built 1922
Triplet RC	6441/2/3J	LNER Dias. 12/13/14, Built 1924
Third	364J	ECJS Dia. 34, built 1907
Third	1372	ECJS Dia. 34, built 1907
Full brake	146	LNER Dia. 43, built 1924
Third	61632	LNER Dia. 23, built 1926
Brake	42689	GNR Dia. 218A, built 1911
Composite Brake third	10130N	LNER Dia. 40, built 1925
Third	69J	ECJS Dia. 34, built 1906

The variety of numbering, in the pre-Grouping, post-1923 and post-1925 schemes, is noteworthy, as are the borrowing of non-East Coast stock and the inclusion of some of the older elliptical-roofed stock. Doubtless the general disruption to operations that had arisen during the first week of the General Strike had some effect.

Twin sleeping car Nos. 181/181A

The most interesting of the vehicles in the post-war ECJS building programme was the twin first-class sleeping car. A mock-up of a section of a car was produced and this was inspected by the traffic superintendents in January 1921. They asked for a number of changes to be made. The completed twin sleeper, No. 181/181A, was exhibited at Kings Cross during April 1922, along with 'A1' Pacific No. 1470 *Great Northern* and the ensemble attracted much admiring attention. East Coast sleeping-car design was seen to be well-advanced, and the attention by Gresley and Bulleid alike to interior details demonstrated their keenness to depart from the fussiness of much Edwardian practice.

The twin-sleeper had 20 berths, 16 of which could form double berths with the adjacent berth. There was one lavatory and one attendant's compartment. The overall length of the twin was 113 ft 6 in., the total weight 61 tons 17 cwt and its building cost was £12,628. The connection between the articulated bodies was enclosed by a gangway plate, a feature then used for other articulated stock.

As for the interior fittings, *Engineering* in its issue of 14th April remarked that 'the attention paid to the convenience of passengers without ostentatious display is especially noteworthy, and is an advance on anything previously seen in this or any country'. The corridors were panelled in natural teak, while the sleeping berths had plain mahogany panelling to waist height and, above that, white enamel. Such simplicity of finish even inspired letters to *The Times* to champion the cause of overdecorated Edwardiana.

One other feature of interest in the twin sleeping car was the use of frameless

S.L. 4090.

G.N. AND N.E.J.S. FIRST CLASS DINING CARRIAGE
WITH KITCHEN.
Nos 1. 2.
BUILT DEC. 1905.

DRAWING No 78.

DIAGRAM 1.

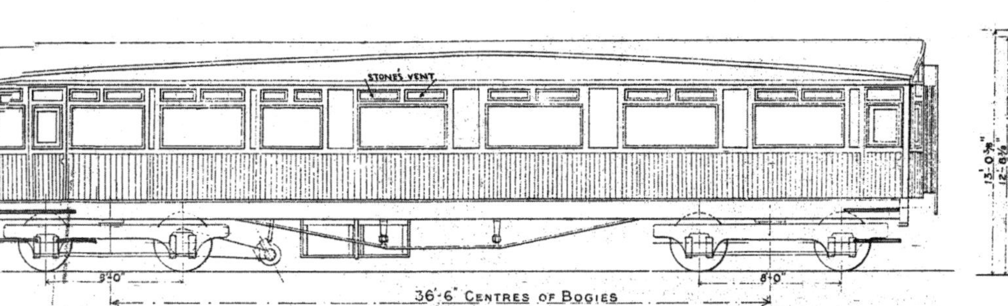

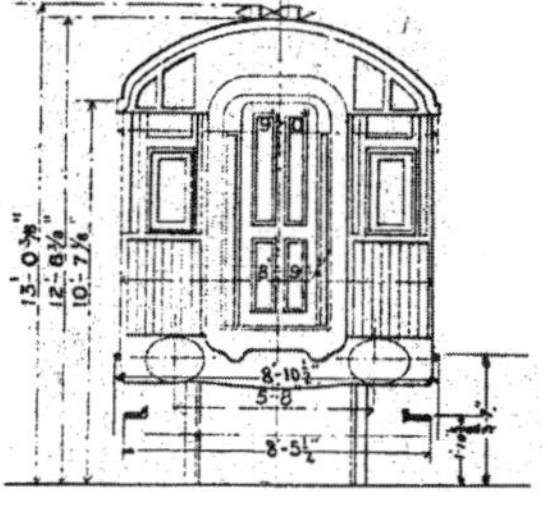

2 COMPARTMENTS - 12 FIRST CLASS SEATS
OR
8 SEATS WHEN DINING
1 COMPARTMENT - 5 FIRST CLASS SEATS
1 OPEN COMPARTMENT - 9 FIRST CLASS SEATS
1 WAITER'S PANTRY
1 KITCHEN
CORRIDORS AND PASSAGES
WEIGHT 33 T. 3 C. 0 Q.

ELECTRIC LIGHT.
STEAM HEATING.
DUAL BRAKES.

GN/NE Joint first-class dining cars Nos. 1/2, to JS Dia. 1. *National Railway Museum*

Plate 37: Compartment side of composite No. 2, in original condition (EC Dia. 2B, built Doncaster, 1911, much later was LNER No. 31152 as a full-third). First-class coupé compartment third from left. Photograph dated April 1911. The axleboxes were cast with the GNR lettering. *National Railway Museum*

Plate 38: Compartment side of brake composite No. 347, in original condition (EC Dia. 47B, built Doncaster, 1911). Photograph dated May 1911. Note that there are sliding doors to the luggage compartment. Running with non-standard 10 ft WB bogies. This was the leading vehicle in the up Aberdeen sleeping-car express involved in the collision at Retford in February 1923, and it was so badly damaged as to be broken up on site. *National Railway Museum*

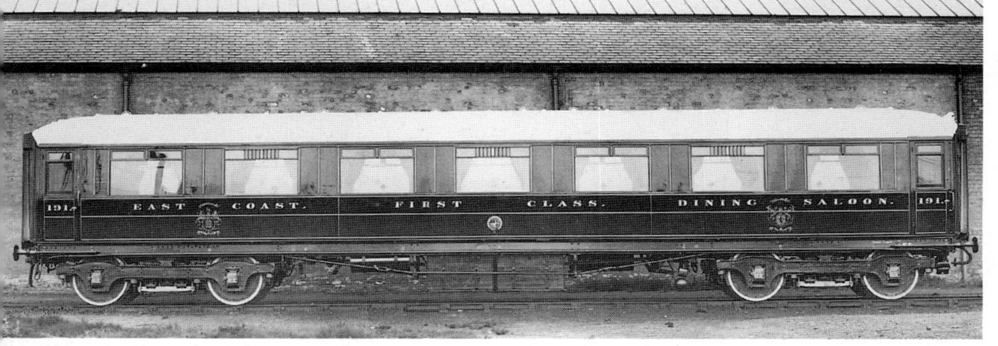

Plate 39: First-class dining car No. 191, in original condition (EC Dia. 75A, built Doncaster). 'Flying Scotsman' sets of 1914 and photographed in the June of that year. This remained in the East Coast fleet as an open first after 1943. *National Railway Museum*

Plate 40: Interior view of first-class dining car No. 191, in original condition (EC Dia. 75A, built Doncaster). 'Flying Scotsman' sets of 1914 . The interior was divided into a smoking and non-smoking saloon, with 1+1 seating. Drinking glasses inscribed 'ECJS Dining Car'.

National Railway Museum

Plate 41: Corridor side of composite No. 78, as SC 7819 E (EC Dia. 3A, built York, 1914). Running on compound-bolster bogies. In BR carmine and cream livery and photographed in July 1957 lying condemned at Craigendoran, having been withdrawn in November 1956. *R.M. Casserley*

Plate 42: Corridor side of brake third No. 41, in original condition (EC Dia. 49A, built Doncaster, into service 31st March, 1920, later was LNER No. 141). Hinged doors to luggage compartment and compound-bolster bogies. Unlike the earlier ECJS vehicles built at Doncaster, note that the bogies have step-boards; from 1914 a second step-board had been fitted under the doors of GNR-manufactured carriages as they passed through shops. Like the other one-off brake vehicle - No. 347 - which was a replacement for an accident victim, No. 41 was involved in a destructive accident and wrecked in the Welwyn Garden City accident of 1935. Perhaps the fates were being tempted. *National Railway Museum*

Plate 43: Corridor side of third No. 180, in original condition (EC Dia. 31A, built York, 1921, much later was LNER No. 52081). Similar style to the York-built composites of 1914, with the louvred ventilators to some corridor windows. Note the use of the pressed-steel 8 ft WB bogies, replaced by the compound-bolster type in December 1924. Photograph dated August 1921. *National Railway Museum*

Plate 44: Corridor side of third No. 177, as E 52079 E (EC Dia. 31A, built York, 1921). Running on compound-bolster bogies and in BR carmine and cream livery. Photograph dated August 1956. *R.M. Casserley*

Plate 45: Luggage van No. 158, in original condition (EC Dia. 39B, built York, 1914, much later was LNER No. 5262). Sliding double doors and unusual guard's ducket. Five tons payload. ECJS circlet only. Photograph dated 1914. *National Railway Museum*

Plate 46: Luggage van No. 219, in original condition (EC Dia. 39C, built York, 1921, much later was LNER No 5268). Sliding double doors and older, GNR pattern of guard's ducket to which the ECJS reverted. ECJS circlet only. Photograph dated June 1921. Eight tons payload and fitted with a modified type of bogie with additional springing. *National Railway Museum*

Plate 47: Twin articulated sleeping-car, showing corridor side of No. 181A and compartment side of 181, in original condition (EC Dia. 68, built Doncaster, 1922). ECJS circlet only on lower body panels. *National Railway Museum*

Plate 48: Diagram 68 twins were built after the Grouping to the LNER's 1923 Building Programme, cost per twin, £9,000. Twin articulated sleeping-car, showing corridor side of No. 198J and compartment side of 199J, in original condition (EC Dia. 68, built Doncaster, 1923). Standard LNER livery, lettered 'Sleeping Carriage'. *National Railway Museum*

Plate 49: Ten-berth first-class sleeping car No. 159J, in original condition (EC Dia. 64B, built York, 1923, later LNER No. 1159). The cost of each of these cars was £5,917 and they were built to allow for the introduction of new services and 'to compete more effectively with the West Coast . . .' says a memo from the LNER's Traffic Committee dated 22nd February, 1923. Vehicle carrying destination board lettered: 'London Kings+ Cross & Dundee via Forth & Tay Bridges'. Later examples of this design were built up to 1925 on what was later referred to as LNER Diagram 17. This photograph seems to have been taken after No. 159J had been outshopped in late March 1924 following the customary winter overhaul of East Coast sleeping cars, involving examination, lifting and washing. The photograph was taken at York which is strange as these York-built cars were scheduled to be maintained by Doncaster.

National Railway Museum

Plate 50: There seem to be remarkably few pictures of the GN/NE Joint expresses in action. Even this picture dates from 1925, but it shows the 5.30 pm down climbing Holloway bank behind 'C1' four-cylinder Atlantic No. 3279. The leading vehicle is brake third No. 15 (JS Dia. 8, built Doncaster, 1907); then a third to JS Dia 7, built York, 1907; a 1906, York-built slab-sided third to JS Dia. 4, and then the restaurant car set of open third, restaurant third and open first, all built by Doncaster in 1907/8. *Rail Archive Stephenson*

Plate 51: At least it's an excuse for including an 'A4' in the book! No. 4492 *Dominion of New Zealand* heads a down Newcastle express past Hatfield in the late 1930s. Second in its train is the one of the distinctive-looking JS Dia. 7 thirds, by then fitted with compound-bolster bogies. All six had been transferred from East Coast stock in 1933/4. *RAS Marketing*

Plate 52: The interior of GN/NE Joint restaurant first to JS Dia. 1, built 1905. There were two dining saloons, the nearest seating nine, the smaller one, five. *National Railway Museum*

Plate 53: GN/NE Joint third No. 8 (JS Dia. 4, built York, 1906 and much later LNER No. 52056). Note the deep channel-section underframe. The ventilators were of decorated, ground-glass.
National Railway Museum

Plate 54: GN/NE Joint brake first No. 9 (JS Dia. 5, built York, 1906 and much later LNER No. 2318, having changed identities twice!). *National Railway Museum*

Plate 55: Here is what GN/NE Joint No. 9 looked like at Skegness in 1954 when it was a full-third, E 2318 E! It still seems to have varnished body panelling and, for its 49 years, looks in remarkably good shape; many of the later Gresley carriages had bowed bodywork at a much younger age. *R.M. Casserley*

Plate 56: Another testimony to York's standard of carriage building comes from this picture of third No. 7 (JS Dia. 7, built York, 1906) when running as E 52057 E, again at Skegness in 1954. It appears to be in the teak brown paintwork applied by York up to the early 1950s and carries a Shopping Proposal date of 1955. *R.M. Casserley*

Plate 57: One of the four GN/NE Joint sleeping cars, No. 12, in original condition (JS Dia. 17, built Doncaster, 1909). These had the 10 ft wheelbase bogies with outside springs. One curiosity of these - and the York-built GN/NE Joint sleeping cars - was that there was just one door on each side of the body, almost amidships. All four came near to completing their projected lifespan of 28 years. *National Railway Museum*

Plate 58: There are few official photographs of vehicles transferred from East Coast stock to the LNER Areas so this excellent example, from Gorton Works, is of particular value for depicting GN/NE Joint third No. 16 (JS Dia. 7, built York June 1907), in GC Section stock as 52058. The carriage has been running on compound-bolster bogies since 1924 or so. It was revarnished and given new transfers in the summer of 1933 by Gorton although it had received an overhaul in the February of that year. *National Railway Museum*

Plate 59: GN/NE Joint brake third No. 15 (JS Dia. 8, built Doncaster, 1907 and much later LNER No. 52086). Photograph dated October 1907. *National Railway Museum*

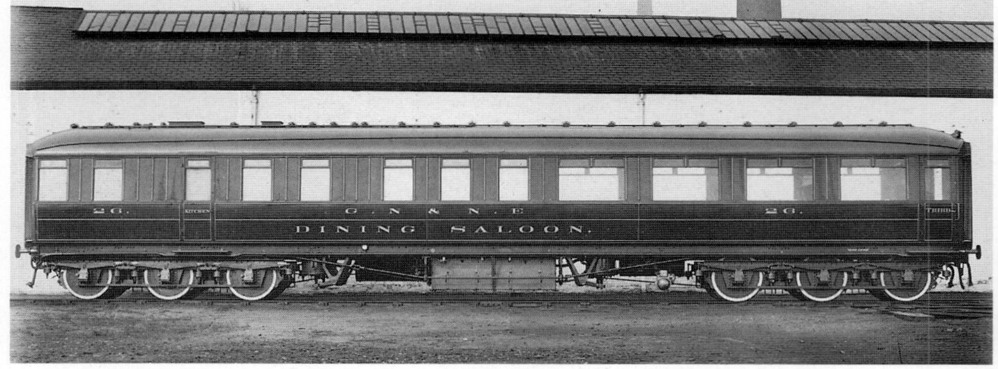

Plate 60: GN/NE Joint third-class dining car No. 26 (JS Dia. 10, built Doncaster, 1907 and later LNER No. 1426, then 1436). Photograph dated October 1907. *National Railway Museum*

Plate 61: GN/NE Joint open first No. 31 (JS Dia. 11, built Doncaster, 1907 and much later LNER No 7122). Photograph dated October 1907. From 1925, these open firsts were lettered 'Restaurant Cars'. Note how these GN/NE carriages have dark-painted roofs, possibly red oxide. *National Railway Museum*

Plate 62: GN/NE Joint first No. 29 (JS Dia 6, built York, 1907), as SC 784 E in BR carmine and cream livery. Under the LNER 1934 Carriage Building Programme, the two firsts to this Diagram, and that on Dia. 34, were transferred to the Northern Scottish Area as thirds for use on the Aberdeen - Inverness service. *RAS Marketing*

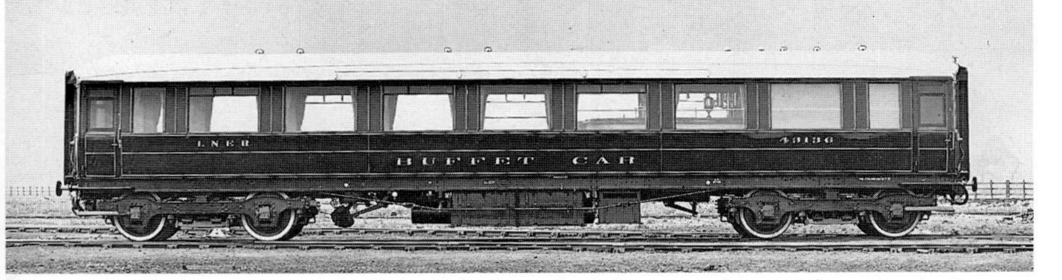

Plate 63: GN/NE Joint open third No. 25 (JS Dia. 9, built Doncaster, June 1908), newly rebuilt at Doncaster in July 1933 as a buffet car for the GN Section, No. 43136. At a cursory glance, this could well have been a brand-new LNER standard vehicle. *Robert Humm Collection*

Plate 64: A spruce-looking GN/NE Joint open third No. 23 (JS Dia. 9, built Doncaster, 1907), as buffet car E 43134 E, in BR maroon livery at Stratford in September 1957. This shows the 'other' side to No. 43136, with the kitchen at the left-hand end. *R.M. Casserley*

Plate 65: The typical 1930s' LNER interior of one of the former GN/NE open thirds converted as a buffet car, looking towards the kitchen end. *Robert Humm Collection*

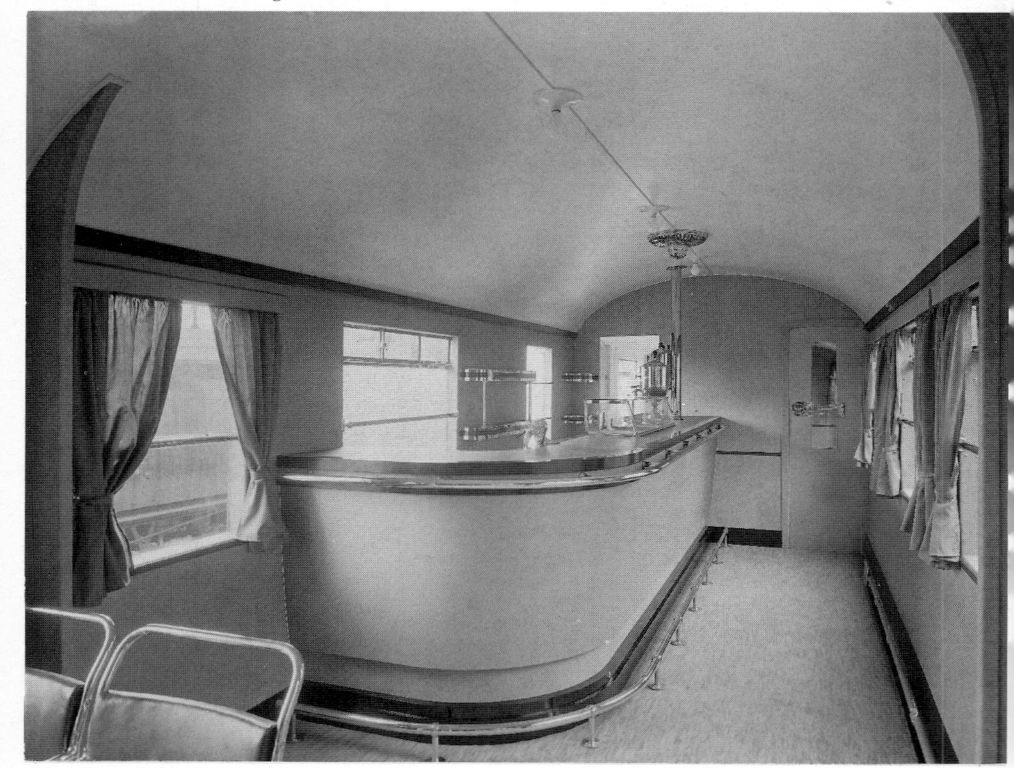

Plate 66: GNR Sheffield Stock brake third No 3049, in original condition (GNR Dia. 256, built Doncaster, 1906). Photograph dated July 1906. This carriage is carrying one of the 'London (Kings +) Sheffield Manchester (Central)' destination boards. *National Railway Museum*

Plate 67: GNR third-class dining car No. 3037, in original condition (GNR Dia. 68, built Doncaster, 1906). Photograph dated September 1906. *National Railway Museum*

Plate 68: GNR Sheffield Stock composite dining car No. 3040, as a full kitchen car and in BR livery as E 2334 E. The dining saloons were converted into pantry and larder accommodation. The conversion of this and a sister car came about because in 1933 Gresley was opposed to building a new gas-equipped kitchen car for excursion work in the North Eastern Area. New restaurant cars were built for the Southern Scottish Area which displaced the former 3040/1 for their rebuilding as kitchen cars in 1936/7. The photograph shows E 2334 E at Heaton in June 1957 when painted in BR maroon livery. It was reported working from Leeds - Kings Cross in September 1959 and was withdrawn the following year. *S.J. Brown*

Plate 69: GNR Sheffield first-class dining car No. 3034 (GNR Dia. 46, built Doncaster, 1906), as restored for the exhibition to mark the centenary of Kings Cross station in October 1952. It was not to last long in this condition as it was converted to a cafeteria car in April 1953. *C.R.L. Coles*

Plate 70: Interior of one of the saloons of Sheffield Stock open third No. 3046, as built (GNR Dia. 224, built at Doncaster, 1906). Generally neat - and electrically-lit - but still featuring the iron-framed seats so popular with Gresley's predecessor, Howlden, and which must have hacked many a shin! The metal-framed parcel racks are a little forbidding and conceal a painted dado. Framed scenic photographs between the windows. *National Railway Museum*

droplights which operated on a rack and pinion and could be wound open, or closed by a small motor-car type handle; this avoided having first to release the window blind to obtain ventilation. There was a louvred glass ventilator above each droplight. Also serving as an indication of the thought that had gone into the design was the grouping by the side of the berth of the switches that controlled the three-lamp roof fitting, the reading lamp and the two-speed electric fan.

One innovation was fortunately forestalled. Bulleid had proposed a bed which tapered inwards in a way that suggested the macabre; the carriage builders placed a chalked notice next to the mock - up which read simply: 'we don't want a coffin'.

Nos. 181/181A were at first used on the Aberdeen service and on 13th February, 1923, the twin was marshalled in the 7.15 pm Aberdeen - Kings Cross when this train collided at Retford with an up goods. Nos. 181/181A were third and fourth in the formation. In this destructive accident, the twin was derailed but remained upright. In his report, the inspecting officer had this to say: 'The behaviour of the articulated twin sleeping car, under so severe a trial, is worthy of note'. His other comments about the way the ECJS carriages absorbed the force of the accident has been referred to in Chapter 3.

Later in 1923, and after repair, Nos. 181/181A were in use between Kings Cross and Newcastle. In subsequent renumbering the twin became Nos. 1181/2. Others were built on the diagram under the LNER's 1923 Carriage Building Programme, and these were numbered (1)198/9 and (1)200/1.

The East Coast Joint Stock immediately before and after Grouping

The requirements for ECJS at Grouping became the responsibility of the Superintendents' and Passenger Managers' Committee. This committee was actually convened before Grouping and its first meeting took place on 14th July, 1921, attended by representatives from the Eastern group of companies. At the meeting of 21st November, 1922, the representatives sent their proposals for the carriages they wished to see completed in 1923 and, so the minutes record, 'urged that the special attention of the general managers should be called to the necessity for a thorough renovation of the East Coast Joint Stock which has been allowed to get into such a bad state that strong complaints are being received from the travelling public'.

This indeed set the tone for the majority of succeeding annual building programmes as the financial affairs of the LNER were often such that the new construction was limited to the renewal of the East Coast stock and little else. With Viscount Grey in the chair, the February 1923 meeting of the LNER's Traffic Committee recommended to the Board a Carriage Building Programme for the twelve months from 1st April, 1923. This provided for the building of stock costed at £545,893 and identified the construction of two twin sleeping cars and six single sleeping cars for the East Coast stock, together with the repair of the underframes and bogie bolsters of 28 clerestory carriages. Although outside the coverage of this book it throws light on the state of the ECJS in the early 1920s.

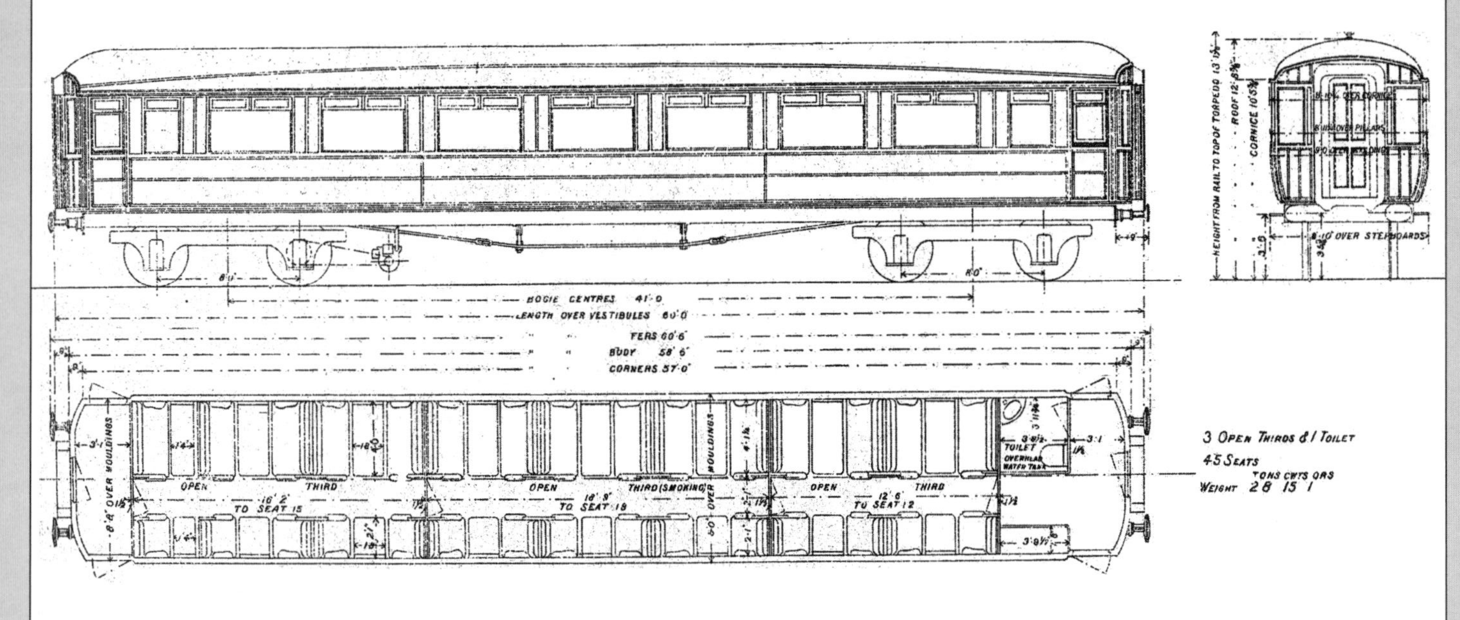

GN/NE Joint open third, to JS Dia. 9, built at Doncaster in 1907/8. *National Railway Museum*

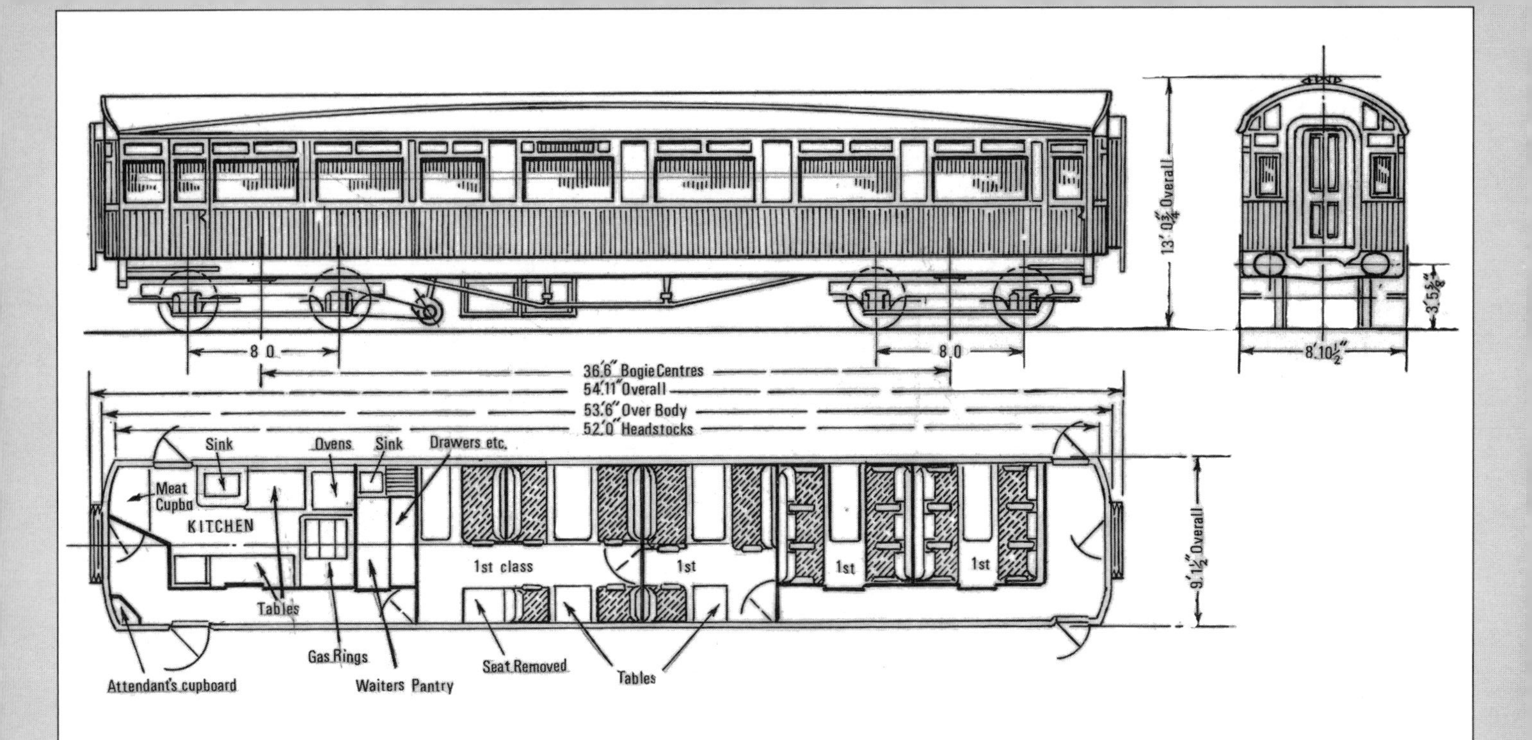

GN/NE Joint first-class dining cars Nos. 1/2, originally to JS Dia. 1 but seen here in a recent redrawing of GC Section Dia. 5R1 which was prepared after the transfer of these cars in 1925. Once on the GC Section they were converted to vacuum braking only and No. 52002 (it had been 2002C) received compound-bolster bogies. Both were condemned *c.* 1938, no doubt being unpopular because of their non-standard layout.

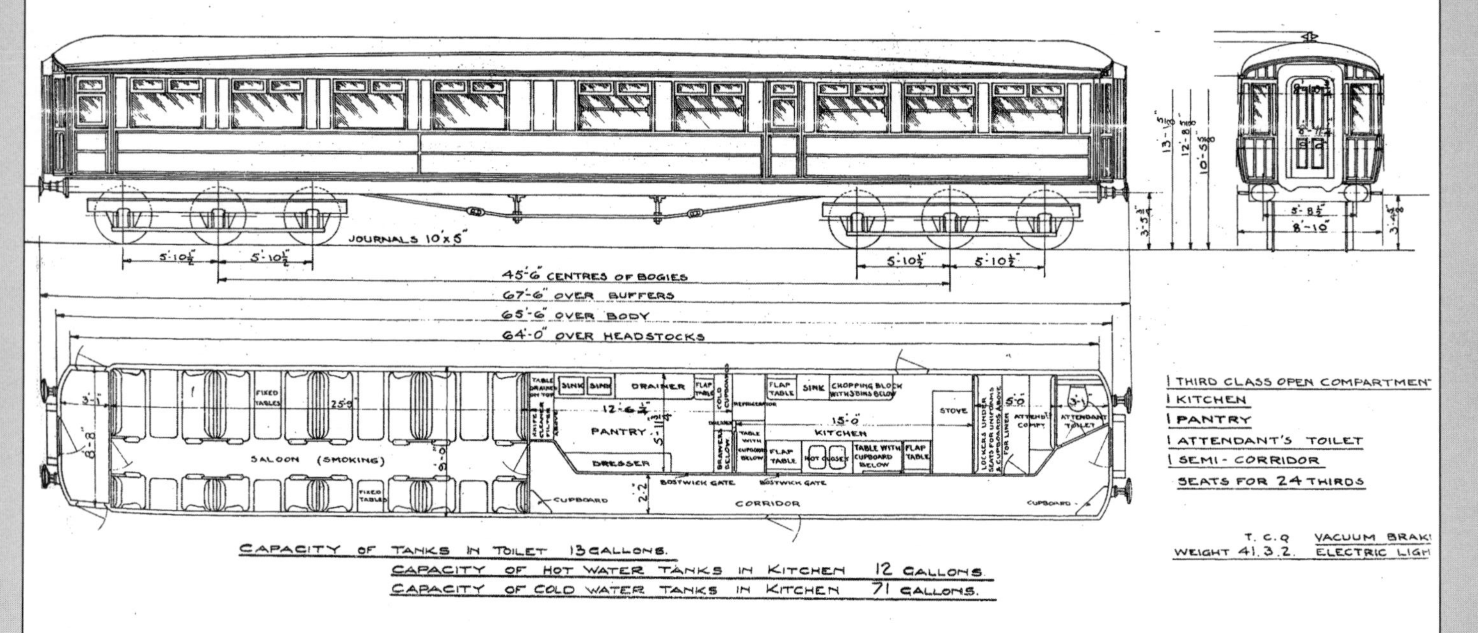

GN/NE Joint third-class dining car, to JS Dia. 10. Again, this is a drawing prepared in the 1920s when the cars had become Nos 1426 - 8; their subsequent renumbering to 1436 - 8 was to clear the way for Gresley post-1923 triplet articulated restaurant cars renumbered under the 1943 scheme.

National Railway Museum

Great Northern/North Eastern Joint Stock

Kings Cross to Newcastle traffic was separated from the Anglo-Scottish workings once the Great Northern and North Eastern railways decided early in 1899 to provide dining and sleeping cars between Kings Cross and Newcastle only. The first such workings, using ECJS vehicles, involved a dining car for Newcastle conveyed on the 6.15 pm Kings Cross - Wakefield and Bradford, and returning the next day on the 12.20 pm York to Kings Cross (through carriages at 7.45 am from Edinburgh). This working commenced as from 1st October, 1903 and meals were served south of York only. From 1st October, 1904, a Newcastle portion, including the dining car from the 6.15 pm, was conveyed on the 5.30 pm Kings Cross - Nottingham and detached at Grantham.

As the original ECJS agreement applied to trains running at least between Kings Cross and Edinburgh, it was not surprising that before long the NBR should object to the use of ECJS vehicles south of Newcastle only. The progress towards a new set of carriages for the Kings Cross - Newcastle service seemed to have moved in stages, with agreement at first in November 1904 for four catering vehicles, then in July 1905 for the remaining carriages. Whereas at first it seems that the intention was that the GNR and NER should own the stock separately, by July 1905 it was agreed that a similar agreement should be reached as for the ECJS stock, with joint ownership, the cost of construction being paid for in proportion to the route mileage worked on the service. Hence new stock was built by the GNR and NER in the proportions 69.25 per cent to 30.75 per cent respectively, so representing the share of each company. All these were built at York. From 1st July, 1905, the breakfast and luncheon cars were allocated to the retimed 8.0 am from Newcastle (formerly the 7.40 am) and the 5.30 pm down.

The 1905/6 vehicles

The new GN/NE vehicles seem to have entered service in December 1905 and comprised two restaurant/kitchen firsts, two restaurant thirds and two brake thirds. These were to the NER's austere slab-sided, matchboard panelled design with elliptical roofs and electric lighting. These vehicles, Nos. 1 - 6 in the joint stock, were followed in April and May 1906 by two thirds and two brake firsts to the same specification. All were prominently lettered in a way that detracted further from their appearance.

Firsts Nos. 1/2 had a kitchen, two dining saloons and two compartments, the last-mentioned also being intended for dining when required. Third-class Nos. 5/6 were dining saloons with a pantry and seated 48 passengers when not used for dining, 36 when they were. All four carriages were classified as restaurant cars in 1924/5. Brake thirds Nos. 3/4 were shown on official diagrams as likely to be used for passengers taking meals.

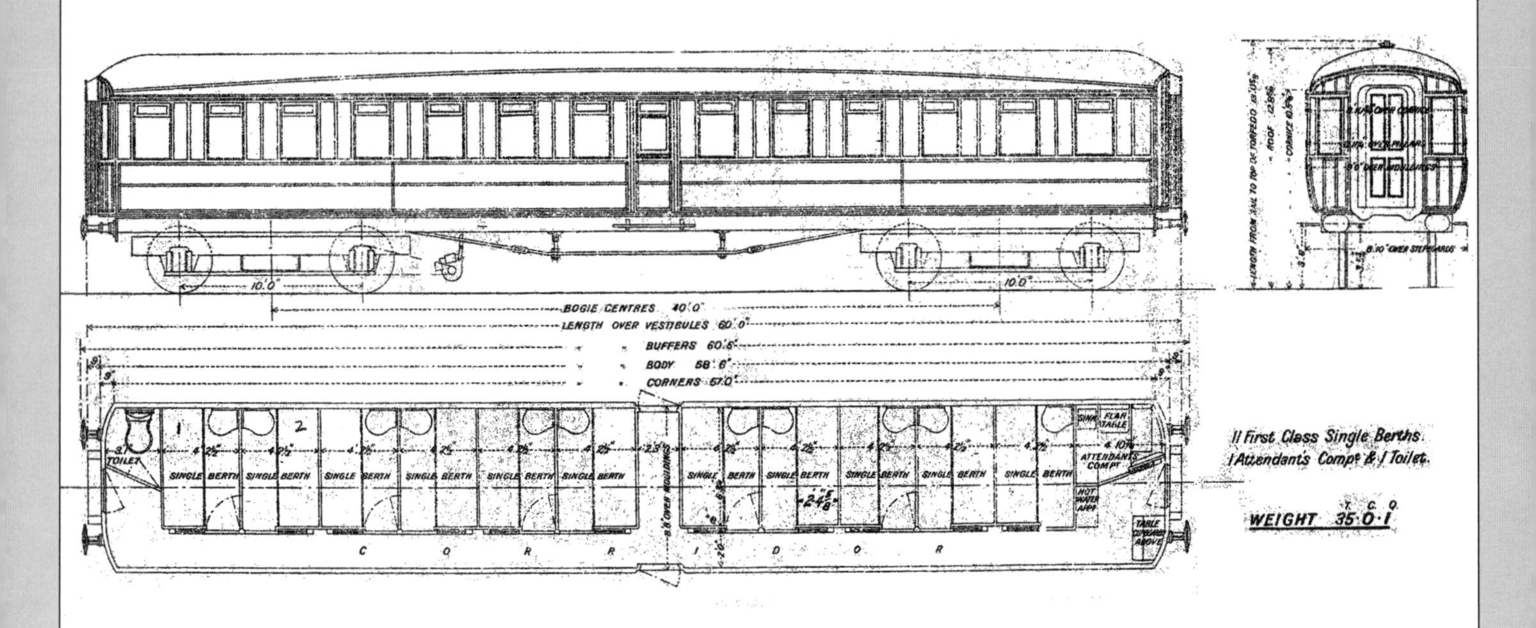

GN/NE Joint first-class sleeping-car Nos. 11/2, to JS Dia. 17. *National Railway Museum*

GN/NE Joint sleeping cars

For the Kings Cross and Newcastle sleeping car service, ECJS cars were at first used but the NBR's perfectly legitimate complaint on this score saw new GN/NE sleeping cars agreed in June 1906 although design work seems to have started earlier that year. There were four cars, Nos. 11 - 14, the first two built by the GNR in 1909 and the other pair by York during the previous year. All four were built to what was by then referred to as 'GN style' as standardised for the ECJS and, although there were differences in specification, all had eleven berths. The cars worked on the 11.45 pm Kings Cross - Newcastle and the 11.20 pm Newcastle - Kings Cross.

GN/NE Joint stock built 1907/8

By the autumn of 1906, the provision of further new stock for GN/NE was under discussion and agreement was reached in December 1906, the GNR Board approving the proposals the following month. In all, there were 21 new vehicles while two existing carriages were converted. What happened was that the 8.0 am Newcastle - Kings Cross was allocated all new vehicles while the existing set, with two vehicles altered and with the addition of six newcomers, was transferred to the 10.30 am from Newcastle. There were also seven carriages built as 'releasing' or spare stock. The 21 new carriages, costing £45,500, entered service between June 1907 and June 1908 and were numbered 15 - 35.

The types built - and builders - were as follows:

Brake third (two compartments)	Doncaster	No. 15	8 am Newcastle
Third (eight compartments)	York	Nos. 16 - 20	One to 8 am, two to 10.30 am, two spare
Open third (three saloons - 45 seats)	Doncaster	Nos. 21 - 25	One to each train, rest spare
Restaurant/ kitchen thirds (12-whl) (one saloon) - 24 seats)	Doncaster	Nos. 26 - 28	One to each train, one spare
Firsts (seven compartments)	York	Nos. 29/30	One to 10.30 am, one spare
Open firsts (two saloons - 26 seats)	Doncaster	Nos. 31 - 33	One to each train, one spare
Brake first (five compartments)*	Doncaster	No. 34	8 am Newcastle
Bogie brake van	Doncaster	No. 35	10.30 am Newcastle

* Converted to seven - compartment first in 1911.

All these vehicles were 58 ft 6 in. over the panels and 9 ft wide, with the exception of the restaurant thirds which, like the Sheffield diners, were 65 ft 6 in. in length, the two brake carriages which were to 8 ft 6 in. width and the full brake which was only 8 ft wide. All were electrically-lit and the open vehicles had large, 4 ft 5 in. width windows.

As to the vehicles converted under the 1906 plans, brake third No. 4 was converted to a full brake in 1908 and brake first No. 9 became a full first.

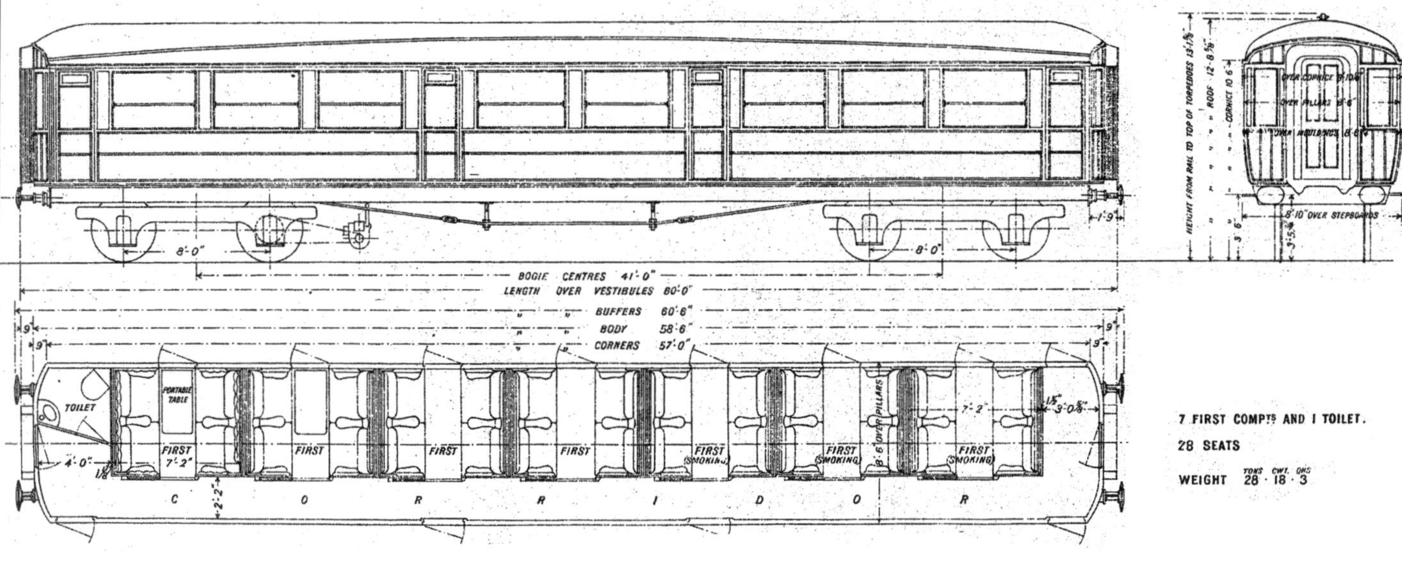

GN/NE Joint first No. 34, to JS Dia. 12, as rebuilt in 1911 from the brake first No. 34, built in 1907. This vehicle was transferred as a full-third to the Northern Scottish Area in 1937.

National Railway Museum

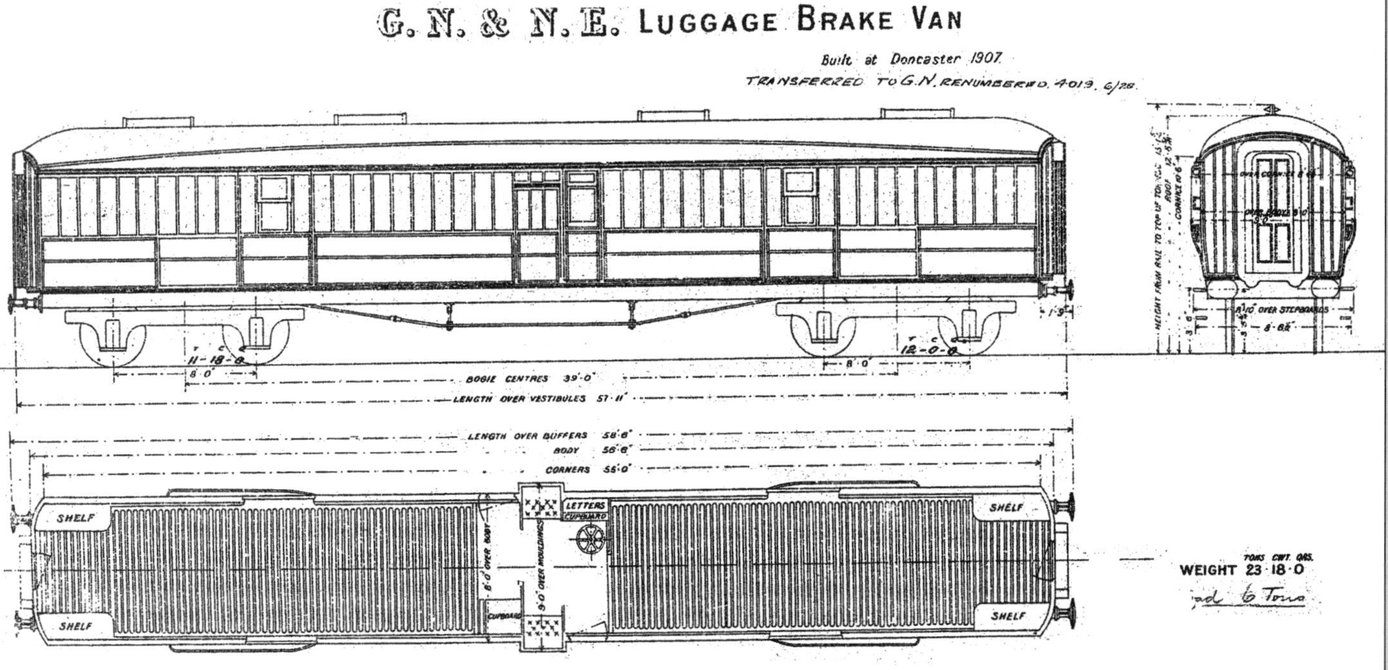

G. N. & N. E. LUGGAGE BRAKE VAN

Built at Doncaster 1907.

TRANSFERRED TO G.N. RENUMBERED 4019. 6/28.

BOGIE CENTRES 39'-0"

LENGTH OVER VESTIBULES 57'-11"

LENGTH OVER BUFFERS 58'-6"

BODY 56'-6"

CORNERS 55'-0"

SHELF

LETTERS CUPBOARD

8'-0" OVER BODY

9'-0" OVER MOULDINGS

CUPBOARD

WEIGHT 23·18·0 (TONS CWT. QRS.)

GN/NE Joint full-brake, to JS Dia. 13, and of interest for indicating that this van was renumbered to 435J at Grouping before becoming 150 in 1926, later passing to the GN Section.

National Railway Museum

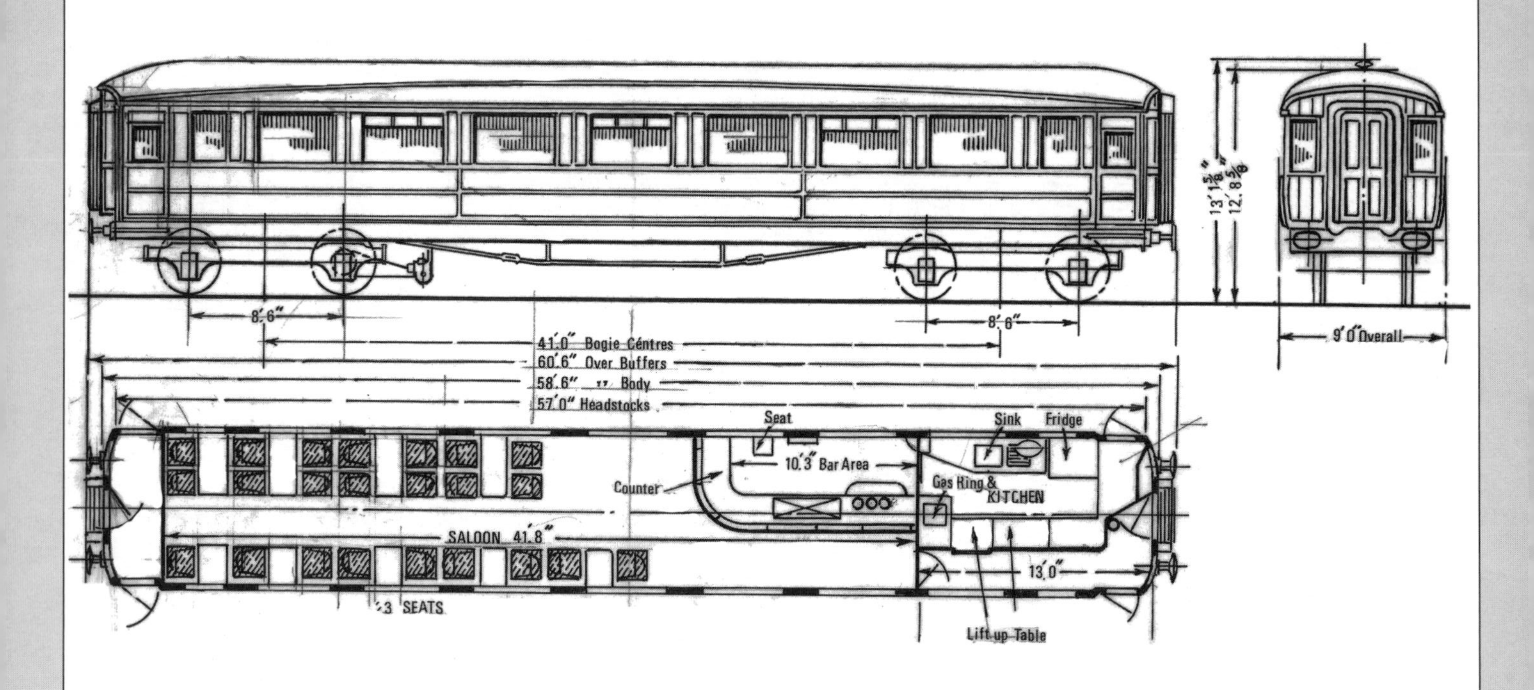

GN/NE Joint open third, to JS Dia. 9, as rebuilt by the LNER in 1933 as buffet cars and shown in a redrawing of Diagram 78V which applied to Nos. 43133/4/7. These were almost similar to their compatriots Nos. 43135/6 (Dia 78T) but the buffet counter was longer. The Diagram numbers were in the GNR Diagram series.

In contrast to the unfavourable comments attracted by the earlier GN/NE vehicles, the railway press was positively fulsome about the new stock. To the *Railway Engineer* writing in 1911, 'one of the best equipped trains that leave London each day is the Great Northern 5.30 pm express to Newcastle' while writing on contemporary British passenger stock in the *Railway Magazine* in 1914, a contributor reckoned that the GN/NE set had 'one of the most attractive dining cars in the country...' Until the arrival of the 1914 'Flying Scotsman' sets, there is no doubt that the Sheffield and GN/NE sets were the best on the East Coast, if not elsewhere.

The vehicles that attracted the most interest were the open firsts with their decor in 'Adam' style, in which all interior panelling was painted white, offset by doors, their framing and the window frames in polished mahogany. The ceiling was painted flat white with Adam-esque figures in relief. The electroliers and net brackets were in 'Adam' style finished in old gold. The seats in the non-smoking saloon were upholstered in green tapestry with Morocco leather used in the smoking saloon.

The third-class cars were panelled in teak and sycamore, the scheme offset by terracotta upholstery which was also used in the third-class compartments. Blue cloth and green Morocco leather were the materials used in the first-class non-smoking and smoking compartments respectively. The interior furnishing consultants used were Warings.

The finish of the Doncaster-built dining cars impressed a commentator in the NER's CME's department, probably our friend Mr Twinberrow, who commented that 'dining cars recently turned out from Doncaster demonstrate that the Chippendale, Sheraton and Adam styles are more suitable for such interiors than the Bizarre patterns of carved and mixed woodwork. I think we should find an improvement in appearance...' Indeed, Gresley took a close interest in the interior finish of rolling stock and, from this time onwards, generally used commercial designers or furnishers for the decor of prestige vehicles. He and Bulleid showed a preference for plain, painted surfaces rather than varnished woodwork.

The formation of the 8 am at or about 1907, and after receipt of the new stock, survives in an undated diagram in the PRO archives:

Brake third, Third, Open third, Open third, Restaurant/kitchen third, Open first, Brake first

Originally, the destination boards fitted to the GN/NE carriages were made of iron but they became the standard type in 1911 and were lettered London (Kings Cross) and Newcastle.

GN/NE Joint Stock after 1910

Brake first No. 34 became a full first in 1911 and a new full brake was built in 1912 at Doncaster - No. 36. As a result of travellers' superstitions, sleeping car No. 13 changed numbers with first No. 10 in 1922. At Grouping, the GN/NE carriages at first had their numbers increased by 400 and from 1925 they were renumbered into the East Coast series as 1401 - 3/5 - 34, the bogie brakes becoming 150 - 152 in the EC van series.

As to carriage workings, the set forming the 8 am Newcastle - Kings Cross returned as the 5.30 pm from Kings Cross. As shown in the train formations taken from the 1914 ECJS carriage workings, other GN/NE vehicles came up on the 10.28 am from Newcastle (10 am Sundays) which included ECJS stock worked on the 7.45 am from Edinburgh - Newcastle. The GN/NE catering vehicles were at one stage returned on the 10.35 am Kings Cross - Edinburgh, as far as Newcastle, but in the summer 1914 timetable reached Newcastle by stages as empty stock, beginning with attachment to the 5.20 am Kings Cross - Doncaster slow train. The other vehicles were dispatched from Kings Cross as empty stock to York (before their return to Newcastle) on the 8.45 am semi-fast, or on the 1.40 pm express.

The GN/NE Joint stock after Grouping

As with other Doncaster-built vestibuled stock of the period, compound-bolster bogies were fitted in place of the 8 ft wheelbase variety in 1924/5, namely on Nos. 1403/10-5/20-5/9/30. Four of the catering vehicles, Nos. 1401/2/5/6, were transferred to the GC section in 1925 and other transfers from East Coast stock took place from the early 1930s. By 1930/1, the air braking equipment was stripped from the ex-GN/NE stock.

The sleeping cars received compound-bolster bogies in 1924 and the folding washbasins of Nos. (1)410/4 were replaced by the pedestal type at the same time. All four cars survived until 1935 - 7.

Under the LNER's 1933 Carriage Building Programme, open thirds Nos. 1421 - 5 were transferred from East Coast stock to the GN section and converted to buffet cars as Nos. 43133 - 6 while what became No. 43137 was originally allocated to the GE section. As rebuilt, they featured a kitchen, buffet counter and seating for 23 passengers. Typical duties in 1933 included working on the 8.45 am Kings Cross - Doncaster and back, the 9.35 am Kings Cross - Cambridge and back, and in the Cleethorpes portion of the 4 pm Kings Cross, to return south at 9.10 am the next day. No 43135 was modified in 1941 and the seating reduced by two. All five cars survived into the mid/late 1950s, Nos. 43133 - 5 being recorded on the Lowestoft - York through train at dates between 1955 - 8. Their demise was sealed with the decision to eliminate catering vehicles with oil-gas cooking equipment by the end of the summer 1961 timetable.

The 1935 Carriage Building Programme provided for the transfer from East Coast stock to the North Eastern Area of the last straight-sided GN/NE vehicles, Nos. 1403/9/13 and van 151. No. 1409 was reclassified as a third and No. 1403 was converted to a full brake while later vehicles Nos. 1429/30/4 went to the Northern Scottish Area in 1936/7. Next in the fleet to go from the East Coast allocation were open firsts Nos. 1431 - 3, transferred under the 1939 CBP as open thirds to the Northern Scottish Area. The restaurant thirds remained in the East Coast allocation, being renumbered under the 1942 scheme and Nos. 1436/7, at least, lasted into 1960, No. 1437 having been repainted BR maroon.

REPRODUCTIONS FROM EAST COAST RAILWAYS THROUGH CARRIAGE WORKING instructions for the period July - September 1914 inclusive.

Throughout the reproductions, please note that all vehicles are ECJS, except where specified to the contrary; those shown as * are non-vestibuled and those in italics had loading instructions for luggage, mails etc, not reproduced here.

In column 4, the 'class' refers to the carriage with the lowest number of that type. A key is given only for the elliptical-roofed carriages. Hence, '97' = EC Dia 49A; '78' = EC Dia 3A; '1' = EC Dia 2B; '192' = EC Dia 29A; '190' = EC Dia 75A; '211' = EC Dia 80A; '76' = EC Dia 2B; '24' = EC Dia 34; '155' = EC Dia 39B; '80' = EC Dia 45; '98' = EC Dia 49; '122' = EC Dia 58; '19' = EC Dia 35; '120' = EC Dia 63; '90' = EC Dia 69; '165' = EC Dia 64.

From	To	Vehicles in order from Engine.	Class.	Pairs of Wheels	Weight. Tons	Weight. Cwt.	Seats. 1st.	Seats. 3rd.	Up Working.
	9.50 a.m.								
King's Cross	**Edinburgh**... (arr. 6.0 p.m.)	*Brake Third* ...	280	6	34	2		24	10.0 a.m. from Edinburgh.
		Third	93	4	28	16		42	
		Third ...	93	4	28	16		42	
		Open Third ...	354	6	38	0		47	
		Pantry Third	313	6	37	4		42	
		Kitchen First	310	6	37	14	20		
		Corridor First	86	4	30	0	36		
		Brake Van ...	45	4	23	2			
		Leaving King's	Cross	40	257	14	56	197	
	10.0 a.m.								
York .. ... (dep. 1.53 p.m.)	**Edinburgh**... (arr. 6.15 p.m.)	G.P.O. Van ...	N.E.	4	26	2			7.45 p.m. from Edinburgh.
King's Cross	**Glasgow** .. (arr. 7.35 p.m.)	*Brake Third* ...	97	4	27	6		18	8.40 a.m. from Glasgow and 10.15 a.m. from Edinburgh.
		Compo. ...	78	4	31	0	10	27	
"	**Edinburgh**... (arr. 6.15 p.m.)	Compo. ...	1	4	29	17	10	30	10.15 a.m. from Edinburgh.
		Third D Car	192	4	29	10		42	
		Kitchen	211	4	35	7			
		First D Car	190	4	29	10	24		
"	**Perth** ... ... (arr. 7.52 p.m.)	*Compo.* ...	76	4	34	0	10	24	8.35 a.m. from Perth and 10.15 a.m. from Edinburgh
"	**Aberdeen** .. (arr. 10.5 p.m.)	Compo. ...	1	4	29	17	10	30	6.15 a.m. from Aberdeen and 10.15 a.m. from Edinburgh.
		Third	24	4	31	15		48	
"	"	*Brake Van* ...	155	4	25	15			
		Leaving King's	Cross	40	303	17	64	219	

The 9.50 am and 10.0 am 'Flying Scotsman' from Kings Cross - Edinburgh. The former was the relief train which ran during the summer and, in 1914, until and including October; earlier practice was to run one train only in each direction after 1st October, but to duplicate them when required. The 9.50 am consists of clerestory vehicles, and the 10.0 am, a 1914 set of elliptical-roofed carriages for this train. Some of these were older than 1914. The working of the North Eastern Railway TPO van next the engine north of York was a regular feature of the 'Flying Scotsman's' operation. The down and up 'Flying Scotsman' were duplicated to/from Newcastle at times, e.g., on Mondays and Fridays in May, and weekdays during June 1914. *Public Record Office*

From	To	Vehicles in order from Engine.	Class.	Pairs of Wheels.	Weight. Tons	Weight. Cwt.	Seats. 1st.	Seats. 3rd.	Up Working.
	10.35 a.m.								
Bristol ...	Newcastle (arr. 5.29 p.m.)	Brake Third ...	*Mid.	4	24	0			Locally.
		Compo. ...	*Mid.	4	28	0			
		Brake Third ...	*Mid.	4	24	0			
King's Cross	Glasgow ... (arr. 10.29 p.m.)	*Dual Brake Cpo.*	342	6	36	6	8	12	11.0 a.m. from Glasgow and 12.25 p.m. from Edinburgh.
		Dual Third	38	4	27	5		42	
"	Edinburgh (arr. 8.46 p.m.)	Compo. ...	301	6	38	18	12	28	2.30 p.m. from Edinburgh.
		Pantry Third...	64	4	32	3		34	7.30 a.m. Edinburgh to Perth following day. 12.30 p.m. from Perth, & 2.30 p.m. from Edinburgh.
		Compo. D. Car.	362	6	41	9	12	18	
		Third ...	38	4	27	5		42	7.45 a.m. from Edinburgh.
		Brake Van ...	45	4	23	2			10.25 a.m. from Edinburgh.
"	Cromer ... (arr. 2.51 p.m.)	Semi-open Third	G.N.	4	28	18		48	
		Brake Compo.	G.N.	4	27	12	10	24	
		Brake Van ‡ ...	G.N.	3	12	16			
Grantham ...	Doncaster ...	Brake Third ¶	G.N.	3	13	12		18	Locally.
		Third ¶	G.N.	3	17	8		24	
Newcastle (dep. 5.45 p.m.)	Alnmouth ... (arr. 6.33 p.m.)	Brake Compo...	*N.E.	4	25	10	11	24	
		Brake Third ...	*N.E.	4	24	9		40	
	Leaving	King's Cross ...	...	45	295	14	42	248	
	11.20 a.m.								
King's Cross	Edinburgh (arr. 8.5 p.m.)	*Brake Third*	262	6	31	19		24	10.35 p.m. from Edinburgh.
"	Perth... ... (arr. 10.37 p.m.)	Compo. ...	298	6	38	17	12	30	12.30 p.m. from Perth and 2.30 p.m. from Edinburgh.
"	Montrose ... (arr. 12.12 a.m.)	*Dual Compo* §...	17	4	29	9	8	18	10.20 a.m. from Aberdeen and 2.30 p.m. from Edinburgh.
		Dual Third §...	38	4	27	5		42	
"	Edinburgh (arr. 8.5 p.m.)	Pantry Third...	64	4	32	3		34	12.25 p.m. from Edinburgh.
		Compo. D. Car	316	6	33	17	12	12	
		First	89	4	28	16	36		
		Brake Van ...	45	4	23	2			
	North Berwick (arr. 8.3 p.m.)	*Dual Brake Cpo.*	80	6	37	-	8	18	12.30 p.m. from North Berwick.
Keswick ... (dep. 12.35 p.m.)	Newcastle (arr. 5.9 p.m.)	Brake Compo. ‡	*N.E.	4	26	10	9	18	Locally.
	Leaving	King's Cross ...	...	44	287	8	76	178	

§ To be worked locally to Aberdeen. ‡ Commences July 11th.
¶ Sats. only Commences July 11th.

The seasonal 10.35 am Kings Cross - Edinburgh and 11.20 am Kings Cross - Edinburgh, in each case conveying interesting non-ECJS through carriages such as Bristol - Newcastle (Midland stock); Kings Cross - Cromer (GNR stock) and Keswick - Newcastle (NER stock) via Stainmore and Darlington. All the ECJS vehicles were clerestories, with the exception of the dual-fitted brake composite for North Berwick which was one of the EC Dia. 45 carriages, chosen for their large luggage compartment. Neither train ran after September.
Public Record Office

FROM	TO	Vehicles in order from Engine.	Class.	Pairs of Wheels.	Weight. Tons	Weight. Cwt.	Seats. 1st.	Seats. 3rd.	UP WORKING.
	2.20 p.m.								
King's Cross	**Edinburgh** (arr. 10.45 p.m.)	*Dual Brake 3rd* ‖	98	4	27	18		36	12.0 noon from Edinburgh, Sunday.
		Brake Compo ...	239	6	34	16	8	12	7.45 p.m. from Edinburgh.
		Third... ...	24	4	31	15		48	
		Dual Compo ‖	246	6	35	18	12	24	12.0 noon from Edinburgh, Sunday.
		Third... ...	24	4	31	15		48	2.0 p.m. from Edinburgh.
		Open Third ...	14	4	29	18		42	
		Pantry Third	304	6	39	4		42	
		Kitchen First	332	6	40	12	18		
		First	122	4	29	12	28		
		Brake Van ...	19	4	24	4			
	Newcastle (arr. 8.3 p.m.)	*Brake Van* § ...	*49	3	12	17			Locally to Edinburgh & 6.25 p.m from Edinburgh
		King's Cross ...		41	274	13	54	192	
	7.55 p.m. (Sats. and Sundays excepted.)								
King's Cross	**Inverness** ... (arr. 9.8 a.m.)	*Brake Van* ...	45	4	23	2			Loc'llytoP'rth. 7.55 p.m. from Perth & 10.35 p.m. from Edinburgh.
		Third	24	4	31	15		48	
		Third	24	4	31	15		48	5.0 p.m. from Inverness and 11.15 p.m. from Edinburgh.
		Sleeping Car †	120	4	32	19	10be	rths	
		Compo. ...	17	4	29	9	8	18	
		Brake Van ...	19	4	24	4			
	Fort William (arr. 9.42 a.m.)	Third	38	4	27	5		42	5.5 p.m. from Fort William & 10.55 p.m. from E'burgh
		Sleeping Compo	90	4	31	16	6 berths	12	
		Brake Van ...	259	3	14	4			
	Leaving	King's Cross ...	...	35	246	9	24	168	

‖ Saturdays only. § Attached at Newcastle to 11.45 p.m. from King's Cross. Will be a G.N. South end brake compo on Sats. to return 11.19 p m. from Newcastle Sats. † Will go through to Strathpeffer *if* required.

The 2.20 pm Kings Cross - Edinburgh, the afternoon 'Scotsman'. Despite the number of elliptical-roofed carriages apparently in the Joint Stock by this date, this train includes a mixture of these and clerestory vehicles. Although the down afternoon 'Scotsman' (or Scotch express, as the GNR tended to call it) was not regularly duplicated, its up line counterpart ran in the summer timetable as the 2 pm and 2.30 pm from Edinburgh, respectively the main train from Edinburgh only (but gaining a through GNR carriage from West Hartlepool - Kings Cross), and the through carriages from Perth, Aberdeen and Glasgow. The 2 pm usually ceased running after the end of September. The 7.55 pm was the first part of the year-long 8 pm down and conveyed the Fort William and Inverness portions of that train. *Public Record Office*

From	To	Vehicles in order from Engine.	Class.	Pairs of Wheels.	Weight. Tons	Weight. Cwt.	Seats. 1st.	Seats. 3rd.	Up Working.
	8.15 p.m. (Sats. & Suns. excpd)								
Newcastle (dep. 1.33 a.m.)	Glasgow ... (arr. 5.35 a.m.)	Dual fitted Brake Third § (South end)	263	6	31	19		24	9.35 p.m. from Glasgow and 11.15 p.m. from Edinburgh.
King's Cross	"	*Brake Van* ...	19	4	24	4			5.0 p.m. from Glasgow.
"	Edinburgh (arr. 3.55 a.m.)	*Brake Van* † ...	19	4	24	4			4.0 p.m. from Edinburgh.
"	Aberdeen ... (arr. 7.22 a.m.)	*Brake Van* ...	19	4	24	4			
		Third ...	24	4	31	15		48	7.35 p.m. from Aberdeen and 11.15 p.m. from Edinburgh.
		Third ...	24	4	31	15		48	
		Sleeping Car ...	165	4	32	19	10	berths	
		Brake Compo. ...	239	6	34	16	8	12	
"	Montrose ... (arr. 6.24 a.m.)	*Brake Third* ... (South end)	262	6	31	19		24	7.50 p.m. from Montrose and 10.55 p.m. from Edinburgh.
	Leaving King's Cross ...		...	36	235	16	18	132	

*§ Leaves King's Cross 4.20 p.m. and Doncaster at 9.35 p.m.
† To be vestibuled both ends.

The 8.15 pm Kings Cross - Edinburgh, with the Aberdeen portion forward on the 4.0 am from Edinburgh Waverley. This was the main part from the winter 8 pm down sleeping car express. The 8 pm down was duplicated at Christmas and other holidays, the first portion for Aberdeen and Inverness, the second, for Newcastle, Edinburgh and Glasgow. On both the 7.55 pm and 8.15 pm down the sleeping cars are elliptical-roofed. In the winter 1914/5 timetable, the Inverness and Fort William cars on the 8 pm down did not run throughout the year and were EC Dia. 70A vehicles. The East and West Coast companies ran through carriages and sleeping cars on alternate days from Kings Cross and Euston respectively. The East and West Coast sleepers for Inverness were a 'Q' working to/from Strathpeffer. *Public Record Office*

From	To	Vehicles in order from Engine.	Class.	Pairs of wheels.	Weight. Tons	Weight. Cwt.	Seats. 1st.	Seats. 3rd.	Up Working.
Week days	**8.45 p.m.** (Sats. excepted.)	**and Sundays**							
King's Cross	**Hull** ... ... (arr. 1.32 a.m.)	*Brake Van* § ...	* G.N.	3	12	16			As required.
"	**Leeds** ...	Mail Van ...	* G.N.	2	10	9			Locally.
"	**Newcastle** (arr. 2.58 a.m.)	Mail Van ...	G.N.	3	15	5			7.27 a.m. from Newcastle, and 9.50 p.m. from York.
"	"	Mail Van ...	G.N.	3	15	5			
"	"	Pantry Third †	GN&NE (5 class)	4	31	3	Ety.		10.0 a.m. from Newcastle, Sundays.
"	"	Kitchen First †	GN&NE (1 class)	4	33	3		Ety.	
"	"	*Brake Van* § ...	GN&NE	4	25	5			10.38 a.m. from Newcastle.
Newcastle .. (dep. 3.8 a.m.)	**Edinburgh** (arr. 5.53 a.m.)	G.P.O. Van ...	N.E.	4	26	2			Locally.
King's Cross	**Glasgow** ... (arr. 7.23 a.m.)	*Brake Compo.*...	239	6	34	16	8	12	1.0 p.m. from Glasgow and 2.30 p.m. from Edinburgh.
		Third... ...	24	4	31	15		48	
"	"	Sleeping Compo	147	4	31	8	6 berths	12	Locally to Edinburgh and 7.45 p.m. from Edinburgh.
"	**Edinburgh** (arr. 5.53 a.m.)	*Brake Third* ...	98	4	27	18		36	10.25 a.m. from Edinburgh.
		Twin Compo...	202	6	37	9	16	30	
		Brake Third ...	262	6	31	19		24	
		Leaving King's	**Cross.**	45	274	5	30	162	

§ Sundays excepted. † Sundays only.

The 8.45 pm Kings Cross - Edinburgh, incidentally showing one empty stock working for GN/NE vehicles, with a couple of elliptical-roofed vehicles. The 'class 147' sleeping composite was a clerestory vehicle and the winter train did not have a sleeping car for Glasgow. *Public Record Office*

From	To	Vehicles in order from Engine.	Class	Pairs of Wheels	Weight. Tons	Weight. Cwt.	Seats. 1st.	Seats. 3rd.	Up Working.
King's Cross	11.30 p.m. (Saturdays only.) Aberdeen ... (arr. 11.28 a.m.)	*Brake Compo.*	342	6	36	6	8	12	3.30 p.m. from Aberdeen. 7.45 p.m. from Edinburgh, Sundays.
		Third ...	38	4	27	5		42	
		Sleeping Car...	125	6	36	6	10 b'ths		Locally to Edinburgh.
	Perth ... (arr. 8.40 a.m.)	Sleeping Car ...	120	4	32	19	10 b'ths		Locally from Perth and 10.50 p.m. from Edinburgh, Sundays.
		Third ...	24	4	31	15		48	7.55 p.m. from Perth and 10.35 p.m. from Edinburgh, Mondays.
		Compo. ...	17	4	29	9	8	18	4.10 p.m. from Perth and 7.45 p.m. from Edinburgh, Sundays.
		Third ...	38	4	27	5		42	
		Brake Van ...	45	4	23	2			7.55 p.m. from Perth and 10.35 p.m. from Edinburgh, Mondays.
	Leaving	King's Cross ...	...	36	244	7	36	162	

The 11.30 pm Saturdays only Kings Cross - Edinburgh, with modern vehicles in the Perth portion. In the winter 1914/5 timetable the weekday Glasgow section had a EC Dia. 69 sleeping car and there was an older sleeper composite in the Perth portion. One of the EC Dia. 64 cars ran to Dundee. *Public Record Office*

From	To	Vehicles in order from Engine.	Class.	Pairs of Wheels.	Weight. Tons	Weight. Cwt.	Seats. 1st.	Seats. 3rd.	Up Working.
Week days	**11.45 p.m.** Saturdays excepted	**and Sundays.**							
Newcastle...	**Edinburgh**	Brake Van ‡...	*49	3	12	17	Ety.		6.25 p.m. from Edinburgh.
King's Cross	**Glasgow** ... (arr. 9.5 a.m.)	*Brake Compo* ...	342	6	36	6	8	12	9.35 p.m. from Glasgow, and 10.55 p.m. from Edinburgh.
		Brake Third ...	98	4	27	18		36	
		Sleeping Car ...	235	4	30	19	10 berths		
"	**Edinburgh** (arr. 7.25 a.m.)	*Brake Third* ... (South end)	262	6	31	19		24	7.45 p.m. from Edinburgh.
"	**North Berwick** (arr. 9.8 a.m.)	Dual Sleeping Car §...	235	4	30	19	10 berths		Locally to Edinburgh. 10.35 p.m. from Edinburgh.
"		*Dual Brake C'po*§	80	6	37	0	8	18	
	Newcastle (arr. 5.0 a.m.)	Sleeping Car ...	GN&NE	4	35	1	11 berths		11.19 p.m. from Newcastle. Saturdays excepted.
		Third ...	GN&NE	4	29	13		42	
		Brake Van ...	G.N.	4	22	17			
	Leaving	King's Cross ...	...	42	282	12	47	132	
	11.45 p.m. Saturdays only.								
Newcastle	**Edinburgh**	Brake Van ...	*49	3	12	17	Ety.		6.25 p.m. from Edinburgh.
King's Cross	**Glasgow** ... (arr. 10.35 a.m.)	*Brake Compo* ...	342	6	36	6	8	12	9.35 p.m. from Glasgow, 10.50 p.m. from Edinburgh (Sundays).
		Third ...	38	4	27	5		42	
		Sleeping Car ...	165	4	32	19	10 berths		
"	**Edinburgh** (arr. 7.25 a.m.)	Third ...	38	4	27	5		42	10.50 p.m. from Edinburgh Sunday.
		Dual Brake third	280	6	33	3		24	12 noon from Edinburgh Sundays.
"	**Newcastle** (arr. 5.0 a.m.)	*Brake Van* ...	GN&NE	4	25	3			10.28 a.m. from Newcastle (Monday).
		Brake Van ...	G.N.	4	22	17			10.0 a.m. from Newcastle (Sundays)
"	**York** ... (arr. 3.20 a.m.)	*Brake Van* ...	G N	4	22	17			Spare.
	Leaving	King's Cross ...	...	36	227	17	18	120	

§ Attached to 5.50 a.m. from Newcastle. ‡ Mondays excepted.

The 11.45 pm Kings Cross - Edinburgh, of interest for showing the GN/NE Joint sleeping car and third conveyed - Saturdays excepted - on this train and the EC Dia. 45 brake composite working to North Berwick. These vehicles were used on the night service from Kings Cross - North Berwick as late as 1935. Before 1913, the 11.45 pm was generally discontinued January - March inclusive and its vehicles worked on the 11.30 pm down which would be duplicated as required. *Public Record Office*

Formation of Trains conveying East Coast Stock on leaving Edinburgh.

From	To	Vehicles in order from Engine.	Class.	Pairs of Wheels.	Weight. Tons	Weight. Cwt.	Seats. 1st.	Seats. 3rd.	Down Working.
	7.45 a.m.								
Edinburgh	**Newcastle** (arr. 10.19 a.m.)	Brake Compo.	N.E.	4	26	15	9	18	12.12 p.m Newcastle to Edinburgh.
		Compo. D. Car	N.E.	4	30	7	10	15	
	King's Cross (arr. 4.10 p.m.)	Third ...	38	4	27	5		42	10.35 a.m. from King's Cross.
		Third ...	38	4	27	5		42	10.30 p.m. from King's Cross.
		Compo. ...	292	6	39	2	12	27	
		Brake Van ...	45	4	23	2			
	Leaving	Edinburgh		26	173	16	31	114	
	10.28 a.m. from Newcastle.								
Newcastle	**King's Cross** (arr. 4.10 p.m.)	Brake Van ...	GN&NE	4	25	5			8.45 p.m. from King's Cross and 11.45 p.m. Sats.
		First Corridor	GN&NE	4	29	5	24		8.45 a.m. from King's Cross
		Kitchen First §	GN&NE (1 class)	4	33	3	21		5.20 a.m. from King's Cross.
		Pantry Third §	GN&NE (5 class)	4	31	3		36	
		Third Open ...	GN&NE	4	31	3		36	1.40 p.m. from King's Cross.
		Third ...	GN&NE	4	29	13		42	8.45 a.m. from King's Cross.
Edinburgh (dep. 7.45 a.m.)	"	Third ...	38	4	27	5		42	10.35 a.m. from King's Cross.
		Third ...	38	4	27	5		42	10.30 p.m. from King's Cross.
		Compo. ...	292	6	39	2	12	27	
		Brake Van ...	45	4	23	2			
	Leaving	Newcastle		42	296	6	57	225	

§ Will be Open First (31 class) and Kitchen Third (26 class) on alternate days.

Because what went down had to come up, to save repetition and also because the up workings for carriages are shown in the last column of the down train formations, the up train workings are restricted to just one train, the 10.28 am Newcastle - Kings Cross, which appears in the working book by virtue of conveying the ECJS vehicles that had arrived on the 7.45 am from Edinburgh. These ran with a North Eastern Railway dining car on the first leg of the journey and so gave the impression of a through restaurant car express from Edinburgh - Kings Cross. In summer, the GN/NE Joint dining cars on the 10.28 am had previously returned on the 10.35 am King's Cross - Edinburgh, as far as Newcastle.

Public Record Office

Chapter Five

GNR Vestibuled Stock including dining cars and articulated stock

The Sheffield stock - 1906

This well-known corridor stock comprised the first set trains to be built by Gresley and is significant in that its general outline and features were to become standardised for Gresley GNR and LNER stock until 1941. The carriages had several fine features and at the time of introduction must have been strong rivals with the GWR 'Dreadnought' and LNWR American Boat Stock as the best elliptical-roofed carriages of the period. In design, however, they could claim to be more advanced than either of these, having Pullman gangways and buckeye couplers; from them was derived a standard vehicle that served both GNR and LNER whereas the other railways' examples were reserved for specialised use.

It is worth quoting a somewhat typically anti-Americanism from the *Railway Magazine* of December 1906. Suitably impressed by Doncaster's product it pronounced:

> We are glad to see that the exterior of the vehicles are furnished in the well-known GNR style of bold panelling instead of the matchboarded design to be seen in some vehicles running into Kings Cross. [This was a reference to the NER-built carriages in the 1905 GN/NE Joint set train.] These latter suggest the idea that they have been built in an American lumber yard rather than in a down to date British railway carriage works.

The first Sheffield stock carriages appeared in July 1906, the GNR Traffic Committee having recommended on 29th June, 1905 the construction of three new trains on capital stock and six additional dining cars. The train sets made their debut in the winter service of 1906, one set working down on the 6.5 pm Kings Cross - Manchester and 3.26 pm return, the second used for the 6.35 pm Sheffield - Kings Cross, to return on the 10.20 am Kings Cross - Sheffield. As with some of the other GNR expresses, these were light formations of four carriages, made up initially of a brake first, composite dining car, open third and brake third of the new stock.

Apart from the dining cars, these carriages were 58 ft 6 in. over the end panels in length and 8 ft 6 in. wide. The dining cars were 65 ft 6 in. in length and 9 ft wide. All were carried on strongly-trussed steel underframes, the dining cars running on 11 ft 9 in. wheelbase six-wheeled bogies, the other carriages on standard 8 ft bogies, later exchanged for the 8 ft 6 in. compound-bolster type. Some vehicles had Stone's train lighting, others the Vickers-Maxim type.

As to the bodywork, the saloon compartments had large bodyside windows extending up to the cant-rail, with small opening lights, hinged at the top and opening outwards. The side-corridor compartments had bodyside doors to each compartment and toplights to the quarterlight windows. These features were to become widely used for the Gresley GNR corridor stock.

The first-class seated two-a-side only and featured mahogany and sycamore panelling in the compartments, with tapestry upholstery while the third-class had teak panelling and velvet pile upholstery. The first-class dining car had saloon panelling in harewood and satinwood and a flat-white ceiling with Carton Pierre ornaments. The lighting was most striking and modern with the 'Lino Light' lamps hidden behind the ceiling cornices illuminating the ceiling with diffused light. There were also table lamps. The loose seating comprised chairs upholstered in 'high-class' Blenheim tapestry, there was hand-made carpet on the floor and the interior fittings were in a dull silver finish. To the staff writer in the *Railway Gazette* of 15th March, 1907, the 'interior appointments and comfort of these cars left nothing to be desired . . .'

The Sheffield stock comprised twelve carriages, made up initially into the three sets, one of which was spare, the vehicles being numbered 3039-50. In 1910, an additional open third was built, No. 3223, presumably to act as a spare for the Sheffield stock. The composite dining cars, Nos. 3039-41, had a central kitchen with the dining saloons each side. This was an arrangement which was not later followed by Doncaster for GNR, ECJS, GN/NE or LNER dining cars. Generally, either a semi-open first ran with a third-class restaurant car or else there was a first-class car paired with a pantry third. No doubt the Sheffield cars were an exception in view of the lightweight formations run on this service.

There were also the six first-class (Nos. 3033 - 5) and third-class (Nos. 3036 - 8) dining cars for general service which had all the general features of the Sheffield stock composite diners. Nos. 3036 - 8 were what were termed by the LNER as restaurant pantry cars. Nos. 3036/7 had two saloons seating 24 and 18 while No. 3038 had three saloons seating 12, 12 and 18; in each case the pantry was at one end.

Subsequently, there were few changes to the carriages which for convenience will all be referred to as Sheffield stock, although the open thirds appear to have been converted to two-a- side seating at some date and some of the windows of the first-class dining cars received glass louvred ventilators. Composite dining cars Nos. 3040/1 were transferred to the Southern Scottish Area in April 1927 and duly renumbered; possibly the GN section could find no use for their limited seating capacity. In 1936, the two cars were transferred to the North Eastern Area and rebuilt as kitchen cars at Dukinfield in 1936/7, becoming 2334/5; they remained in service until 1960. No. 3039 was transferred to the North Eastern Area in 1933 and renumbered 22262. It was rebuilt as a kitchen car at Dukinfield in 1936.

The Sheffield stock remained on front-line workings through the 1930s when Nos. 43033/6 were used on the 'Scarborough Flyer'. Brake first No. 43042, for instance, was in the Hull portion of the 5.45 pm from Kings Cross as late as 1935. The first to be withdrawn was probably diner No. 43033 which was condemned in July 1948 but the other carriages lasted into the 1950s.

No. 43034 was restored to its original GNR exterior appearance in October 1952 as part of the celebrations to mark the centenary of the Kings Cross station. The restaurant car's restoration was carefully undertaken at Doncaster using enlarged sections of the original works' photographs for guidance on the lettering. It was not to stay for long in this condition as during the next year it was converted to a cafeteria car. No. 43035 was also converted in 1953 as a cafeteria car and both survived into the early 1960s. For further details of the conversion of former GNR dining cars as cafeteria cars, see page 99.

GNR general service vestibuled stock 1905 - 22

Although Gresley's appointment as carriage and wagon superintendent saw the adoption of modern carriage designs and construction at Doncaster, unlike the parallel situation at Swindon with G.J. Churchward this did not presage a major carriage building programme. Nor did it bring standardisation of types. For between 1905 and 1922 only 210 general service vestibuled carriages were built for GNR services and they were to no less than 38 different designs. The largest number under one Diagram was 21 and these were corridor thirds built over a period of ten years. For purely GNR services the maximum number of vestibuled carriages built in one year was no more than 41. So the Gresley GNR elliptical-roofed carriage was hardly a mass-produced product.

But there were standard features such as the application of buckeye couplers and Pullman type gangways, as well as a consistent outline. The first elliptical-roofed vehicles were the railcar carriage portions but the first elliptical-roofed vestibuled carriage was No. 2977, a corridor composite (GN Dia. 101) completed in December 1905. This was 63 ft 6¼ in. long with large corridor - side windows and body end lights and running on 11 ft 9 in. six-wheel bogies. Building at the same time was a batch of ten open thirds (GN Dia. 248H), to the same body length and on the same bogies. These were subsequently modified to become four-wheeled bogies having lost their centre wheelsets. The third type of elliptical-roofed carriage turned out at Doncaster from late 1905 was a brake open third (GN Dia. 270) to an unusual 50 ft 10½ in. length.

Although vehicles to these three Diagrams were the earliest 'Gresley' carriages, they seem to have originated as Howlden clerestory designs which had been altered to take elliptical roofs and so the Sheffield stock and the vehicles built for the ECJS the following year must be regarded as the true prototypes of the Gresley vestibuled carriage.

There were a number of features common to the Gresley GNR vestibuled carriages. The large corridor-side windows extended from the waist to the cant-rail and generally, although not always, were without ventilators. The side-corridor vehicles had doors to the outside of each compartment flanked by quarterlights. Doors and quarterlights had fanlights. For many open carriages the large windows were full height and they had hinged ventilators beneath the cant-rail but others had quarterlights and intervening droplights to each seating bay. A number of brake thirds, brake composites and some earlier composites had body end lights although this was more a feature associated with ECJS vehicles. Brake carriages had neat, smooth-panelled guard's duckets.

A number of thirds and brake thirds as well as four Diagrams of vestibuled composites (GN Diagrams 108/9/14/64) had an equal proportion of third-class accommodation in open bays and compartments. The GNR referred to them as semi-open. A similar arrangement was used by Bulleid in some Southern Railway stock built after 1945.

From 1905, electric lighting was used in this general service stock but there was a reversion to gas lighting subsequently, and it was only after 1914 that all new stock was built with electric lighting. This was despite agreement by the GNR Locomotive Committee in late 1905 that all new GNR carriages to capital or revenue accounts should be so fitted.

At first, the 8 ft wheelbase bogie was used, along with the 11 ft 9 in. six-wheeled design already mentioned. From 1909, the compound-bolster bogie began to be employed and, generally after 1920 and into LNER days, many earlier carriages received them also. A 10 ft wheelbase design was used concurrently and until just before Grouping. There were also experimental bogies such as the French PLM Railway bogies with which composite No. 2705 (GN Dia. 164K) ran for a while and the Skefco roller bearing axleboxes fitted to the bogies of composite No. 955 (GN Dia. 109).

GNR Gresley Vestibuled Carriage Types and Diagrams

Type	*Diagram*	*Length/Width*	*Compartments*	*Seats*	*First Built*
Corridor first	86	61′ 6″ X 8′ 6″	7	28	1912
LNER code: (FK)	87	61′ 6″ X 8′ 6″	7	42	1921

These side-corridor firsts of conventional appearance and layout differed in that Dia. 86 seated two-a-side, Dia. 87 three-a-side and the former were built with 10 ft wheelbase bogies and the 1921 carriages had the 8 ft 6 in. compound-bolster type.

Type	*Diagram*	*Length/Width*	*Layout*	*Seats*	*First Built*
Open third/	224	58′ 6″ X 8′ 6″	2 saloons	42*	1906
open second	229	52′ 6″ X 8′ 6″	3 saloons	42	1909
LNER code:	248A	58′ 6″ X 9′ 0″	3 saloons	45	1911
(TO)	248E	58′ 6″ X 9′ 0″	3 saloons	48	1913
	248H	63′ 6¼″X 8′ 6″	3 saloons	47	1905

* Later 56 seats

Dia. 224 was the Sheffield stock open third, originally seating 2 + 1, later 2 + 2. No. 3223 was an additional vehicle on this Diagram, built in 1910, for less cost than each of those on the first order. Apart from this type, the other GNR open thirds had three saloons.

Dia. 229, also with 2 + 1 seating, had a droplight and quarterlights to each bay and each side, only alternate bays having opening doors. Diagrams 248A/248E were of more attractive appearance with large windows having hinged ventilators to each bay, these two designs being similar, apart from the variation in seating layout.

Dia. 248H was basically a Howlden design, of greater length than the later Gresley types. Of these, only 2975 had an all-steel underframe, the others having wooden underframes. These carriages had originally been composites, built with clerestory roofs on Diagram 104. No 1761 was the other member of the batch and remained with its clerestory roof.

Buffet car conversions from GNR open thirds by the LNER

In April 1932, Nos. 43130/1 of Dia. 229 were converted to provide a buffet counter at one end of the vehicle in order to run in the Garden City and Cambridge Buffet trains introduced from 2nd May, 1932. These new workings were put on in response to competition from road coaches. The original proposal had been to use Sentinel articulated steam railcars but instead Sir Ralph Wedgwood, Chief General Manager of the LNER, recommended the use of conventional trains made up of a brake third, buffet third and composite although such light formations were soon strengthened. For instance, a typical Cambridge Buffet train in 1935 comprised two vestibuled thirds to GN Dia. 248D, a vestibuled composite to GN Dia. 164K, a buffet car and a GN Dia. 257 vestibuled brake third.

Nos. 43130/1 reverted to open thirds in 1936, having proved that the Cambridge buffet expresses were a profitable proposition. In the summer of 1932 Nos. 43130/1 had been used for Kings Cross - Skegness and Cambridge - East Coast excursions, as a result of which the LNER moved to wider introduction of buffet cars.

The buffet cars at first introduced on the LNER were conversions from pre-Grouping open thirds, of NER, GER and GNR (also GN/NE Joint Stock) designs. As far as the GNR examples were concerned, No. 41552 (GN Dia 248E) was converted in 1933 at the same time as the GN/NE open thirds described in Chapter 4. Other 1933 conversions to the same layout included open thirds Nos. 41442/88 which were allocated to the GC section as Nos. 52062/3. The 1935 replacements for Nos. 43130/1 were Nos. 41577 and 41651 and with these - and the conversions mentioned above - a larger kitchen was provided than for 43130/1. In addition there was a larger bar counter and cooking facilities included a grill and a refrigerator. The interior was given Rexine wall finishes and furnished with tubular steel chairs, seating 21.

Type	*Diagram*	*Length/Width*	*Compartments*	*Seats*	*First Built*
Third/ semi-open	219	58′ 6″ X 8′ 6″	2 saloons, four compartments	48	1908
LNER code: (TK)/	220	58′ 6″ X 8′ 6″	2 saloons, four compartments	48	1906
(Semi - TO)	228	52′ 6″ X 8′ 6″	7	42	1909
	248	58′ 6″ X 8′ 6″	8	48	1910
	248B	58′ 6″ X 8′ 6″	2 saloons, four compartments	48	1911
	248C	52′ 6″ X 8′ 6″	7	42	1911
	248D	52′ 6″ X 8′ 6″	7	42	1912

The different diagrams of vestibuled thirds exhibited a full range of side-corridor, and combined side-corridor/open - centre gangway - layouts. Some of the vehicles were originally gas-lit.

Diagrams 219/220 differed by virtue of the window arrangements, with large, ventilator fitted windows to the open sections in the former design, and quarterlights to the open sections for the Dia. 220 vehicles.

The plan for each of these Diagrams was:

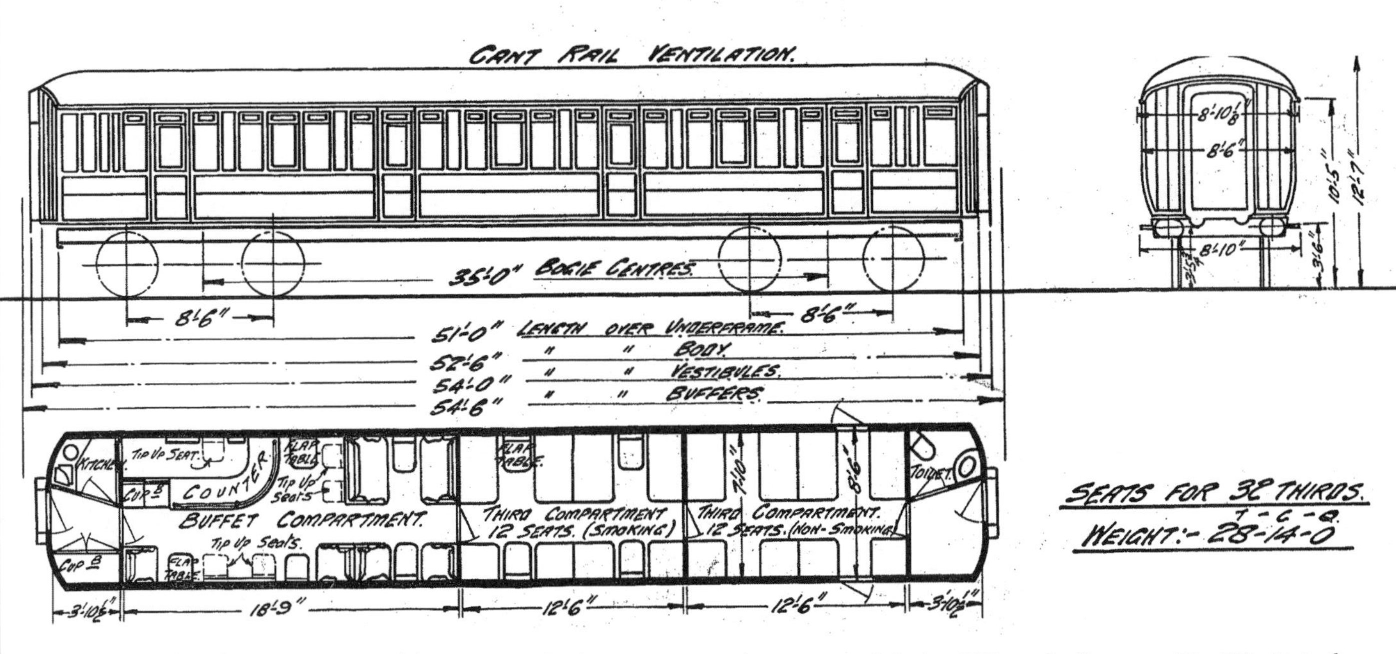

GNR open third (LNER Nos. 43130/1) to Dia. 229 (built Doncaster, 1909), as converted during 1932 to a buffet car on Dia. 78S. Note the reference to 'cant-rail ventilation', by which is meant the hinged toplights or fanlights above the quarterlights. As more suitable converted buffet cars became available, Nos. 43130/1 became spares, by which time they had attracted complaints as a result of 'their lack of comfort and inadequate cooking facilities', according to a report from the Divisional General Manager of the Southern Area in May 1935. Gresley considered that Nos. 43130/1 were unsuitable for upgrading to the standards of the other cars so two more recent ex-GNR vehicles were converted to buffet cars (Nos. 41577, 41651), and Nos. 43130/1 were converted back to open thirds. *National Railway Museum*

Lavatory - open third saloon, 12 seats - open third saloon, 12 seats - three side-corridor - lavatory.
non-smoking smoking compartments

The '248' series could produce the following variants, as well as the different lengths: large corridor-side windows to Dia. 248 and 248D; large windows to both sides of the open sections, including ventilators to the corridor-side windows, and quarterlights to the compartments; large corridor-side windows but with ventilators on the four carriages to Dia. 248C.

The plan for Diagram 248B was:

Lavatory - open third saloon, 12 seats - open third saloon, 12 seats - four side-corridor - lavatory.
non-smoking smoking compartments

Type	*Diagram*	*Length/Width*	*Compartments*	*Seats*	*First Built*
Composite	101	63′ 6¼″ X 8′ 6″	3 1st,	12/33	1905 (as built)
LNER code:			2 3rd class saloons		
(CK)			2½ 1st,	10/31	1914 (as rebuilt)
			2 3rd class saloons		
	108	58′ 6″ X 8′ 6″	3 1st, 2 3rd,	12/27	1907
			1 3rd class saloon		
	109	58′ 6″ X 8′ 6″	3 1st, 2 3rd	12/27	1906
			1 3rd class saloon		
	114	52′ 6″ X 8′ 6″	2 1st,	8/27	1909
			2 3rd class saloons		
	164	58′ 6″ X 8′ 6″	3 1st, 2 3rd	12/27	1910
			1 3rd class saloon		
	164F	58′ 6″ X 8′ 6″	3½ 1st, 5 3rd	10/30	1911
	164K	61′ 6″ X 9′ 0″	3½ 1st, 4 3rd	21/32	1922

As already noted, the composite No. 2977 was the first carriage with an elliptical roof to be built at Doncaster and its layout was more that of a Howlden design, with noticeably cramped lavatories at each end comprising a WC hopper only. On rebuilding in 1914, the lavatories were made full-size with wash-basins, at the expense of a small loss in seating capacity.

Diagrams 108/109 had three-a-side seating in the thirds and their layout was as follows:

Lavatory - two side-corridor - open third saloon, 15 seats - three side-corridor - lavatory
3rd class comps 1st class comps

This was a sensible layout which had the aim of providing third-class smokers with an open section, and with non-smoking accommodation in the compartments. In both Diagrams, the exterior of the open section had quarterlights to each seating bay.

A variation on this layout came with Dia. 114 - notable for the limited first-class seating provided - and this type also differed as there were cant-rail ventilators to the open third section.

Lavatory - two side-corridor - open third saloon, 12 seats - open third saloon, 15 seats - lavatory
1st class comps

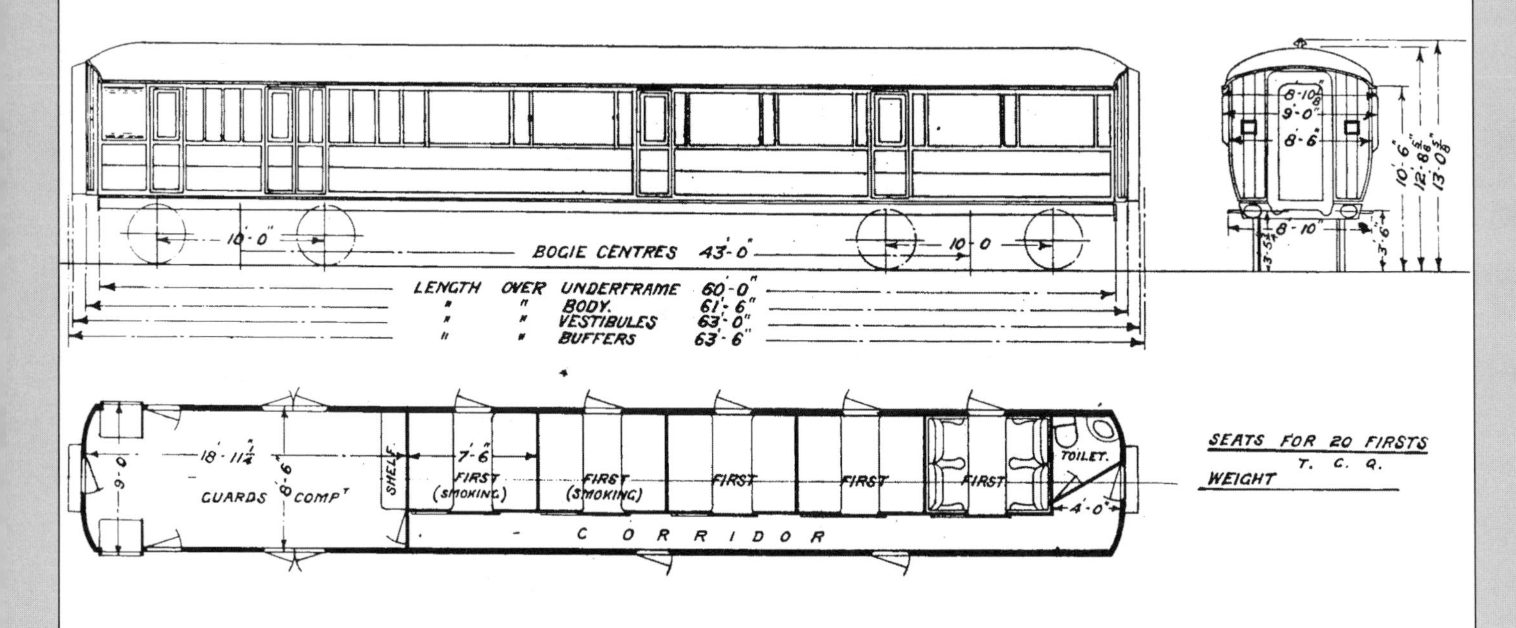

GNR brake first on Dia. 98, built by Doncaster in 1913, and again in 1922. The cost of the one vehicle in 1913 was £2,062, but the pair in 1922 each cost £4,554 - a reflection of the price inflation after 1918.

Dia. 164 had large windows with ventilators to the open section and its layout was:

Lavatory - two side-corridor - open third saloon, 15 seats - three side-corridor - lavatory
3rd class comps 1st class comps

Diagrams 164F and 164K were conventional side-corridor carriage designs, the latter being the only 61 ft 6 in. length design, similar in layout to LNER standard Dia. 7 vestibuled composites which featured in the types built from 1924 onwards.

Type	*Diagram*	*Length/Width*	*Compartments*	*Seats*	*First Built*
Brake first	96	58′ 6″ X 8′ 6″	4	16	1906
LNER code:	97	61′ 6″ X 9′ 0″	5	20	1910
(BFK)	98	61′ 6″ X 8′ 6″	5	20	1913

All three Diagrams represented conventional side-corridor vehicles, 96 being Sheffield stock. No. 3177 of Dia. 97 is shown in the records as being altered to run with the East Coast royal train. As late as 1935, a Dia. 96 vehicle was diagrammed for the Hull section of the 5.45 pm from Kings Cross while one of Dia. 98 worked to Harrogate via Church Fenton on the 1.40 pm Kings Cross - York.

Type	*Diagram*	*Length/Width*	*Compartments*	*Seats*	*First Built*
Brake third	264	52′ 6″ X 8′ 6″	2 saloons	30	1909
open	270	50′ 10½″ X 8′0″	2 saloons	37	1905
LNER code:	271	50′ 10½″ X 8′6″	2 saloons	35	270 altered
(BTO)	274*	58′ 1½″ X 8′6″	2 saloons	42	1907 non-vestibuled
	285A	52′ 6″ X 8′ 6″	2 saloons	30	1912

Most of these carriages appear to have been built for party or excursion work. One saloon was usually designated for smoking, the other for non-smokers. All Diagrams differed to some extent, making these easily the most varied of the Gresley GNR designs. Diagrams 264 and 270 (gas-lit) had an offset gangway within each saloon and 2 + 1 seating. But while the exterior styling of Dia. 264 featured cant-rail ventilation and hinged ventilators to the windows, Dia. 270 had quarterlights to each seating bay, and doors to alternate bays. Dia. 285A (gas-lit) had large windows with ventilators and an interior with the internal gangway to one side linking both saloons.

The layout for all these Diagrams - excepting 274 - was as follows:

Lavatory - open third saloon - open third saloon - brake compartment

Dia. 271 was a modification to 270 with a full lavatory in place of a WC hopper only, with a resultant reduction in seating.

The two batches of carriages built to Dia. 274 were non-vestibuled and possibly intended to work with the non-vestibuled football saloons to Dia. 21. The layout of Dia. 274 was as follows:

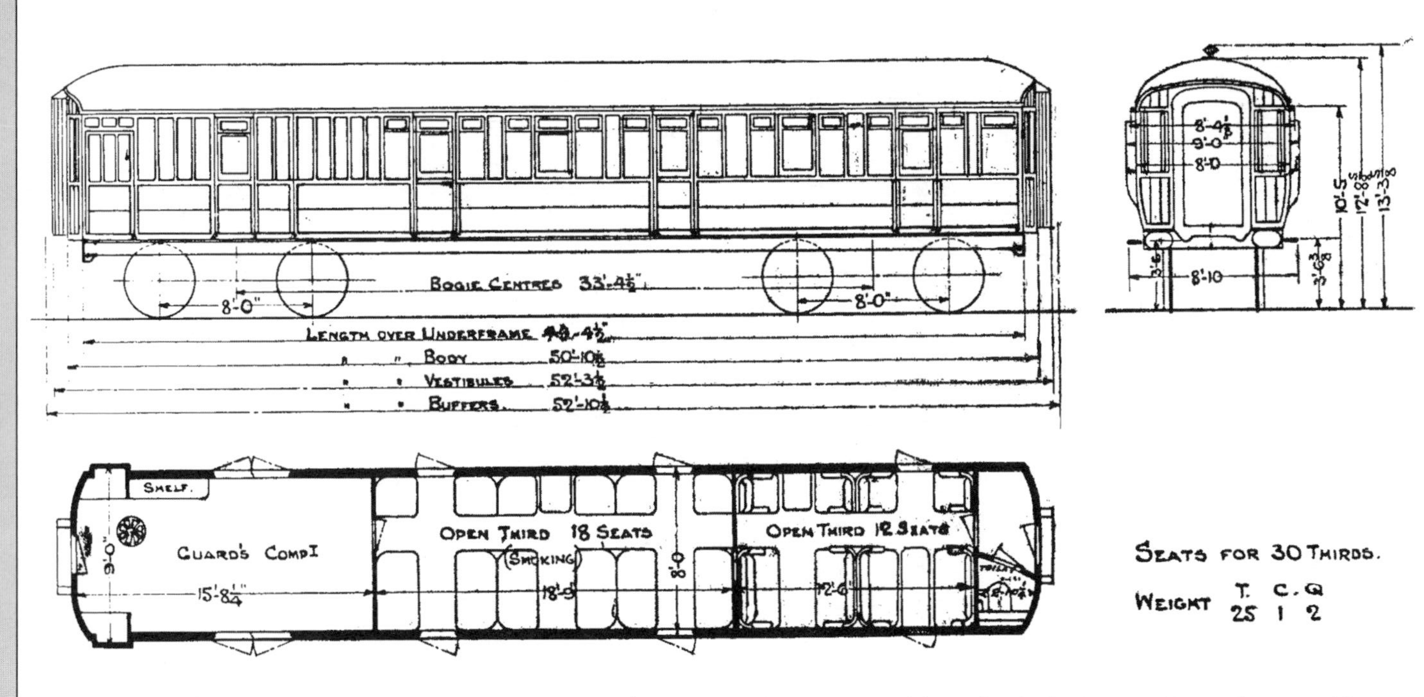

GNR brake third on Dia. 270, built by Doncaster in 1905. The interior is divided, as usual for such vehicles, into smoking and non-smoking saloons. The seating is arranged 2 + 1, with an off-centre gangway and there are exterior doors to alternate bays only. Note the Howlden-type guard's ducket. There are two glazed rectangular panels in the brake compartment end, another feature of these earlier Gresley carriages. The minuscule lavatory was rebuilt to include a washbasin, with the result that the adjoining saloon lost seating for two.

Brake compartment - open third saloon - 2 X lavatories - open third saloon

There were offset internal gangways to the open sections in both saloons.

Type	*Diagram*	*Length/Width*	*Compartments*	*Seats*	*First Built*
Brake third /	256	58′ 6″ X 8′ 6″	5	30	1906
semi-open	257	58′ 6″ X 8′ 6″	5	30	1907
brake third	258	58′ 6″ X 8′ 6″	1 saloon, 3 compts.	30	1906
LNER code:	284	61′ 6″ X 8′ 6″	1 saloon, 3 compts.	36	1910
(BTK), (Semi -BTO)	285	61′ 6″ X 8′ 6″	1 saloon, 3 compts.	36	1911
	285B	58′ 6″ X 8′ 6″	5	30	1914

Of the two types of vestibuled brake third, the straightforward side-corridor design existed in fairly small numbers. Diagrams 256 (Sheffield stock)/257 were very similar, with large windows with ventilators to the corridor side. The others were semi-open but Dia. 258 vehicles had a side-gangway to the open section, the open section being nearer the brake compartment. Dia. 284 had the compartments nearer the guard, a centre gangway to the open section and large windows with ventilators to bays in the open section.

In 1935, a number of these carriages were still diagrammed to principal GN section expresses. A Dia. 256 vehicle worked in the Cromer section of the 3 pm from Kings Cross, one from Dia. 257 in the Peterborough section of the same train.

Type	*Diagram*	*Length/Width*	*Compartments*	*Seats*	*First Built*
Brake composite	171	61′ 6″ X 9′ 6″	3 1st, 3 3rd	18/24	1909
LNER code:	175	58′ 6″ X 8′ 6″	2 1st, 4 3rd	8/24	1908
(BCK)	176	58′ 6″ X 8′ 6″	3 1st, 3 3rd	12/18	1906
	216	58′ 6″ X 8′ 6″	3 1st, 3 3rd	12/18	1910
	218A	61 ′ 6″ X 8′ 6″	3 1st, 3 3rd	12/24	1911
	218BB	61′ 6″ X 8′ 6″	2½ 1st, 3½ 3rd	10/21	1915
	218F	61′ 6″ X 8′ 6″	3 1st, 3 3rd	12/18*	1912
	218G	61′ 6″ X 8′ 6″	3 1st, 3 3rd	12/18	1913

* Later 24 seats.

In the days of numerous through sections on principal trains, composite brakes were a necessity and the different types were probably custom-built for the various GN section expresses. Notice how the first-class in all but Dia. 171 allowed for two-a-side seating although many were probably altered to three-a-side seating in due course.

As with some of the other types described above, it is interesting that so many brake composites remained on top-notch work as late as 1935 although the number of LNER standard carriages specified by the GN section for the Building Programmes of the late 1930s no doubt resulted in the displacement of the veterans. Here is a sample of those diagrammed in 1935:

Dia.	*Section*	*Train*
171	Harrogate	10.10 am Kings Cross - Leeds
176	Hull	10.10 am Kings Cross - Leeds
176	Hull	1.30 pm Kings Cross - Leeds
218A	Hull	1.30 pm Kings Cross - Leeds
176	Bradford	1.30 pm Kings Cross - Leeds
218F	In the Grimsby section and used for the Kings Lynn through carriage on the 3 pm ex-Kings Cross	
171	Saltburn	5.30 pm Kings Cross - Newcastle
175	Lincoln through carriage on the 5.45 pm Kings Cross - Leeds/Bradford	

These tough old carriages, even if well past their best, were at work on main line expresses into BR days. At times it seemed strange that rakes of BR standard stock were allocated to less important trains while the GNR Gresleys, repainted in carmine and cream livery, were prominent in principal workings. Indeed, they were only displaced by the large-scale deliveries during the mid/late 1950s of further BR standard stock. Some of the buffet car conversions lasted until 1961 and had survived to be painted in BR maroon livery.

Family and invalid saloons 1908 - 12

Twelve saloons were built in the 1908 - 1912 period. Of these, there were two 50 ft family saloons (Nos. 3101/2, GN Dia. 9), a 50 ft invalid saloon (No. 3087, GN Dia. 10) and three 52 ft 6 in. family saloons (No. 6, GN Dia. 45C and Nos. 397 and 807 GN Dia. 45D). Accommodation was provided in these vehicles to suit the travelling Edwardian family or invalid plus servants, as the case may be.

Nos. 3101/2 were originally arranged with a first-class side-corridor compartment and two saloons to provide three double sleeping berths or seats for 14 firsts and a third-class compartment for servants seating six. Later, the compartment was redesignated to seat six third-class passengers. Both lost their original 8 ft bogies for the compound-bolster type. They were withdrawn in February 1939 and appropriated for Air Raid Precautions' duty.

No. 3087 had a main saloon including a bed for an invalid, two lavatories, two first-class compartments and an attendant's/luggage compartment. It, too, had the original 8 ft bogies replaced by the 8 ft 6 in. type. Latterly DE 320042 in BR service, it has been at Steamtown, Carnforth since the mid-1970s.

No. 6 (GN Dia. 45C) had two saloons, two lavatories, a first-class and a third-class compartment and an attendant's/luggage compartment. It seems to have been earmarked for use by the aristocracy, and also had a more melancholy role as a royal funeral saloon.

No. 6 was first used in this role for the last journey of Queen Alexandra, in 1925. When King George V died at Sandringham in January 1936, No. 46 (as it had now become) was chosen to convey his body to Windsor via London. The vehicle had all its interior furnishings removed, and the centre partition removed. The saloon interior was lined throughout with black and mauve velvet on the walls, a black velvet carpet covered the floor, and a support for the coffin was erected in the centre. All the windows were painted black, black

Plate 71: 'A1' Pacific No. 2544 *Lemberg* climbs Holloway bank with the 5.45 pm Kings Cross - Leeds in April 1925. As far as can be seen, all vehicles are Gresley GNR, with a Sheffield stock brake first (GN Dia. 96) leading, then a semi-open third (GN Dia. 219) providing third-class dining accommodation next to a first-class dining car of Sheffield stock. *Rail Archive Stephenson*

Plate 72: One of the GN Dia. 271 brake open thirds appears in this photograph of a Skegness evening excursion about to leave Nottingham Victoria behind 'J6' 0-6-0 No 3550, *c.* 1936. This shows more clearly than in the works photograph the Howlden-type guard's ducket, although a side-lamp is no longer provided. The short length of 50 ft and also the 8 ft width are highlighted by comparison with the standard LNER Gresley 61 ft 6 in. vehicles behind. The carriage appears to be either No. 41797 or 41798, by now running on compound-bolster bogies. *Rail Archive Stephenson*

Plate 73: GNR brake open third No. 1797, in rebuilt condition (as GNR Dia. 271, originally built at Doncaster, 1905). Photograph dated April 1914, on conversion and showing the half-bay created at the right-hand end of the body. *National Railway Museum*

Plate 74: The compartment side of GNR first No. 295, in original condition (GNR Dia. 87, built at Doncaster, 1921). With its 61 ft 6 in. length and compound-bolster bogies, this was very near to the specification of the post-1923 Gresley vehicle, apart from the characteristic fanlights above the quarterlights and droplights, and the GNR crest in the lavatory window. Price inflation from 1908 - 22 meant that No 295's cost was 2½ times that of a similar first of 1908. The 'Smoking' labels are on the quarterlights rather than the fanlights. *National Railway Museum*

Plate 75: GNR open third No. 1488, in original condition (GNR Dia. 248E, built at Doncaster, 1913). Photograph dated January 1914. The interior was divided into three saloons. This carriage was later converted to a buffet car, as seen in the next photograph.
National Railway Museum

Plate 76: GNR open third No. 1488, as buffet car BR E 52063 E in maroon livery (originally GNR Dia. 248E). Photograph taken at Stratford in October 1960. Like all others with oil-gas cooking equipment this car was withdrawn during the following year. The kitchen is at the left-hand end. Note that the original hinged window ventilators have given way to the sliding type.

R.M. Casserley

Plate 77: GNR open third No. 2749, as BR E 42749 E (GNR Dia. 248A, built at Doncaster, 1912). Still in some sort of teak livery, but seen as condemned at Stratford, in August 1957.

R.M. Casserley

Plate 78: GNR semi-open third No. 928, in original condition (GNR Dia. 248B, built at Doncaster, 1911). The window arrangement conceals the fact that the left-hand end consisted of two open saloons and the right-hand, four side-corridor compartments; unusually, the corridor windows have ventilators. Photograph dated January 1912. *National Railway Museum*

Plate 79: The corridor side of GNR third No. 761, as BR E 4761 E (GNR Dia. 248D, built at Doncaster, 1920). Similarly still in some sort of teak livery but seen as condemned at Stratford in August 1957. These vehicles were 52 ft 6 in. long and were the most numerous type of side-corridor third, numbering just 18. The compound-bolster bogies were acquired in 1920/1.
R.M. Casserley

Plate 80: The compartment side of GNR third No. 343, as BR E 4343 E (GNR Dia. 248D, built at Doncaster, 1913). This photograph of the vehicle still in traffic, at Stratford in May 1956, shows all too well the unappealing effect of dirty BR carmine and cream livery on a panelled vehicle.
R.M. Casserley

Plate 81: GNR composite No. 1006, in original condition (GNR Dia. 108, built at Doncaster, 1907). This shows the 'corridor' side, a somewhat misleading description, except that there was a lavatory and two side-corridor third-class compartments at the left-hand end, then a 15-seater open third section for smokers, but with quarterlights and droplights rather than large windows, and finally three first-class compartments and a lavatory. The lighting on the July 1907 day when this photograph was obtained shows well the 8 ft pressed steel bogies originally used.
National Railway Museum

Plate 82: The compartment side of GNR composite No. 447, by now downgraded as a third as BR E 447 E (GNR Dia. 164K, built at Doncaster, 1922). In BR carmine and cream livery when photographed at Stratford in September 1957. Note how the square-cornered panelling of the Gresley vehicle contrasts with the rounded mouldings of the ex-GER side-corridor stock still in teak livery. No. E 447 E lasted until September 1959. *R.M. Casserley*

Plate 83: As mentioned in the text, GNR vestibule stock remained in top-line service well into the 1930s on the Southern Area of the LNER (and elsewhere). From the point of view of the traveller, perhaps, there was little external difference to the standard LNER Gresley vestibule stock built until 1941/2. Here class 'C1' 4-4-2 No. 4426 heads an up express at Marshmoor in 1937. Behind the engine is GNR Dia. 176 vestibuled brake composite No. 41812, then a standard LNER vestibuled third, another GNR brake composite, and a semi-open GNR brake third; the tail of the train comprises mostly LNER standard vehicles. The formation as a whole demonstrates the harmonious blend of Gresley-designed vehicles spanning a generation. *RAS Marketing*

Plate 84: An up Cambridge express crosses Welwyn Viaduct in 1938 behind class 'D16/2' 'Royal Claud' 4-4-0 No. 8783. This engine or its companion, No. 8787, normally came up to town on a stopping train. The leading vehicle is a GNR semi-open third brake (either GNR Dia. 284 or 285) running on the 10 ft bogies with outside solebars. *Ken Nunn Collection/LCGB*

Plate 85: GNR semi-open brake third No. 3208, in original condition (GNR Dia. 284, built at Doncaster, 1910). The centre window in the open section, right-hand of the body, was later made a half-drop window to improve ventilation. *National Railway Museum*

Plate 86: The corridor side of GNR brake third No. 3058, as BR E 43058 E (GNR Dia. 257, built at Doncaster, 1907). These were very similar to the Sheffield Stock brake thirds. The GNR could never seem to make up its mind about ventilation! Note how this type had hinged ventilators to the large lights - windows - on the corridor side. *R.M. Casserley*

Plate 87: The 'compartment' side of GNR semi-open brake third No. 2373, as BR E 42373 E (GNR Dia. 258, built at Doncaster, 1906). Nearest the brake van was an open section (two bays), with a side gangway, then three side-corridor compartments. Condemned at Stratford in 1957; the vehicle to its left is an ex- GER restaurant car. *R.M. Casserley*

Plate 88: The compartment side of GNR brake composite No. 2690, in original condition (GNR Dia. 171, built at Doncaster, 1909). The unusual bogies are seemingly the 'alternative' 10 ft wheelbase type used by Gresley for a small number of vehicles and, in this case, having some side-control fitting. Photograph dated April 1910. *National Railway Museum*

Plate 89: A guaranteed excursion sponsored by the *Bradford Telegraph* newspaper, *c*. 1933, is described as an 'Excursion de luxe' for the good reason that it has two, possibly three (clerestory) restaurant cars, third, fifth and (possibly) sixth in the formation. These are paired with open thirds, two of them all-steel LNER vehicles of 1927/8. The leading carriage is a GNR Dia. 218F brake composite, by now LNER No. 432, running on the outside-solebar type 10 ft wheelbase bogies. Next to it is a GNR open third of Dia. 248A, probably No. 41577 which was later converted to a buffet car. And the well-turned out 'C1'? No. 4433 was one of three in the Copley Hill shed Pullman link. *Rail Archive Stephenson*

Plate 90: The corridor side of GNR brake composite No. 115, in original condition (GNR Dia. 218F, built at Doncaster, 1912). Outside-solebar 10 ft wheelbase bogies. Photograph taken December 1912. *National Railway Museum*

Plate 91: There are remarkably few 'in-action' close-up studies of pre-Grouping carriages and this is doubly interesting as the vehicle concerned is still extant, having been preserved by the LNER (SVR) Association. It is GNR brake composite No. 229, as LNER 4229 (GNR Dia. 218F, built at Doncaster, 1912), working as the Halifax through carriage in the 5.45 pm Kings Cross - Leeds/Bradford. The train was photographed near Potters Bar *c.* 1929/30 with class 'A1' No. 4471 *Sir Frederick Banbury* at its head. The official photographs have the disadvantage of depicting the vehicles in 'perfect' condition and it is easy to miss little details, such as the fact that the toplights above the quarterlights were hinged from the top (as were the lavatory windows). The ventilators to the open sections in GNR Gresley carriages were hinged at one side. This is a good example of a carriage in reasonably clean 'in-service' condition, but with the initial sparkle of the varnish having worn off. No. 4229 is still gas-lit and retains the 10 ft wheelbase bogies with which this batch was fitted. Note that No. 4229 is marshalled with the brake compartment trailing, something that was criticised by the Inspecting Officer when reporting on a number of accidents, not least that at Castlecary in 1937. No. 4229 acquired electric lighting and compound-bolster bogies in 1932 and much later passed for departmental use as DE 320700, moving to the Severn Valley Railway in 1977 where there are hopes that it may be restored to running condition. *Rail Archive Stephenson*

Plate 92: The 'compartment' side of GNR brake composite No. 1614, as BR E 41614 E (GNR Dia. 218BB, built at Doncaster, 1920). This type had two coupé compartments: one third-class (where the passenger is looking out) and one first-class, the third from the brake. In BR carmine and cream livery at York, 1957. The bodywork is as straight as a ram-rod, after 37 years' service; No. 41614 was withdrawn the following year. *R.M. Casserley*

Plate 93: The interior of the invalid saloon GNR No. 3087 (GNR Dia. 10, built at Doncaster, 1908). This shows the main saloon, with the invalid's bed. Note the ornate electrolier, also the handles to control ventilation in the false 'clerestoried' ceiling. *National Railway Museum*

Plate 94: A GNR first-class saloon from GNR Dia. 9, and built at Doncaster, 1909. This 1940 photograph shows it converted as an Air Raid Precaution Cleansing Unit, No. 903703, the fortunately unfilled purpose being to serve as a cleansing unit for ARP personnel in attendance at a poison gas attack. Both the Dia. 9 vehicles had been condemned in 1939.

Robert Humm Collection

Plate 95: GNR first-class saloon No. 807, as restored in the mid-1980s (GNR Dia 45D, built at Doncaster, 1912). The close-up shows that it has retained nearly all its original features, possibly the lettering is a little smaller than it should be, but note the full-stop to the number! Seen in Rick Edmondson's prestige charter train, at Ruislip in 1992. *C.R.L. Coles*

Plate 96: The interior of GNR first-class saloon No. 397 (GNR Dia. 45D, built at Doncaster, 1912). This shows the smaller saloon, with the main saloon beyond. Painted Lincrusta below the window level, polished woodwork above and for the partition, but otherwise the carriage has the plain, painted panelling favoured by Gresley. Note the false 'clerestoried' ceiling.
National Railway Museum

Plate 97: Reproduction from the 1936 *Cruises of the 'Northern Belle'* brochure published by the LNER. This interior shot is of the main saloon of GNR first-class saloon No. 6, as LNER No. 46. It was used as the 'Writing Room' in the 'Belle' - but drinks are being served. The inclusive charge for a week's cruise was £20; a good week's wage at the time was £4. *Author's Collection*

Plate 98: The interior of the saloon of GNR first-class dining car No. 3251 (GNR Dia. 75, built at Doncaster, 1911). This was the conventional one of the 1911 pair of cars. The single saloon sat 18. Electric fan and electroliers were fitted. Note the combined coat-hook and hat-peg, a fitting perpetuated in LNER carriages. *National Railway Museum*

Plate 99: GNR first-class dining car No. 1707, as cafeteria car M 41707 E (GNR Dia. 78C, built at Doncaster, 1914). A 'heavy-type' bogie was fitted at the right-hand, kitchen end. BR carmine and cream livery, seen at Llandudno, 1954. *R.M. Casserley*

Plate 100: GNR first-class dining car No. 1697, as cafeteria car W 41697 E (GNR Dia. 78C, built at Doncaster, 1914). By now in BR maroon livery, the car is seen after shopping at York Works, early in 1964. It lasted until May 1965, lying condemned for some time in Hackney sidings, Newton Abbot. It looks to have been fitted with a British Standard gangway for coupling to former GWR vehicles. *David Lowther*

Plate 101: GNR composite articulated twin Nos. 4911 (the third brake, on the left) and composite No. 4912 (its corridor side) (GNR Dia. 218DD, built at Doncaster, 1919). No. 4911 had a pantry next to the brake: the adjacent door is marked 'Kitchen' and the large window is obscured and carries the GNR crest. Next to this is a third-class open section. The composite is a side-corridor vehicle. *National Railway Museum*

Plate 102: Articulated twin brake first Nos. 4931 and 4932 to GNR Dia. 218J as seen in a Leeds Forge official photograph. *Robert Humm Collection*

Plate 103: Most of the photographs of the GNR vestibuled twins show their brake end as they were marshalled that way next the engine on workings such as the 4 pm from Kings Cross. Before electrification of the Manchester - Sheffield via Woodhead main line in 1954, a 'K3' class 2-6-0 No 61910 drifts downhill near Hazelhead, east of Dunford Bridge, with a Manchester London Road - Hull express. Next the engine is a twin composite brake (GNR Dia. 218CC) and, beyond that, a GNR clerestory semi-open carriage. *Rail Archive Stephenson*

Plate 104: There are not that many photographs clearly showing the Leeds quintuplet in service! Rest assured, it is framed between the telegraph poles as the loaned GWR 'Castle' No. 4079 *Pendennis Castle* lifts the quintuplet's normal train, the 10.10 am Kings Cross - Leeds up Holloway bank during May 1925. *Rail Archive Stephenson*

Plate 105: The official 'as built' photograph of the Leeds quintuplet set, with brake third No. 9015 leading (GNR Dia. 78F, built at Doncaster, 1921). The painted destination details read: 'King's Cross & Leeds.'. The GNR Atlantic is No. 1456. *Robert Humm Collection*

Plate 106: A special 'royal' train formation, the photograph coming from a copy negative produced at Doncaster Works in 1953. The engine is Large Atlantic No. 1452 (built 1910), behind which are: royal train equipment van, ECJS No. 82; GNR vestibuled composite No. 3192 (GN Dia. 164F, built 1911); GNR first-class saloon No. 6 (GN Dia. 45C, built 1912); semi-royal saloon No. 3099 (GN Dia. 4, built 1908); 'Harrogate' dining car No. 3250 (GN Dia. 76, built 1912); HM the King's saloon, ECJS No. 395; what looks like either saloon No. 1280 or 1281 and, lastly, an ECJS bogie brake. The date is believed to be 1913, but why this formation? *National Railway Museum*

velvet curtains were hung over the doors, and the exterior was repainted black with the mouldings finished in mauve. The roof remained white. This work was carried out at Stratford Works, and occupied no more than 24 hours. The royal train was used for the journey to London where the public attended the lying-in-state. On 28th January, 1936, the royal train left Paddington for Windsor, and was made up of GNR brake first No. 4188; saloons Nos. 41280 and 43099; the funeral saloon No. 46; royal saloons Nos. 395 and 396; saloons Nos. 43100 and 41281, and brake van No. 109.

No. 46 was included in the formation of the 'Northern Belle' during the summer seasons of 1933-9 and when so used was described as a 'writing-room and lounge'. In February 1952, it was again used as a royal funeral saloon on the death of King George VI and was similarly converted as in 1936, painted black, and worked from Wolferton to London, and on to Windsor.

No. 397 (GN Dia. 45D) differed by having larger saloons and lacked the first-class compartment. As LNER No. 4397, it was furnished with a cocktail bar in 1934 and used as a spare for the LNER 1924-built 'Toilet thirds' Nos. 1007/12 which ran in the 'Flying Scotsman'. The 'Toilet thirds' were the combined hairdressing-saloon, cocktail bar and ladies' retiring-room cars. Nos. 397 and 807 had 8 ft 6 in. bogies as built.

Nos. 397/807 survived to be preserved, the former passing to the Carriage Inn at Jesmond in 1981 after a stint at Steamtown, Carnforth. In latter years on BR it had been departmental saloon No. DE 320206. No. 807 was more fortunate in that it was extensively restored at Steamtown in 1984 and, under the ownership of Rick Edmondson, it has formed part of his exclusive touring train which was used for the 'Queen of Scots' in Scotland during 1990 and has since been employed on main line steam charters. No. 807 has been restored largely to its GNR condition and varnished teak finish and generally serves as a lounge/writing-room.

All the saloons described except for No. 3087 were originally dual vacuum/Westinghouse fitted.

The third-class saloons (GN Dia. 21) followed the general design of the non-vestibuled GNR stock and were 58 ft 1½ in. in length. They were intended for parties travelling to football matches and included luggage space at each end, two lavatories amidships and the seating for 56 passengers faced inwards to longitudinal, centrally placed tables.

General service dining cars - 1912 - 14

There were twenty GNR restaurant car workings in 1913 and the majority of vehicles in use were Howlden clerestories, supplemented by the nine Gresley 65 ft 6 in. diners built in 1906. Four 52 ft 6 in. long first-class dining cars were built in 1912 and 1914 and had 4 ft 6 in. width saloon windows, the centre one of which was of the drop-type and had glass louvred ventilators. The interior was arranged with an entrance lobby at one end, a dining saloon, pantry, kitchen and lavatory. All four vehicles were mounted on the 8 ft 6 in. bogies, the heavy type being used under the kitchen end on Nos. 1697/1707.

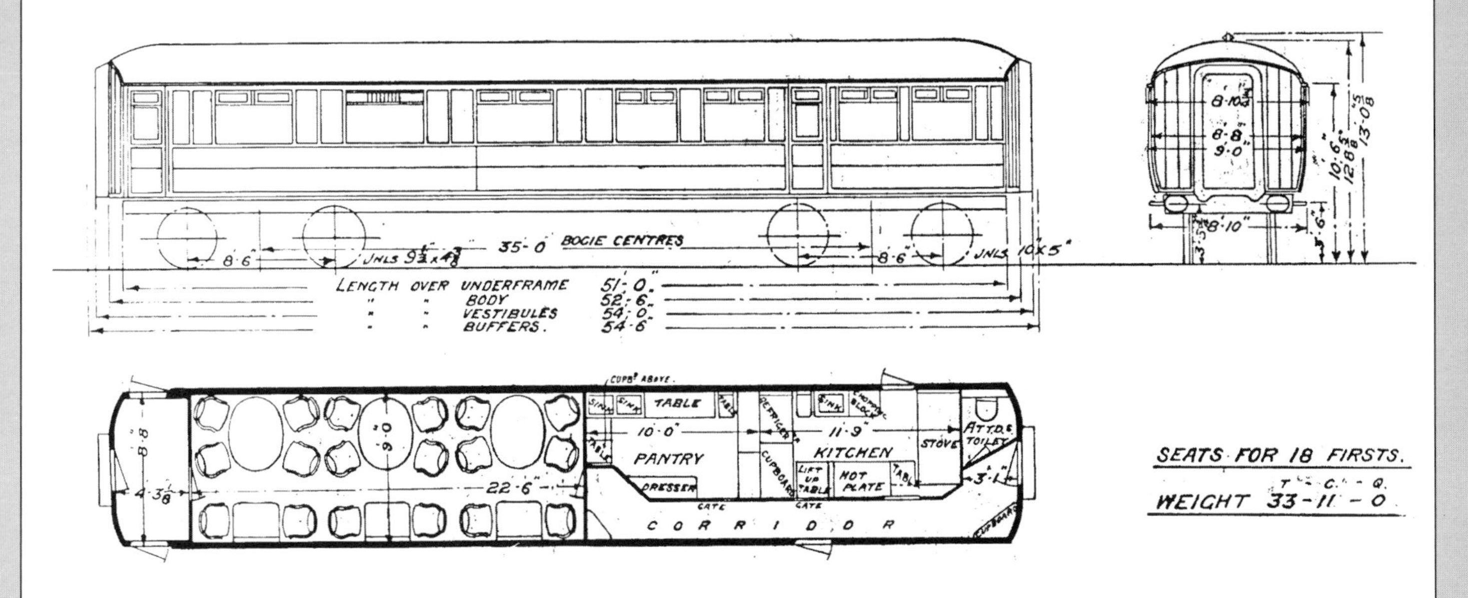

GNR first-class dining car No. 3250 on Dia. 76, built by Doncaster in 1912. This was sometimes referred to as the 'Harrogate car', having been built for the through service from King's Cross. Accordingly it was dual-fitted. This shows the car as originally built with the oval dining tables, each seating four.

No. 3250 entered service in the autumn of 1912 on the Kings Cross - Harrogate workings and was equipped with dual brakes. It is of particular interest for its internal layout although as this was not perpetuated it may have proved a disappointment. The eighteen diners were seated at a choice of large, oval mahogany tables on one side - each with four chairs - and, on the other side, tables seating two, also with chairs. Until then, seating in dining cars had been fixed, and in the GNR's case usually iron-framed, so that the concept of movable chairs was certainly novel. Another attempt was made in LNER days to adopt chairs in place of bench-type seats in restaurant cars but was successfully resisted by the train catering staffs.

The interior decor in No. 3250 was also distinctive, with light-grey panelling from floor to the base of the windows and striped grey, satin-finish wallpaper above to the cornices. The ceiling and bulkheads were covered in Tynecastle linen decorations, in the Adam-esque style then in favour with Gresley. All wood panelling was in mahogany, except in the lobby which had oak matchboarding below and sycamore panels above. A tasteful colour scheme was set off by grey silk rep curtains, chairs upholstered in green tapestry, a green carpet and metal fittings in an oxidised silver finish. There was no shortage of lighting: three ceiling bowl fittings were supplemented by wall-brackets and table lamps, all with silk shades. The design treatment constituted an interesting departure from the heavy and overdecorated interior schemes of so many contemporary dining cars and typified Gresley's attempts to evolve a more sophisticated environment for carriage interiors.

The other three cars - No. 3251 of 1912 and Nos. 1697 and 1707 of 1914 - had conventional seating, again for eighteen diners; No. 3250 was in due course altered to suit. Nos. 1697/1707, on GN Dia. 78C, originally had a saloon with seating for 12 arranged in 1+1. At an unknown date they were altered to seat 18 diners, with 2+1 one seating. These two cars were fitted with compound-bolster bogies, with a heavy type bogie at one end. All four cars were to be long-lived though not in their original form, as described below.

Conversion of GNR dining cars to cafeteria cars by BR

The reason for the surprising longevity of some of the GNR catering vehicles is a result of their conversion to cafeteria cars.

In the early 1950s, the Railway Executive was critical of the unprofitability of some train catering operations using traditional restaurant cars. In early 1952, Riddles submitted a proposal for what was described as a 'prototype party catering vehicle' to the RE. He was working to a specification at the request of the Hotels Executive which at the time was responsible for train catering. This prototype was to be converted from an existing vehicle at an estimated cost of £2,500 and would provide a bar counter as well as seating accommodation for 56 passengers. This prototype was a former LNER open third to Dia. 186, numbered E 13369 E, and it was placed in service early in 1952. The Hotels Executive were so pleased with it that they decided to ask the Railway Executive to proceed with the conversion of a further 49 party cars. The RE duly authorised the conversion of that number of party cars in April 1952, and by April 1953 16 had been outshopped, or were in the process of being rebuilt.

Selected for conversion in the first part of the conversion programme of what were now referred to as cafeteria cars, classified by BR as CAFs, were the four ex-GNR 52 ft 6 in. dining cars Nos. 41697, 41707, 43250 and 43251, as well as two 12-wheeled 65 ft cars Nos. 43034 and 43035. The cost of conversion at Eastleigh Works for the first four was just under £2,500 apiece and all four were ready during May 1953, one month after the emergence of Nos. 43034/5 which cost £3,500 each to rebuild.

The point of these conversions was to provide vehicles for use on advertised or guaranteed excursion trains. On these, restaurant cars usually had been provided, but were no longer profitable. However, early experience showed that a development of the cafeteria car with a kitchen able to provide hot meal service could be used on booked trains as well; the car involved was former Great Eastern Railway restaurant car E 672 E. Somewhat confusingly, both this and the other conversions afterwards tended to be referred to as RCAFs.

The programme of conversions of a motley selection of largely life-expired restaurant cars was reported in April 1953 as having exhausted the available vehicles surplus to needs. The cost of conversion proved higher than expected as it was noted that the cars were 'fairly old' - none of the ex-GNR cars was less than 39 years old! Whatever the merits of the programme, the CAFs found another role when they were employed on the overnight cheap fare 'Starlight Specials' introduced between St Pancras and Glasgow, and Marylebone and Edinburgh as from April 1953. Indeed, No 43034 worked out of Marylebone on the first 'Starlight Special' of the 1954 season.

However, of the former GNR cars converted to CAFs, only Nos. 43034/5 were allocated to the Eastern Region. No. 41697 went to the Western Region and the other three to the London Midland Region. All were allocated for maintenance to the Eastern Region. No. W 41697 E survived until as late as 1965 on the Western while during the 1950s the London Midland had found work for M 43251 E in the 'North Wales Land Cruise' train.

Proposed all-steel vestibuled carriage - 1914

It is rather puzzling that the LNER persisted with teak-bodied carriages until as late as 1941/2 when Gresley had experimented with the use of alternative materials. Among the surviving GNR rolling stock records in the national archives is a letter dated 21st July, 1914, signed by Gresley and submitted to the GNR's Locomotive Committee. It reads:

> In view of the development and more extended use of steel carriages I think the time has now arrived when we might with advantage obtain a carriage constructed in this way in order to get some information as to how such vehicles would compare with the ordinary type of wooden coaches, both as regards comfort in running and the cost of maintenance.
>
> I have obtained from the Leeds Forge a quotation for the construction of a 57 ft

corridor composite brake. They quote £650 for one such vehicle, the price including underframe and body, and all outside panelling, steel linings and beadings, but excluding bogies, drawgear, doors, and all interior upholstery, decorations etc which could be fitted at Doncaster.

I estimate that the complete cost of the vehicle would amount to £2,070. Similar vehicles of wood on a steel underframe cost £1,700 each.

I suggest one such vehicle be constructed as part of the renewal programme for next year.

Consideration of Gresley's proposal was deferred by the Locomotive Committee meeting on 23rd July, 1914, just over a week before the outbreak of World War I. Thirteen years were to elapse before contractors were to build all-steel passenger stock to Gresley's designs for the LNER.

Articulated GNR vestibuled stock 1915 - 1921

Many of the characteristic Gresley design features were evolved during his first ten years at Doncaster: the elliptical-roofed, bow-ended passenger carriage, the compound-bolster bogie, careful attention to interior design and, not least, articulation.

The first carriages to be articulated were a pair of Howlden ECJS side-corridor six-wheelers, Nos. 202/206, in January 1907. A standard 8 ft bogie was used for articulation and alterations to the underframe comprised no more than the stiffening of the adjoining headstocks with channel sections so that these could take the centre castings and brackets which served as the top-side friction blocks for the bogies.

There then followed conversions of 40 non-vestibuled GNR six-wheelers. In due course, ECJS stock was dealt with. The process continued until by 1915 99 twins, 13 triplets and 18 quads had been produced from Howlden era stock. That year also saw the production of a quintuplet set. These conversions lasted well, the twins until the 1937-9 period, the triplets until 1946-8 and a quad until 1940. New construction of non-vestibuled articulated stock began in 1910, as described in Chapter 6.

General service stock

Between 1915 and 1919 three different batches of vestibuled articulated twins were built for general service. The 1915/6 batch, GN Dia. 218CC, the first new articulated vestibuled stock to be built in this country, comprised brake open third/side-corridor composite pairs with 49 ft 3 in. bodies seating ten first and 48 third-class passengers. Standard compound-bolster bogies were used, the 8 ft 6 in. type for the outer bogies, the 8 ft type for the articulation bogies.

In 1917 two all first-class twins appeared (GN Dia. 218J), also with 49 ft 3 in. bodies. These were allocated to Leeds expresses and in 1933 were to be found on this service, 44921/2 next the triplet restaurant car in the Leeds Flyer set and 44871/2 in the Leeds portion of the 4 pm ex-Kings Cross and 9 am return.

The 1919 twin composites (GN Dia. 218DD) had detail differences from the 1915 batch, having one less seating bay, its space being taken up by a pantry. They were used on the 4 pm Kings Cross - Leeds to serve light refreshments but were not lettered as restaurant cars. From mid-1924 until 31st December, 1925 both twins were used to provide light breakfast and afternoon tea service for the first time on Liverpool - Hull workings. From May 1926 they were allocated to the York - Swindon train which conveyed the Aberdeen - Penzance through carriages. In 1939 they were displaced by new buffet/restaurant cars and returned to the GN section, having been technically on loan for fourteen years or so to the North Eastern Area.

The layouts of the three types were as follows:

Twin-composites Dia. 218CC
Vestibuled brake open third + Vestibuled composite
Brake - open third saloon, - open third saloon, + lavatory - three side-corridor, - 2½ side-corridor, - lavatory
Compt 18 seats 12 seats 3rd class comps 1st class comps
(smoking) (non-smoking)

Twin composites Dia. 218DD
Vestibuled brake pantry open third + Vestibuled composite
Brake - pantry - open third saloon, + lavatory - three side-corridor, - 2½ side corridor, - lavatory
Compt 12 seats 3rd class comps 1st class comps

Twin firsts Dia. 218J
Vestibuled brake first + Vestibuled first
Brake - two side-corridor - lavatory + lavatory - six side-corridor,
Compt 1st class comps 1st class comps*

* The compartment next to the brake first was oddly-shaped to allow access to the gangway and sat three only.

Quintuplet set for the Leeds service - 1921

This five-coach set carried on six bogies was the first noteworthy design to appear from Doncaster Works after World War I. In the autumn of 1921 it went into service on the 10.10 am Kings Cross - Leeds and 5.30 pm from Leeds, remaining on this working consistently, at least until 1939. It replaced a set previously in use on these services formed of brake third No. 3048, third-class dining car No. 3038, first-class dining car No. 3034 and clerestory brake first No. 260. The quintuplet set comprised a three-compartment brake first, a single-saloon first-class dining car, a kitchen car, a single-saloon third-class diner and a four-compartment brake third. For a total length of 239 ft 8 in the set weighed 118 tons 3 cwt and seated 128 passengers. The quintuplet was shorter in overall length, weighed less and seated more passengers than the displaced four-car set. Its other significance was the use for the first time in Britain of all-electric cooking equipment in the kitchen car. The quintuplet cost £19,435 to build.

There were no new features when it came to construction of the coachwork, except that the vehicles were built to the full extent of the GNR's loading gauge at 9 ft 6 in. and heavy-type 8 ft 6 in. bogies were used throughout. The seating in the brakes at each end was in side-corridor compartments, four-a-side in the third-class, three-a-side in the first-class. The two dining cars originally had single saloons, but these were later divided into two, smoking/non-smoking When new, the quintuplet's riding qualities were much praised but twice during 1921-3 the bogie springs were replaced and, yet again, in 1928.

Earlier in this chapter the use of an all-steel kitchen car with gas cooking in the 1914 'Flying Scotsman' sets was noted as an attempt to reduce the risk of fire. By introducing electric cooking, thereby countering the fire hazard, and employing articulation Gresley saved something like 30 tons in weight with the quintuplet as compared with a five-car set of conventional stock including an all-steel catering vehicle.

The interiors in the quintuplet do not appear as stylish as the best of the prewar dining cars, such as those for the GN/NE Joint service and the 52 ft 6 in. dining cars, but there was a simplicity in finish of the woodwork, something that was to become a feature of Gresley rolling stock in the 1920s. In the first-class saloons the walls were panelled in plain, natural mahogany, without mouldings or panels, while the ends and ceilings were finished in white enamel. Armchair type seats were fitted in the saloons of both classes.

The pioneer electric cooking equipment was designed and installed by J. Stone & Co. under Bulleid's consultation and direction. As batteries alone would not provide sufficient current for cooking while the train was stationary, mains power points were provided at Kings Cross and Leeds. On departure, the mains were disconnected and a throw-over switch brought in axle- driven dynamos to charge the batteries. Other electric fittings included large extractor fans in the saloon ceilings instead of fans on the bulkhead, the latter first used in the 52 ft 6 in. dining cars. A refrigerator was fitted in the kitchen in August 1926.

Between November 1930 and 31st December, 1933, radio reception equipment was fitted to the set and passengers could hire headphones to listen to programmes, but patronage was seldom very encouraging. In late 1935 the first-class dining car was retrimmed in the prestigious blue trellis design tapestry, and fitted out with the blue heather carpet otherwise used only in the principal East Coast vehicles, a measure of the quintuplet's status even after some years' service. At the outbreak of World War II, the set was taken out of service, but from June 1940 returned to its old working. Later it was stored at Nottingham.

In post-war years, the quintuplet worked in the 9.55 am Leeds - Kings Cross and 6.18 pm return, and then, from 1950, in the 9.18 am Kings Cross - Leeds and 2.57 pm return. It was condemned in July 1953 following damage in a shunting accident, but in any case it is unlikely to have survived very much longer, in view of its age and the restrictions on its operations.

As the quintuplet was built to the loading gauge limits it was not possible to fit standard carriage destination boards. As a result the legends were painted on the sides of the roofs and were of gold characters, shaded blue and red in GNR style. This distinction remained with the quintuplet until its demise.

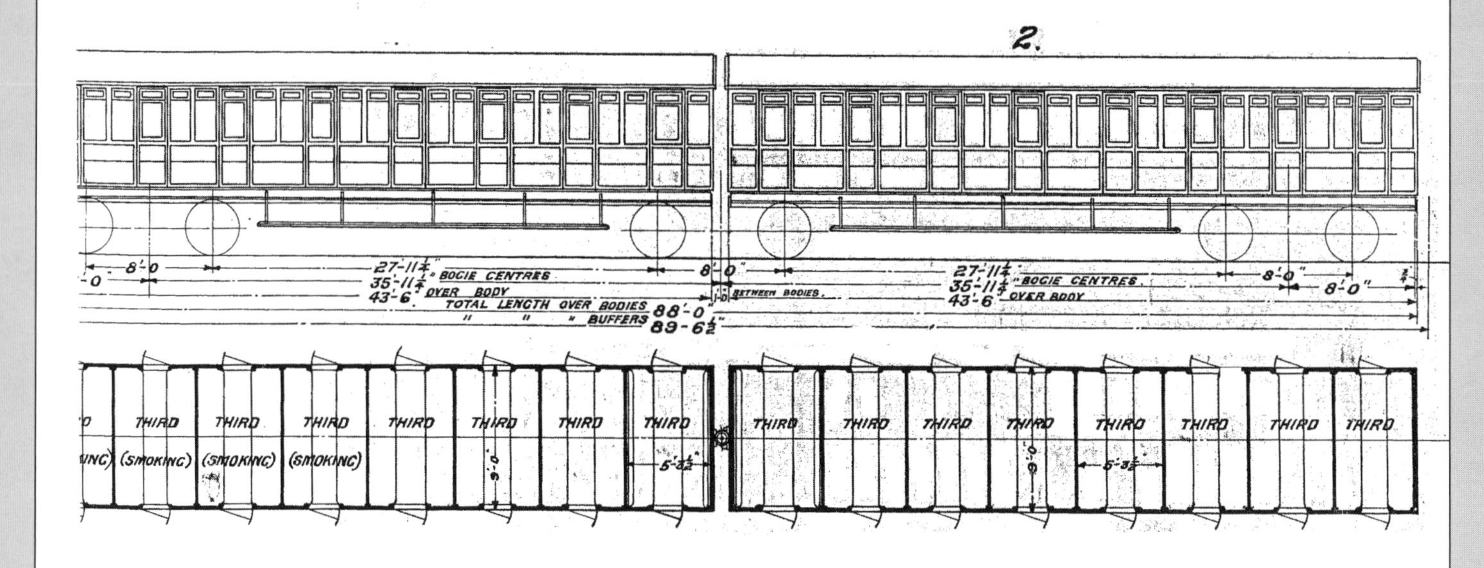

Part of GNR suburban articulated twin third to Dia. 440 (built Doncaster, 1912).

Chapter Six

GNR Non-Corridor and Suburban Stock including the steam railcars

Non-vestibuled stock 1907 - 1912

The GNR did not have intensive local services other than in the London area and, to a lesser extent, in the West Riding and around Nottingham. The Howlden six-wheelers were used to a great extent outside London up until 1939, together with articulated sets made up from Howlden stock. There was not much need for suburban block sets, except in the London area, and the limited number of non-vestibuled carriages was built mainly for semi-fast services.

The first elliptical-roofed non-vestibuled brake thirds, composites and brake composites appeared at the end of 1907 and formed a ten-coach set for the 4 pm Kings Cross - Leeds semi-fast which conveyed through portions for Bradford, Grimsby and Sheffield. These vehicles were of a handsome, high-roofed, screw-coupled design with 58 ft 1½ in. bodies and ran on standard 8 ft GNR bogies. Their main distinction was that although without gangways all passengers - first and third-class alike - had access to lavatories. The bodies were flat-ended, doors were provided to each compartment and the quarterlights all had the usual type of fanlights. Internally, most first-class compartment seated four-a-side with reading lights for each seat while the thirds were five-a-side or four-a-side with gangway. Other internal details were unremarkable.

From 1908 onwards, part-sets with a different compartment layout were allocated to the Cambridge semi-fast trains. This stock disappeared from service from the mid-1950s.

With similar 58 ft 1½ in. by 8 ft 6 in. bodies to the semi-fast stock, the GNR built for itself two batches of non-vestibuled third-class saloons in 1908/9, generally described as 'football saloons'. These are described along with family and other non-royal saloons in Chapter 5.

Stock built for the Cheshire Lines Committee, 1911/2

Through its involvement in the Cheshire Lines Committee, the GNR had some responsibility for the provision of rolling stock for the Committee's services.

At the meeting of the Directors of the Committee at Kings Cross on 1st February, 1910, a report on the state of the rolling stock was tabled by the CLC's carriage and wagon superintendent. He was none other than J.G. Robinson, chief mechanical engineer of the Great Central Railway. In his report he recommended the renewal of 41 old CLC carriages, all of which were over 25 years old, some older. He proposed that the Committee should consider their replacement by a similar number of new carriages, comprising one first-class saloon, 12 brake thirds and 14 each of thirds and composites.

Robinson raised the matter again in his report submitted to the CLC Directors' meeting of 26th July, 1910. On this occasion, the Directors, acting on the recommendation of the Midland, Great Northern and Great Central railways' General Managers, asked for tenders from the CLC's parent companies for the supply of 24 carriages to make up four trains of six carriages for the Liverpool and Manchester service where, as Robinson had noted, 'competition with other companies is so keen.' Tenders were received from the GNR and GCR only and the GNR won on price, being just £8 cheaper in its bid for the 24 vehicles - eight each of brake thirds, thirds and composites. These were delivered by midsummer 1911, at the tendered price.

Except for their shorter length, the new carriages followed most of the design features of the Gresley GNR non-vestibuled stock, were electrically-lit and ran on the standard pressed steel 8 ft wheelbase bogie. There were two types of composite, as illustrated in this Chapter.

There remained 17 vehicles due for replacement and, at the CLC Directors' meeting on 7th February, 1911, approval was given for their renewal and it was agreed that the GNR would tender for the new stock. This tender was accepted by the Committee the following month, the order comprising three brake thirds, seven thirds, six composites and the one saloon. These vehicles were delivered by July 1912.

Numbered within the CLC series 310 - 49, the 1911/2 carriages took the numbers of the four/six-wheeled vehicles they replaced. The new stock was mostly used on the tightly-timed Liverpool and Manchester fast trains. After nationalisation, control of the CLC lines and their stock passed to the London Midland Region and, from 1950, the passenger vehicles were renumbered in the LMS numerical series for non-vestibuled stock.

The non-vestibuled saloon, No 201, 51 ft 1½ in. over the end panels, was fairly typical of its type and featured two saloons, a third-class compartment, two lavatories and a luggage compartment. It was supplied dual-brake fitted and became vacuum-only in 1932. This vehicle was usually based at Liverpool and, as M997E, it survived at Edge Hill until as late as August 1966, by which time it carried BR maroon livery.

Non-vestibuled articulated stock 1923

Early examples of a non-vestibuled type later to be produced in fair numbers by the LNER were two batches of twin brake thirds and composites to GN Dia. 218QQ and 218RR. These formed part of the GNR's 1922 building programme and were completed in 1923, appearing in LNER livery. Dia. 218QQ comprised four twins seating 22 first-class and 88 third-class passengers; the six twins to Dia. 218RR had more third-class seats and less first-class. Each composite had four lavatories. The carriage bodies had the customary fanlights to the quarterlights and the GNR - style guard's duckets. Their duties included Cambridge line semi-fast and GN main line stopping trains.

Articulated stock for the London suburban services 1911 - 1923

From mechanical and operating points of view the articulation of the Howlden rolling stock had proved successful and in 1910 H.A. Ivatt, the GNR's locomotive engineer, proposed to the GNR Board that renewals for two trains of four-wheeled stock should be of articulated stock. Four twins would make up each train as follows: brake third + third, third + third, 1st/3rd composite + 1st/2nd composite, second + brake second. These trains would each accommodate 372 third-class, 180 second-class and 80 first-class passengers - 632 in all. There was also the option of an extra compartment in each brake vehicle.

The bodies of the outer brake twins were only 38 ft 1¼ in. long, the other carriages being 43 ft 6 in., these unusual dimensions being chosen so that a complete train could be accommodated within the platforms at Moorgate station on the Widened Lines. Each eight-coach train was of 330 ft 5 in. length, with a tare weight of 147 tons 4 cwt. Standard GNR 8 ft bogies were used throughout.

The first train of elliptical-roofed articulated twins appeared in September 1911, the vehicles being numbered 3232 - 3239. The bodywork followed most Doncaster conventions with square panel mouldings, window fanlights and characteristic guard's duckets. To accommodate the maximum number of seated passengers, the distance between compartments was minimal and the seat padding likewise; there was just four cwt of hardware for each seated passenger. Each articulated twin was close-coupled to its neighbour.

The general effect of these trains was summed up in their usual nickname of the 'sit-up and beg' sets. Yet they were a considerable advance on the existing close-coupled, low-roofed Howlden four-wheelers and were the prototypes for numerous sets of quad- and quint-arts built for the LNER in succeeding years. At the time of their introduction, the technical press noted that there was 'particular attention paid to heating, lighting and ventilation'; there was certainly the facility of adjustable heat control in each compartment, to add the luxury of heating in the first place for suburban stock! The carriages had gas lighting. Interior finish was simple and unadorned and, except for the first two sets, the third-class seating originally comprised wooden, slatted seats. All doors were fitted with wedge locks, safety catches and inside handles, some advance on the awkward door handles of the Howlden stock.

The second set appeared in December 1912, with carriages numbered 3252 - 9 and during the following year three further sets were delivered. At about the same time, four spare bodies were built, one for each type of twin and numbered 3354 - 7.

Under the GNR's 1918 renewals programme it was decided to convert the five eight-coach sets of twins into ten eight-coach trains of quad-arts by making up the balance with 40 new carriage bodies. Tenders were invited from contractors and Cravens won the contract in October 1920. Apart from building new bodies and underframes, the manufacturers were required to rebuild some of the bodies of existing twins, fit the underframes with inner truss rods and carry out general repairs. The delivery of the new and rebuilt stock was at the rate of two new carriages a week beginning in February 1921, and was completed that August. Roughly 80 per cent of the total cost of £157,000 was charged to the government and comprised part of the wartime compensation due to the GNR.

As part of the conversion work five second-class carriages were rebuilt as five-compartment brake seconds and five seven-compartment thirds as five-compartment brake thirds. The 40 new carriages consisted of equal numbers of composites, seconds, seven- and eight-compartment thirds. The resultant quad-arts were numbered and formed as follows:

Brake third	Conversion*	Brake second	Conversion**
Third (7 compt)	New	Second	New
Third (8 compt)	New	Composite	New
Third (8 compt)	Conversion	Composite	Conversion

* Five ex-thirds

Above numbered 8XX1 - 8XX4 in order
Number series of these quads:
8451 - 4, 8461 - 4, 8471 - 4, 8481 - 4, 8551 - 4, 8561 - 4, 8571 - 4, 8581 - 4, 8591 - 4, 8601 - 4.

** Five ex-seconds

Above numbered 8XX1 - 8XX4 in order
Number series of these quads:
8411 - 4, 8421 - 4, 8431 - 4, 8441 - 4, 8491 - 4, 8501 - 4, 8511 - 4, 8521 - 4, 8531 - 4, 8541 - 4

The conversions were on GN Diagrams 467/467A (all-third quad-arts) and 475/476 (composite quad-arts). In 1921 - 3 the 'rebuilt' sets were supplemented by eleven new quad-arts to the same diagrams and these were virtually identical, the last of the series not entering service until after Grouping. By 1929, the GN inner suburban services were worked entirely by 48 bogie quadruplet sets, 20 of the GNR gas-lit variety and the rest, LNER electrically-lit stock.

The Doncaster Works photographic records, now held at the National Railway Museum, include an interesting print which shows a complete fracture of the articulation bogie under carriages 8671/2. It is reasonable to link this occurrence with the decision to use the heavy-type compound-bolster bogies for the sets built in 1924, that type of bogie until then having been restricted to main line stock. In addition, the 1923 sets had electric lighting which increased the tare weight of the vehicles. There was sufficient space at the brake end for another compartment to be added and the underframes at the outer ends of the sets were designed to take motor bogies should the Inner Suburban services be electrified.

Although the GNR quad-arts spent the majority of their lives allocated to the Inner Suburban services, from time to time they were used on excursions to resorts such as Skegness, as indeed had their four-wheeled predecessors. On occasions in LNER days they were loaned to other sections and for example were used in the Hull area. In later days the six - coach vestibuled sets from the Cambridge service would be used at peak periods for main line extras and the 'sit-up and beg' sets substituted.

By 1954 the GNR sets were becoming a cause for public complaint and before long came the first of the BR standard non-vestibuled sets, their modernity scarcely compensating for a greatly reduced seating capacity.

Steam railcars Nos 1 and 2 - 1905

The Doncaster-built coachwork on Ivatt's first two steam railcars represented Gresley's initial carriage design, following his appointment in March 1905 as carriage and wagon superintendent. The next year the standard Gresley carriage outline appeared, together with other design and constructional innovations, to bring to an end the 'high Victoriana' of the Howlden period.

At the time, the Gresley-designed coachwork of railcars Nos. 1 and 2 made little impact on the technical press. The most noticeable features were the high-arched elliptical roof and the large, fixed bodyside windows extending up to the cant-rail. The interior was divided into three saloons, two third-class and one first-class, with a driving cab at one end and the luggage compartment next to the engine unit. The total seating capacity was 53. The body was pivoted at one end to the engine unit and there was a 8 ft bogie at the other end.

It is recorded that Ivatt intended giving the order for all six GNR steam railcars to contractors but instead decided to save money by building Nos. 1 and 2 at Doncaster. Cars Nos. 5/6 were built by Kitson and Nos. 7/8 by Avonside, with bodywork by Birmingham Carriage and Wagon and Bristol Coach and Wagon Works respectively. These four cars had bodywork to the contractors' designs, with shallow, three-arc roofs.

The six railcars were introduced on a new local service between Louth and Grimsby, six additional halts on this section being opened in late 1905. They also worked between Hitchin and Baldock and Finchley (Church End) and Edgware. By 1917 they were out of traffic and, although they seemed to have worked intermittently after Grouping, all were lying at Doncaster Works by 1925, the engine units being officially withdrawn soon afterwards.

The carriage units from all cars were to survive for longer, the three pairs of cars becoming articulated twins, a new bogie being provided in each case for articulation. Those units from Nos 1 and 2 were converted in 1930 to become carriages 44151/2 respectively, the bodies being extended in length and gaining an extra compartment in place of the space formerly taken up by the cab of the engine unit. No. 44151 was all-third and 44152, a composite with one compartment and the saloon as first-class. This twin was withdrawn in 1937, after sustaining accident damage.

The carriage portions from the other railcars were converted from 1925, those from Nos. 7/8 becoming Nos. 44141/2 in that year and Nos. 5/6 in 1927, as Nos. 44161/2. These survived in traffic until 1958/9 respectively.

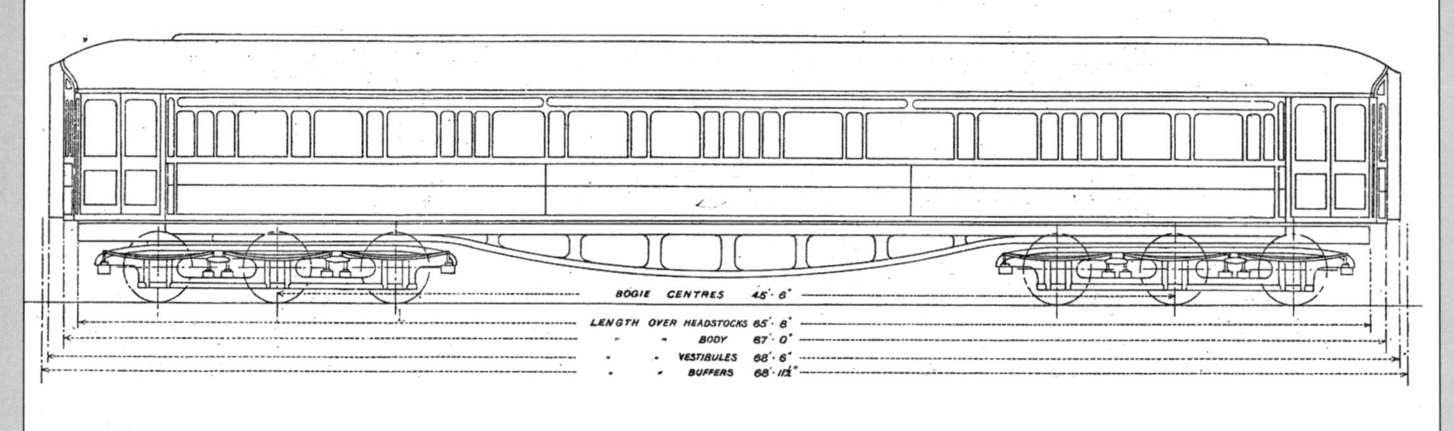

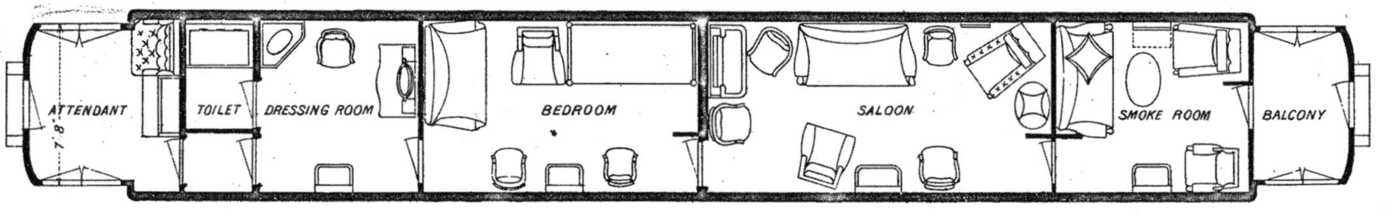

HM the King's Saloon, before the LNER alterations.

Chapter Seven

The East Coast Royal Train

First proposals

New royal saloons for the East Coast companies appear to have been first proposed by Oliver Bury, the GNR's General Manager, at a meeting of the GNR's Traffic Committee in December 1905. He referred to recent royal journeys to the Dukeries and suggested the provision of two new royal carriages by the East Coast companies. In 1903/4 the Great North of Scotland Railway royal train had been used but the following year King Edward VII travelled in the LNWR royal train which had been lent to the GNR. This loan may have raised the question of stock of comparable standard being available to the East Coast companies. The Traffic Committee authorised the General Manager to say at a forthcoming East Coast meeting that the GNR would be prepared to share the cost of the new vehicles with the NER and the NBR.

From the start, the drawing offices of both the GNR and NER were involved and arrangements were made early in 1906 for design personnel to study the LNWR and GWR royal trains.

For the NER, J. D. Twinberrow, the chief carriage & wagon draughtsman, undertook the preliminary work. By 17th May, 1906, he had prepared alternative proposals for two saloon carriages for the King and Queen. The designs were for a 65 ft 6 in. vehicle, 9 ft in width and of 12 ft 8¼ in. height and running on 10 ft wheelbase four-wheeled bogies. The immediate novelty was that the vehicles were proposed as having no opening windows, and would have forced air ventilation only.

But, with even more originality, Twinberrow presented alternative proposals for the royal saloons, the sketches being drawn by his sister who received a £20 fee for her work. One proposal featured a steel underframe with a teak body, 'built on ordinary ECJS lines', commented Twinberrow, but the other was for the royal saloons to be of integral all-steel construction with body and underframe combined. Had this design been adopted, it would have predated any such application in normal British service, apart from the tube railways in London. Twinberrow drew attention to the use of all-steel carriages by French, German and North American railways. Acknowledging that the all-steel bodies would have plain, flat panels, Twinberrow had suggested that any austerity in appearance would be relieved by painting the royal saloons either dark-green with arms and appointments in solid bronze, or a rich cream with gilded lining-out and arms. His daring and innovatory proposal was rejected by Oliver Bury.

In retrospect, it would have been interesting had the East Coast companies chosen to put into service these all-steel pioneers, but instead they opted for vehicles comprising a teak body on a steel underframe. The drawings for the bodies were the responsibility of Doncaster and those for the underframes were prepared at Gateshead. When consulted, Buckingham Palace had no comments to make about the construction of the vehicles nor about their external appearance, but instructed that the interior should be as simple as possible, preferably with white enamel used for interior surfaces, and that no baths were required to be fitted. Waring's were engaged as the interior furnishers.

At Gresley's suggestion, the NER design of underframe, as currently used for the new East Coast sleeping cars being built at York, was adopted for the royal saloons which were to run on six-wheeled bogies; this type was chosen as the distance between axle centres was not exceed 33 ft 9 in. on account of the length of the locking bars then in use by the East Coast companies.

The underframes and bogies were built complete at York, the design of underframes being of a most distinctive pattern involving the use of an inverted bowstring girder. 'Gresley desires Mansell wheels', noted Twinberrow in a surviving letter to Raven dated November 1906. A meeting was held at York on 8th April, 1907 with Gresley, Raven and Stamer present and on this occasion most of the details of the two saloons were finalised. Both vehicles were to be heated by electricity only and no steam heating was to be provided, although steam heating pipes ran beneath the underframes to take the supply through to adjoining vehicles. The dynamos and cells to supply current to the heating system were carried in a brake van running in the royal train. The royal saloons saw the first application of J. Stone's heating and ventilating system, later developed for the LNER's prestige rolling stock of the 1930s.

Both royal saloons were built in 1908 but Her Majesty's seems not to have entered service until the following year. The GNR undertook to build the accompanying saloons and standard ECJS brake vans to make up the royal train and, as completed, the East Coast royal train remained in more or less the same formation for over 50 years. No. 395 was maintained by Doncaster Works and No. 396 passed from York to Doncaster's care as from August 1923.

No 395, as His Majesty's saloon

No 395, as numbered in the ECJS list, made its first journey conveying King Edward VII on 7th September, 1908, working from Kings Cross to Ollerton.

The body construction of both Nos. 395/6 was similar to that for other teak bodied stock with bowed ends and the roof sloping down at each end. However, insulation was increased as compared with standard stock with the use of thick felt packing and rubber padding between body and underframe. The length over the body ends was 67 ft. The ventilation system originally adopted meant that the lack of roof ventilators gave an unbroken line to the roof which was slightly higher than other ECJS vehicles. The recessed double doors at each corner opened inwards. The body panelling was of very fine, carefully matched, figured Javan teak. The fixed windows were of bevelled plate-glass. The mouldings around the body panels and windows were of gilt-brass while the grip handles at the side of the double doors were finished in gilt, those on No. 395 being more elaborate. On both vehicles the royal arms were displayed on the centre panels with ciphers - the King's or Queen's as appropriate - on the entrance doors.

The interior layout, moving from left to right on the plan commonly shown for No 395 which was ECJS Diagram 81, comprised an attendant's compartment, complete with electric kettles (a relative novelty for that date?), urns and a lighting/heating switchboard. The King's dressing room came next, including lavatory, then the bedroom, 14 ft in length, a large day saloon, 17½ ft long, and finally a smoke room leading to the end balcony.

The white enamel surfaces recommended by the Palace were to be found in the dressing room and bedroom, but the day saloon was decorated in Louis XVI style with highly polished sycamore panelling inlaid with pewter and the smoke room was furnished in Jacobean style with inlaid oak panelling. In the bedroom, the furniture was of inlaid mahogany covered with rose-coloured silk damask upholstery. This room was designed so that, with the bed removed, it could be converted to provide a dining-room for daytime journeys. The furniture in the day saloon comprised a variety of easy chairs, a settee and writing desk. Carpeting in all rooms was plain rose-coloured Saxony pile with green silk curtains and blinds, the interior schemes being the work of Messrs Waring's.

There was a major innovation with the electric heating and ventilating system which was developed by J. Stone & Co, current being supplied from one of the brake vans running with the royal train set. One reason for the high, domed roof became apparent as the void between the roof boards and ceiling housed two air ducts running the full length of the body, one duct supplying air to the saloons below, the other extracting it. There were intakes in the roof and the incoming air passed through a purifying tank and then was blown through ducts into the interior by fans located in the ceiling above the attendant's compartment. Stale air was extracted through ceiling vents into the exhaust duct running the length of the vehicle, drawn by an exhaust fan fitted on the underframe. In short, it was an early form of pressure ventilation. There were also electric radiators. As in the GNR's Sheffield stock restaurant cars of 1906, there was concealed electric lighting in the day and smoking saloons, with rows of tubular lights behind the cornices.

No 396, as Her Majesty's saloon

There were some differences to the general specification for the two vehicles, so far as the heating and lighting were concerned, but their nature is unknown. Otherwise Nos. 395/6 were very similar in construction and external finish, but their interior layout and furnishings were different. As built, No. 396 provided separate suites for the Queen Alexandra and for Princess Victoria. Its ECJS diagram number was 82.

At one end, a balcony led to the Queen's day saloon, 14 ft 9 in. in length. Next to this was a dual-purpose room, either serving as the Queen's bedroom when a movable partition provided privacy, or else as a full-width dining room seating six. Beyond this room was a side corridor past a dressing-room, lavatories and the dressing-room and bedroom of Princess Victoria's suite. At the other end of the carriage was an attendant's balcony.

The interior decor comprised much white enamel panelling, offset by an

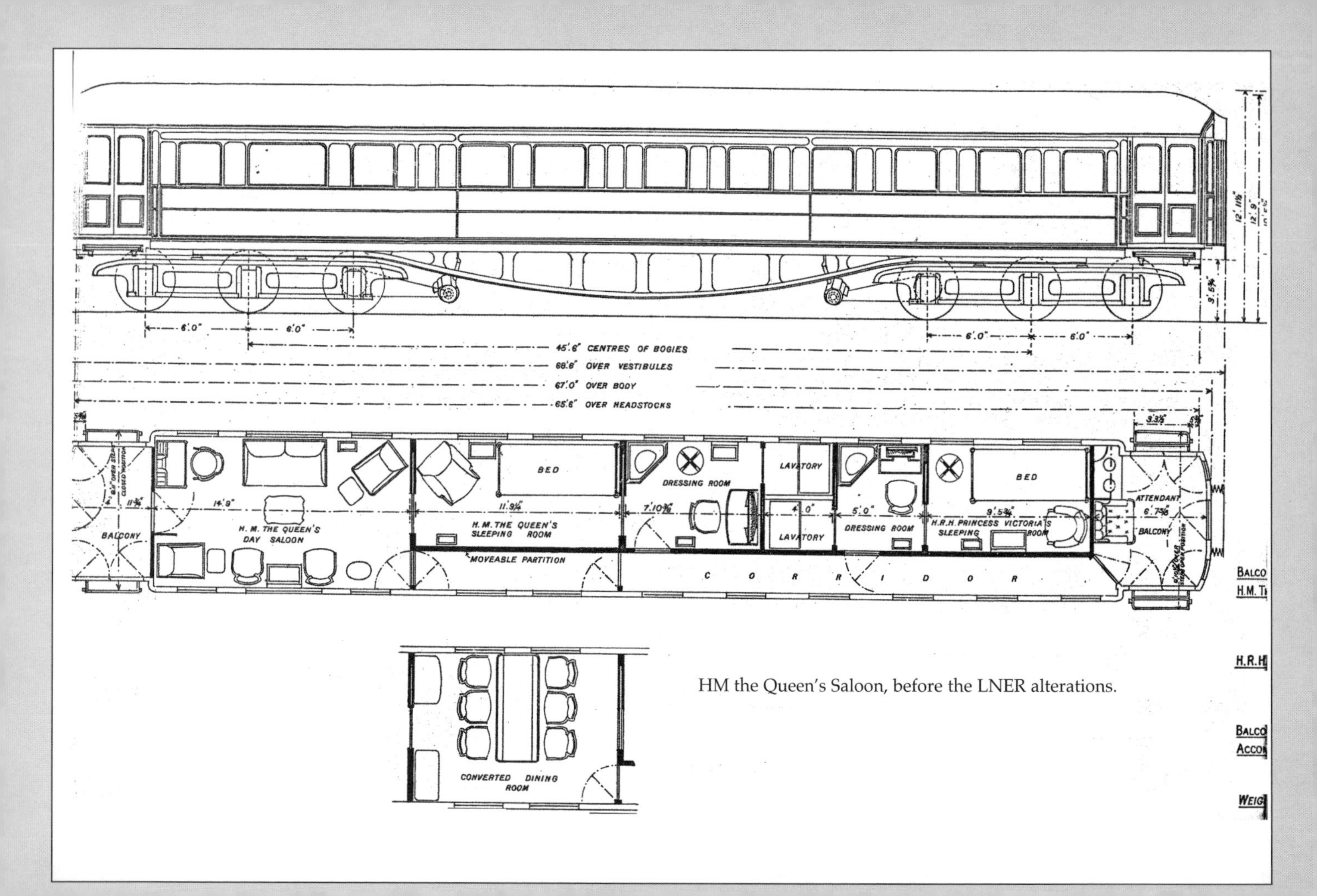

HM the Queen's Saloon, before the LNER alterations.

ivory painted ceiling. The furniture in the day saloon was of inlaid harewood, upholstered in pale, watered silk and residing on a red Wilton carpet. The metallic fittings were mercury gilt. As in No. 395, there was concealed main lighting, supplemented by wall brackets. The furniture used in the dining room was inlaid satinwood, upholstered in striped satin. The Princess's suite had grey carpeting and the corridor alongside was teak panelled, the windows having green silk spring blinds and white curtains.

After Edward VII's death in May 1910, the East Coast authorities approached Buckingham Palace to see if the new Queen wanted changes to be made to the interior of No. 396. The answer was that no alterations were to be made 'at present' but, in due course, electric fans and a Chesterfield were installed.

One interesting footnote to the history of royal saloons on British railways has been so far unpublished. During 1920, the East Coast traffic superintendents noted that as the royal saloons were 'being unused' they might be converted for normal service. By the time the matter was next considered, the Railways Act of 1921 was about to come into force and the East Coast General Managers agreed that the 'conversion of the royal saloons should stand over due to the current position of the railways.' Some preparatory work was done. Drawing No 11019 in the NER Darlington drawing office register is dated 21st January, 1921 and - as reproduced here - is titled 'ECJS - Conversion of HM the Queen's Royal Saloon'. The proposals were for the vehicle to become either a 30-seater first-class dining car, or a 10-berth sleeping car.

Nos 395/6 after Grouping

During 1924, the LNER reviewed the two royal trains it had inherited - the seven vehicles of the GER set and the eight-vehicle ECJS train. The recommendations made to the Board by the Traffic Committee in July 1924 were that the GER royal train should be disbanded and its vehicles converted for normal traffic while the East Coast train should be made suitable for all the journeys that members of the royal family were likely to make on the LNER. This involved the provision of a bath and dressing-room in both Nos. 395/6, baths having been specifically excluded when the Palace had been asked to specify facilities in Edward VII's days! In addition, all the furniture and furnishings were to be renewed, the interior redecorated and the vehicles' running gear given a general overhaul. Not only that but No. 396 was to be converted to Their Majesties' Saloon.

Although the official record says that Nos. 395/6 were to be made suitable for all journeys on the LNER, in fact both were remodelled for daytime journeys only, the LMS royal train being used for all overnight journeys made by the royal family. The total value of work approved on 31st July, 1924 was £6,750 and White Allom's were engaged for certain interior alterations and the supply of new furnishings and fittings, other structural and conversion work being the responsibility of York, Doncaster and Stratford workshops. In addition, the ventilating and heating system was removed from the roof space above the end vestibule in each carriage, to make way for a water tank to supply the bath,

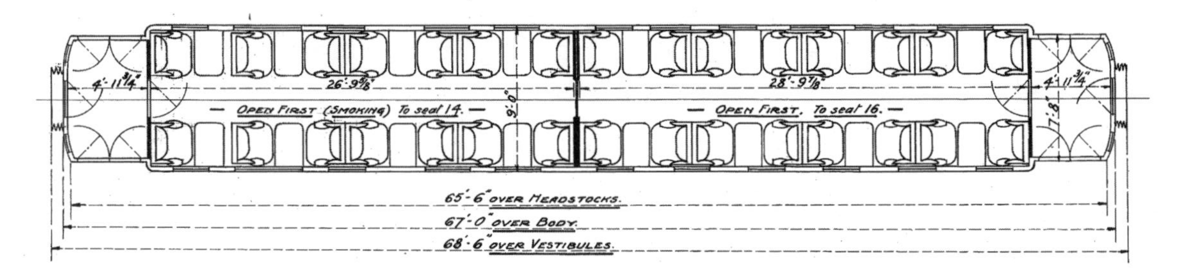

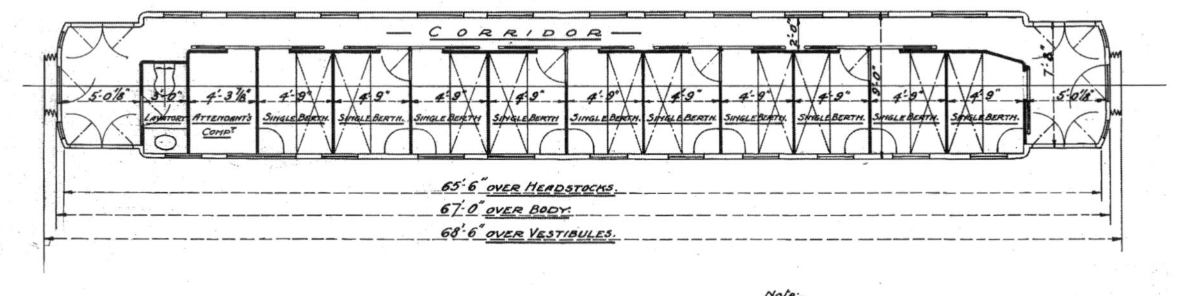

Proposals for the conversion of HM the Queen's Saloon to a sleeping car or a dining car, as shown in a drawing (No. 11019) prepared by the NER's Darlington drawing office in 1921. *National Railway Museum*

heating coming from the train's steam supply, backed up by an electric heater. Steam heating pipes were fitted to the interior of No 395/6, suggesting that the pressure ventilation had not perhaps proved satisfactory.

The vehicles chosen for the LNER royal train were as follows:

King's Saloon; Queen's Saloon; semi-royal saloons Nos. 3099/3100; saloons Nos. 1280/1; equipment vans Nos. 82/132

No. 396, as Their Majesties saloon, later used by HM the Queen and HRH the Duke of Edinburgh

This was the first to be dealt with and it went into York Works on 7th August, 1924. After a somewhat complicated set of arrangements involving a movement to Stratford Works and back, it was outshopped from York on 9th October the same year. As remodelled, No. 396 made its first royal journey to Wolferton a week later.

The interior was altered to provide a saloon, largely as before, and a private sitting-room in place of the bedroom/ dining-room while the remaining rooms alongside the internal corridor became the Queen's dressing-room and the King's bath and dressing-room. White Allom's refurbishment scheme included painting the interior panelling French grey where it was not polished wood and white-painted ceilings. This effect was offset by furniture reupholstered in grey material, a light-green carpet, white and green curtains and all interior fittings in gilt. In the main saloon the concealed lighting was replaced with ceiling light fittings and an extractor fan.

The exterior was revarnished and the King's coat of arms replaced those of Queen Alexandra's and the Queen's ciphers were removed from the balcony doors.

No. 395, as HM the Queen's saloon, later HM the Queen Mother's saloon

No. 395 was sent to Doncaster Works for modifications to be carried out in February 1925. Outshopped in the June of that year it was back again for detailed changes to be made in December, finally being released in July 1926. There is more than a suspicion that HM Queen Mary had fairly strong views on the furnishings in her saloon!

The attendant's balcony was reduced in length, a new toilet provided next to it, and the dressing-room remodelled entirely and given ceiling mounted light fittings, with wall lights over the dressing table. A private saloon was created from the bedroom and included a day couch and new dining table. The day saloon and end balcony were little altered, apart from new light fittings and new or reupholstered furnishings. White Allom adopted a different colour scheme for No. 396, with green trellis pattern carpet, the walls and ceilings in dull jade paintwork (existing woodwork was left, but repolished) and upholstery in green, uncut velvet.

All windows were replaced with new glass carrying HM Queen Mary's cipher. The subsequent changes made at Doncaster from the end of 1925

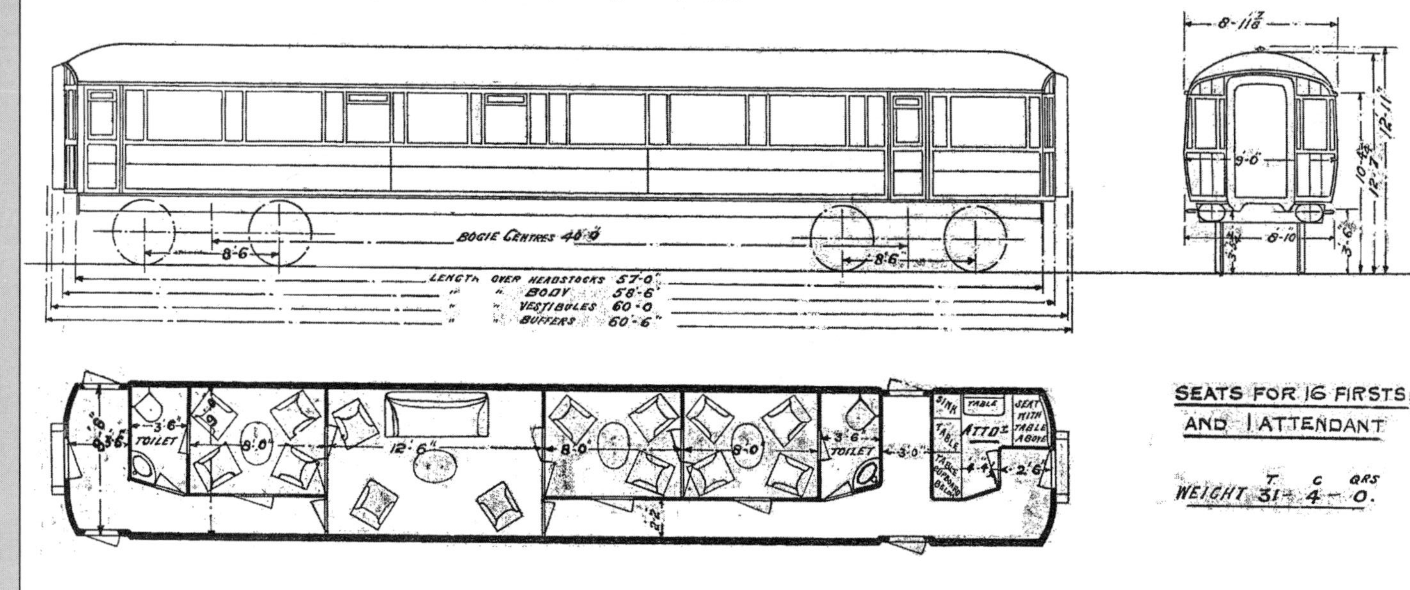

GNR first-class saloon No. 3100 on Dia. 5, built by Doncaster in 1908. This is not the vehicle's original condition but after it had been re-bogied. Later it was altered - perhaps in 1925 - so that the second of the adjoining 8 ft long saloons was converted to a service compartment and the seating was shown as 12 only. No. 3100 was then described as a 'Saloon for Ladies in Waiting and Private Secretaries'.

included altering the balcony doors to open outwards, replacement of the bed/couch, a new settee for the day saloon and an increase in the length of the balcony at the expense of the saloon.

At, or about this time, the story goes that No. 395 was at Doncaster Works for attention, including the renewal of the flooring. Inflammable fumes from the adhesives being used were ignited by the gas-lighting in the shops, with the result that some exterior panels on No. 395 were scorched. An exhaustive search worldwide failed to locate matching teak so the old panels were reversed and cleaned up.

After the death of King George VI, No. 395 became the royal saloon for HM Queen Elizabeth the Queen Mother and it was refurbished to her directions. No. 395 was also designated for the use of other members of the royal family when running in the complete royal train.

Nos. 395/6 in BR days

Both vehicles remained substantially in their condition as rebuilt in 1924-6 until 1954. It was then decided for some reason to bring the livery of the East Coast vehicles into line with those of the former LMS royal train. The result was that the LNER royal train vehicles were repainted into the dark-claret livery with black and vermilion lining out.

Although in itself a handsome finish, the instruction to do so almost brought tears to the Doncaster paintshop staff who had lovingly maintained the fine, matched teak panels with their varnished finish for nearly 50 years. Further refurbishment seems to have taken place at this stage, involving the repainting of interior panelling and reupholstering.

With the disbandment of the former LNER royal train after 1961, Nos. 395/6 were used in shorter formations such as for the annual royal excursion to Tattenham Corner for the Derby, and for use by visiting heads of state between Gatwick Airport and Victoria station.

During 1970 No. 396, with 395, was repainted at York Works and this was probably their final major attention in BR days. No. 395 was last used in 1972. With the entry into service of the new royal train in 1977, Nos. 395/6 were no longer required and were claimed for the National Collection by the National Railway Museum and handed over in 1979. No. 396 is currently on loan to and on display at the Bressingham Steam Museum.

The other saloons in the East Coast royal train

GNR saloons Nos. 3099/3100 - 1908

These two vehicles (GN Diagrams 4/5 respectively) were designated as first-class saloons but would seem to have been built for the royal train in which they were used by ladies-in-waiting and attendants.

With bodies 58 ft 6 in. over the panels, Nos. 3099/3100 followed the usual Gresley GNR lines with elliptical roofs sloping down to bow ends and with the large bodyside windows having hinged ventilators. Both vehicles had electric

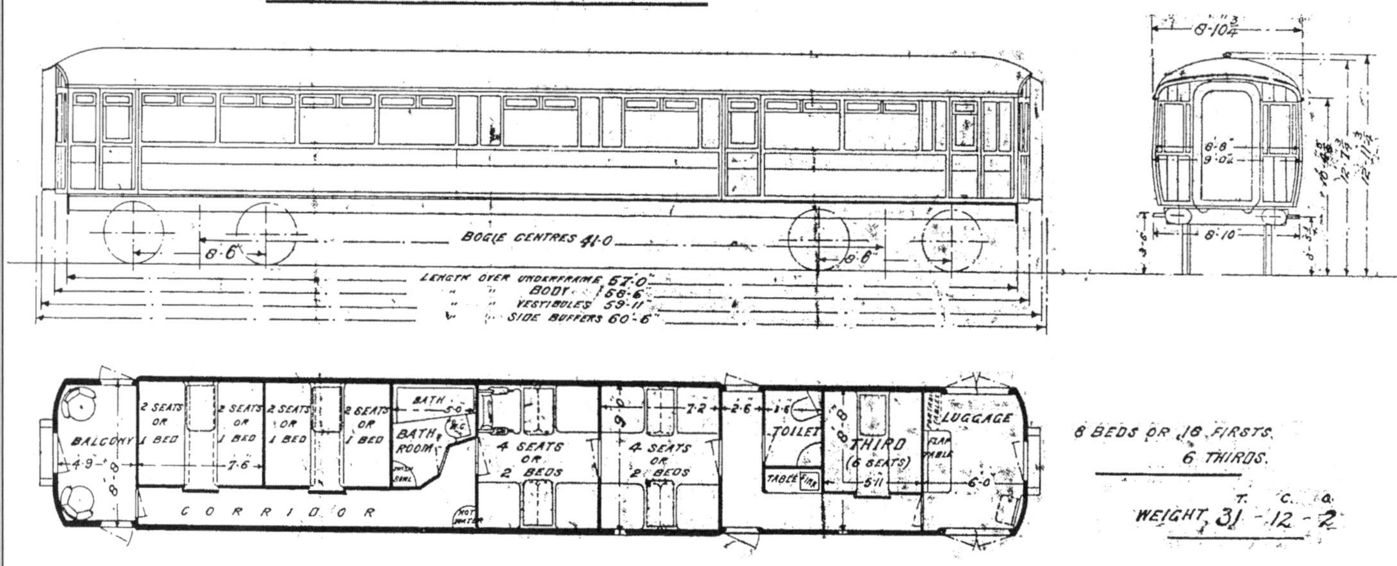

GNR first-class saloon on Dia. 6, built by Doncaster in 1906 and showing 8 ft wheelbase bogies, later exchanged for the compound-bolster type. In royal train use from 1908, both vehicles were altered, No. 1280 having a service compartment in place of the compartment at the right-hand end, and No. 1281, an office in place of the right-hand end compartment with a typist's office in place of the luggage compartment.

lighting. No. 3100 (at least) is shown as having originally 8 ft bogies, later changed for the 8 ft 6 in. standard.

Although as built No. 3099 is shown as accommodating twelve passengers and No. 3100 had room for six servants in addition, at some stage before Grouping they were altered. No. 3099 then had four saloons, seating 17 in all, with two lavatories, while No. 3100 had three saloons - one large - seating 17 and with two lavatories, a bathroom and a service compartment. Most interior panelling was enamelled white while the remainder of the woodwork was polished mahogany. The seating comprised easy chairs upholstered in green tapestry. Both carriages could be converted to provide sleeping accommodation.

Modifications were made to their interiors in 1924/5. At some date after 1928 the then No. 43099 is shown as seating 22 and having had the bath removed. In their final days, No. 43099 was classed as 'Saloon for equerries and ladies in waiting' and No. 43100 as 'Saloon for ladies in waiting and private secretaries'. Both were withdrawn in 1961.

GNR saloons Nos. 1280/1281 - 1906

These were among the first elliptical-roofed carriages of Gresley design and were built as first-class saloons, 58 ft 6 in. over body panels and 8 ft wheelbase bogies. As first built, they seem to have been identical, with seating for 16 first-class passengers and six thirds, the first-class seating being convertible to beds so that eight beds could be made up. Both were electrically-lit. In an article appearing in the *Railway Engineer* for February 1911, No. 1281 is described as 'a convertible saloon (first-class) designed for taking private parties, day or night.'

Probably coincident with their allocation to the royal train, the internal layout of both vehicles was changed. Both then had a balcony/vestibule, two compartments, each with four seats convertible to two beds in each compartment, a bathroom with gas-heated water supply, two open bays, each providing either two beds or four seats and a lavatory. The former third-class compartment in No 1281 was changed to an office while the end luggage space became a typist's office. The bathroom in No 1281 featured a full-size bath, the hot water temperature being thermostatically controlled. No 1280 was reclassified Dia. 6A and the former third-class compartment and luggage space became a service compartment which had revolving chairs.

In both vehicles, the panelling throughout was in sycamore and mahogany, the chairs being upholstered in silk damask and the compartment seating trimmed in Blenheim moquette. Unspecified alterations were made to Nos. 1280/1 in 1924/5.

In their final days, No. (4)1280 was designated 'Saloon for royal household staff and railway officers' and (4)1281, 'Saloon for royal household staff'. Both were withdrawn in 1961.

Royal train equipment/brake vans

To accompany Nos. 395/6. a special 56 ft 6 in. bogie brake van was built in 1908. This was No. 82 in the ECJS list and it was otherwise very similar to the earliest batch of ECJS bogie brakes. One of its purposes was to house the dynamos and cells to supply current to the heating/ventilation system in Nos. 395/6; after the 1924/5 alterations to these vehicles No. 82 retained a back-up facility in case of electrical failure. No. 82 also had a telephone, a sink and a staff lavatory. Another purpose was that it was kitted out with cleaning materials for keeping No. 395 looking spick and span. The instruction in pre-Grouping days was that No. 82 must work with No. 395 (or 396) when dispatched to Scotland and, should it have not worked north with one or other of the royal saloons, it must be in position before the return journey was made.

In 1927 No. 82 was converted from gas to electric lighting - until then it had been the only gas-lit vehicle in the royal train - and it was renumbered 109 in 1929. It survived the cut-back to the royal train in 1961 and became an internal user vehicle - No. 040880 - at Wood Green, serving as an equipment store for Nos. 395/6. It was claimed for the National Collection in 1976 and restored to its varnished teak finish as LNER No. 109.

From 1908 - 26, standard ECJS full brake No. 132 ran in the royal train. It was displaced by a new and similar vehicle dating from 1922, No. 135, which had been allocated to royal train from, as early as late 1925. No. 135 had electric lighting and was fitted with a lavatory for royal train duties in March 1926, in which condition it was to EC Dia. 39E.

Formation of the royal train

A pre-Grouping formation was:

Bogie brake No. 82, saloon No. 1281, saloon No. 3100, royal saloons Nos. 395/6, saloon No. 3099, saloon No. 1280, bogie brake No. 132.

Apart from the substitution of 135 for 132 this was to remain the arrangement for the time that the full royal train was operated.

A November 1925 diagram showed the numbering then to be:

82J - 1280N - 3100N - 396J - 395 - 3099N - 1281N - 135

There were strict rules about the formation of the train so that, for instance, the service compartment of No. 1280 was always next to No. 82.

A list held at Doncaster Works of the royal train vehicles and dated 17th February, 1961 showed the following:

109 - 41280 - 9171 - 396 - 43100 - 135 - 395 - 41281 - 43099

No. 9171 was a standard LNER restaurant first (Dia. 236) with anthracite/electric cooking, allocated, it would seem, from 1954 for royal train use and painted that year in royal claret livery.

The last time that a complete East Coast royal train was operated was on 8th June, 1961 to convey HM the Queen to the wedding of HRH the Duke of Kent at York Minster. The formation was unique and comprised the following vehicles:

135 - 395 - 396 - 9171 - open first 11135 (LNER Dia. 289) - twin open first (LNER Dia. 229) - a Gresley LNER restaurant first - 41280 - 109

Subsequently, all vehicles from the royal train fleet, except Nos. 395/6 and 109, were withdrawn and scrapped. Some artefacts survived for preservation at Wolferton Station Museum.

Until 1939, the royal train vehicles were stabled at Wellington sidings, Highgate. With the 1935 - 40 London Transport New Works programme in connection with electrification of the LNER line to High Barnet, the royal train stock was transferred to Doncaster Works. From 1962, the remaining vehicles were held at Wood Green, but in 1973 Nos. 395/6 were transferred to join the other royal train vehicles at Wolverton Works.

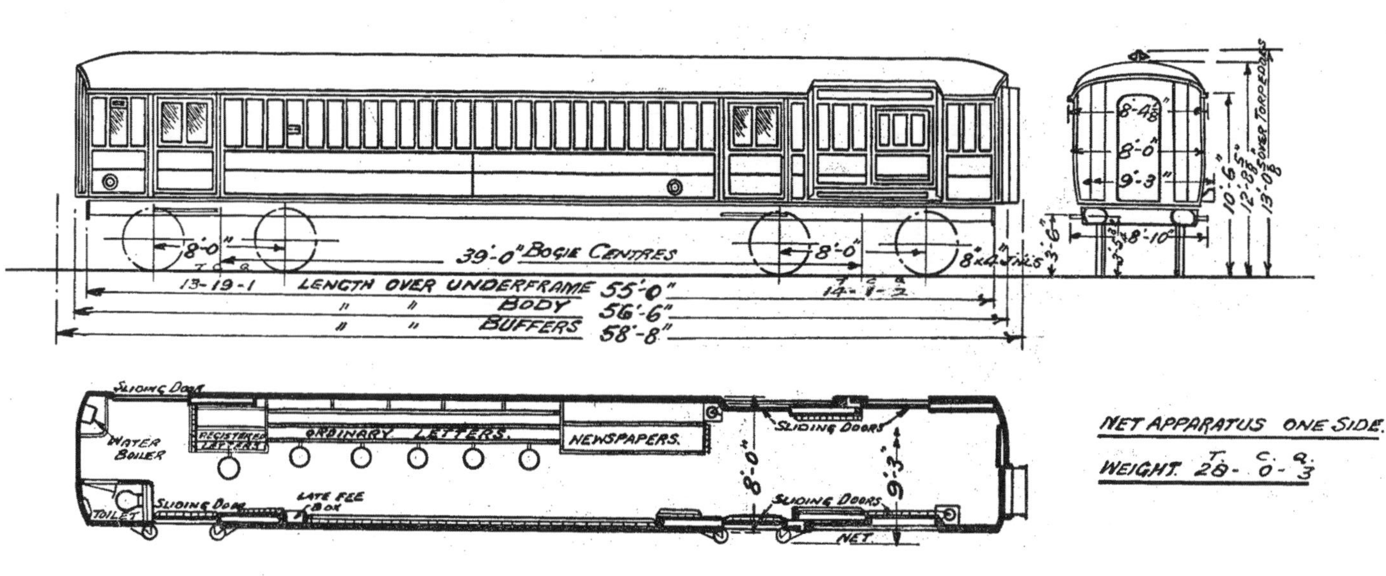

GNR TPO van No. 1969 (GNR Dia. 312, built Doncaster, 1913). Note that one end has no gangway, while the other is centrally-positioned.

Chapter Eight

GNR and ECJS Passenger Brake Vans, TPO, Luggage and Milk Vans

Passenger brake vans, luggage and milk vans 1905 - 23

There were effectively two types of passenger vans for ECJS and GNR service: a 56 ft 6 in. by 8 ft bow-ended vestibuled brake van with side lookouts and a 51 ft 1½ in. by 8 ft 3 in. high-arched roof non-vestibuled luggage or milk van. These were covered by the following diagrams:

56 ft 6 in. by 8 ft vestibuled, 8 ft bogies:

ECJS EC Dias 33A(later 39B), 39B and 39C
GN/NE Joint Stock vehicles JS Diagrams 13/18 - Nos. 35/6
GNR Diagrams 286/7/308

51 ft 1½ in. by 8 ft 3 in. non - vestibuled, 8 ft bogies:

GNR Diagrams 293/307/9
GNR Diagrams 310/325A/326 for milk traffic

The vestibuled design first appeared in March 1906 with the ECJS van No. 126, on EC Dia. 33A. These passenger brake vans featured steel underframes, the new standard elliptical roof with sloping ends and Pullman type gangways. The basic design was to remain the standard for the next 35 years or so but there were differences. The pre-Grouping vans had raised skylight type ventilators in the roof, rather than the familiar cant-rail toplights later used. Two pairs of sliding doors were fitted to the earlier vehicles but, after 1923, hinged pairs were standard. After 1911, vehicles were altered or built new with a slightly cambered floor to facilitate cleaning. The long guard's duckets which extended the full height of the bodysides and carried side-lamps were replaced in later designs by a neater, faceted type. In due course, some of the old-style duckets were removed.

ECJS Dia. 33A was unique for the bodyend lights but these were soon displaced by wooden panels. ECJS Dia. 39B and subsequent batches had electric lighting, as did GN Dia. 308 *et seq*. Generally, these passenger brake vans were intended to carry a maximum distributed load of eight tons. The GNR designs to Diagrams 286 were originally limited to a six-ton payload, but on fitting with heavy duty 8 ft bogies (with the 9½ X 4⅜ in. journals) after 1914 they were able to carry eight tons.

Originally, the GNR brakes were allocated general series numbers but after 1922 most were renumbered in the 4XX series. The ECJS vans were originally numbered in the same series as the carriages but from 1925 were allocated numbers in a new van stock series, from 10 - 19 and 100 - 199.

Few changes affected the non-vestibuled GNR luggage and milk vans which were built between 1909 and 1922. These designs had four pairs of double doors each side and guard's duckets. The general outline was similar to the non-vestibuled semi-fast stock. Vans for milk traffic had a maximum carrying capacity of ten tons (48 milk churns), luggage vans being labelled for seven tons weight, except for those to Dia. 309 which could be loaded to ten tons. Dia. 307 luggage van No. 1566 was altered in 1917 to work as a mail van between Grimsby and Peterborough.

GNR TPO vans

The GNR was responsible for running TPO vans on three main services in the late 1900s:

The 'Great Northern Sorting Carriage' (Day): 5.5 am Kings Cross - Doncaster - Leeds, empty to York and 9.18 am next day York - Kings Cross
The 'Great Northern Bag Tender' (Night): 8.45 pm Kings Cross - Newcastle, empty to York and 9.50 pm York to Kings Cross
The 'Great Northern TPO Midday Mail': 1.30 pm Kings Cross - York and 5.43 pm return

Subsequent changes saw the 'Great Northern Bag Tender' become an operating TPO from 1910 and the 'Midday Mail' working ceased entirely on and from 6th November, 1915.

Three sorting vans were built by the GNR after 1905: No. 2407, later 4202 in the van series, on GN Dia. 313 in 1907; No. 1858, later 4203, same diagram but built in 1909, and No. 1969, later 4201, on GN Dia. 312 and built in 1913. All had 56 ft 6 in. bodies without gangways, nets on both sides, a staff lavatory, gas lighting and dual braking. No. 2407 usually worked on the 'Great Northern Bag Tender', No. 1858 on the 'Midday Mail' and No. 1969 on the 'Great Northern Sorting Carriage' working.

From 1917-9, Nos. 1858 and 2407 were altered for and loaned to the Admiralty Mail Office for naval postal traffic passing to/from the naval bases servicing the Grand Fleet in the north of Scotland and the Orkneys. They were used between Edinburgh Waverley and Inverness. As a result, British Standard gangways (supplied by the London & North Western Railway) were fitted at each end in December 1917, one centrally positioned, the other offset. The traductor arms were removed and some internal changes were carried out, the displaced items being stored at Doncaster Works until the vehicles were returned to normal traffic by the GNR in June 1919.

After Grouping, No. 4201 was used on the Leeds 'Sorting Carriage' and Nos. 4202/3 on the main Kings Cross - York - Edinburgh circuit. The collection net was removed from No. 1858 in April 1924, that on No. 2407 in October 1924.

After prolonged pressure from the General Post Office to replace the six-wheeled ex-GER TPO vans, built 1886-95 and used on the 7.56 pm Ipswich - London and 4 am return, Nos. 4202/3 were transferred to the GE Section in July 1933 where they became Nos. 6133/4 respectively. The latter worked on the Norwich - Liverpool St TPO and was rebuilt with a side gangway at one end, retaining its original centrally positioned one at the other. The Kings Cross - Leeds TPO ceased entirely as from 21st September, 1940 but all three sorting carriages were to be long-lived.

Appendix

List of GNR and ECJS Carriages Built 1905 - 23

Introduction

Numbering schemes

Great Northern Railway

The numbering scheme used by the GNR for passenger carriages, passenger brake vans, milk vans and TPO vehicles ran from 1 upwards without any distinction for types of carriage or van, other than for articulated stock. New vehicles were allocated the lowest vacant number.

In the early 1900s, a new series commencing at 3001 was being used and had reached 3229 in 1910, after which lower numbers were again applied, excepting the articulated stock noted below. New articulated vehicles assumed numbers higher than 3230, and at first both articulated bodies carried the same number (e.g., suburban twins were numbered 3233/3233 etc). The series for articulated carriages was as follows:

3231 - 3283, 3354 - 7, inner London suburban twins.

After 1913 or so, new series were allocated for articulated vehicles, as follows:

4001 - 5022 twin carriages, of which 4001 - 92 were London suburban twins, 4861 - 4931 vestibuled twins. The inner suburban trains were renumbered from the '32XX' series; in the list that follows some unconfirmed numbers are shown as ? 4161 etc.
6001 - 6543 triplet carriages
8001 - 8984 quadruplet carriages
8121 - 4, 8451 - 4 *et seq.* were suburban twins converted to quadruplets.
9001 - 9205 quintuplet carriages
of which 9011 - 5 comprised the Leeds quintuplet set.

After 1922, the majority of vestibuled and non-vestibuled bogie vans were renumbered in a new van series from 400 upwards. The general series were as follows:

41 - 49, 400 - 499, 4001 - 4210 for luggage brake vans, mail vans etc.

300 - 492 were allocated to carriage trucks and 500 - 864 for horseboxes and special cattle boxes.

For the numbering applied after 1923 to former GNR vehicles, see below.

East Coast Joint stock

This stock was numbered in its own series, independent of the companies involved. This was continued after 1923, but from 1925 a separate series were allocated to passenger brake vans which until then had received numbers in the main ECJS range. Otherwise there was no distinction between types, nor as to the works maintaining the vehicles. The principle of numbering was that new vehicles were allocated the lowest vacant number. Replacements of carriages destroyed in accidents were allocated the number of the defunct vehicle. During the late 1900s the highest numbers in the ECJS series were in the 380 - 399 range. Older vehicles dispersed to GNR, NER and NBR fleets were renumbered on transfer from the ECJS fleet.

The articulated sleeping car twin of 1922 was numbered 181/181A as built, later

1181/2. This was in line with ECJS practice for the bodies of an articulated twin.

A separate East Coast stock number series was maintained up until nationalisation and afterwards, some new vehicles receiving East Coast numbers as late as 1952. Existing carriages continued with their numbers into the late 1960s and 1970s.

GN/NE Joint stock

Thirty-six vehicles, carriages and vans, were built between 1905 and 1912 and numbered between 1 and 36. After 1923, several GN/NE carriages at first had their numbers increased by 4xx, with a J suffix, eg, 404J, 435J etc but were then numbered within the East Coast stock series as 1401 - 34 and the vans, 150 - 2.

LNER numbering schemes 1923 - 1925

It was decided in January 1923 that there would be no central control of passenger rolling stock, with the consequence that the individual sections or Areas would be responsible for their own stock and as a result would maintain their own number series. Instructions were issued during April 1923 concerning the numbering of coaching stock taken into the new organisation. All vehicles would retain their pre-Grouping numbers but a suffix letter would be added to denote the section to which they were allocated and which would be responsible for their maintenance.

The suffixes allocated were: East Coast stock - J; North Eastern Railway/Area - Y; North British Railway/Southern Scottish Area - B; Great Northern Railway/section - N; Great Central Railway/section - C; Great Eastern Railway/section - E; Great North of Scotland Railway/Northern Scottish Area - S.

LNER numbering scheme 1925 - 43

The new scheme was introduced in April 1925 and dispensed with the use of suffixes to pre-Grouping numbers. From now onwards the owning Area or section was denoted by the first digit in the number, this prefix being added to the existing number. This was in similar manner to the locomotive numbering scheme brought in from early 1924 and the effect was as follows:

Section/Area	*April 1923 numbers*	*April 1925 numbers*
East Coast	12J/123J	112/1123
North Eastern	12Y/123Y/1123Y	212/2123/21123
Southern Scottish	12B/123B/1123B	312/3123/31123
Great Northern	12N/123N/1123N	412/4123/41123
Great Central	12C/123C/1123C	512/5123/51123
Great Eastern	12E/123E/1123E	612/6123/61123
Northern Scottish	12S/123S	712/7123

The numbers shown above are only for the purposes of illustration.

New standard stock was allocated the lowest available number in the various three, four and five-digit series but other isolated blocks of numbers were used in the five-digit ranges. Individual numbers gave no indication of age. Numbers were reused so that destroyed or transferred vehicles' numbers might be allocated to their replacements.

The new scheme included five separate ranges of numbers:

Plate 107: GNR lavatory brake third No. 3083, in original condition (GNR Dia. 274, built Doncaster, 1907). Photograph dated February 1908. The GNR non-vestibuled stock was screw-coupled. The interior comprised two open sections, divided by lavatories. In most of the GNR carriages of this period, the fanlight above the door droplight was of coloured glass lettered 'Smoking' when providing access to smoking accommodation. *National Railway Museum*

Plate 108: GNR lavatory composite No. 3074, in original condition (GNR Dia. 121, built Doncaster, 1907). Photograph dated February 1908. The GNR non-vestibuled stock was screw-coupled. The interior comprised two open sections, divided by lavatories.

National Railway Museum

Plate 109: An up express near Greenwood, north of New Barnet. 'A1' Pacific No 2549 *Persimmon* carries Class 'A' headlamps for a somewhat varied train which includes Howlden bogie stock. Leading is a Gresley non-vestibuled lavatory brake third (by now with compound-bolster bogies), followed by a lavatory composite. *RAS Marketing*

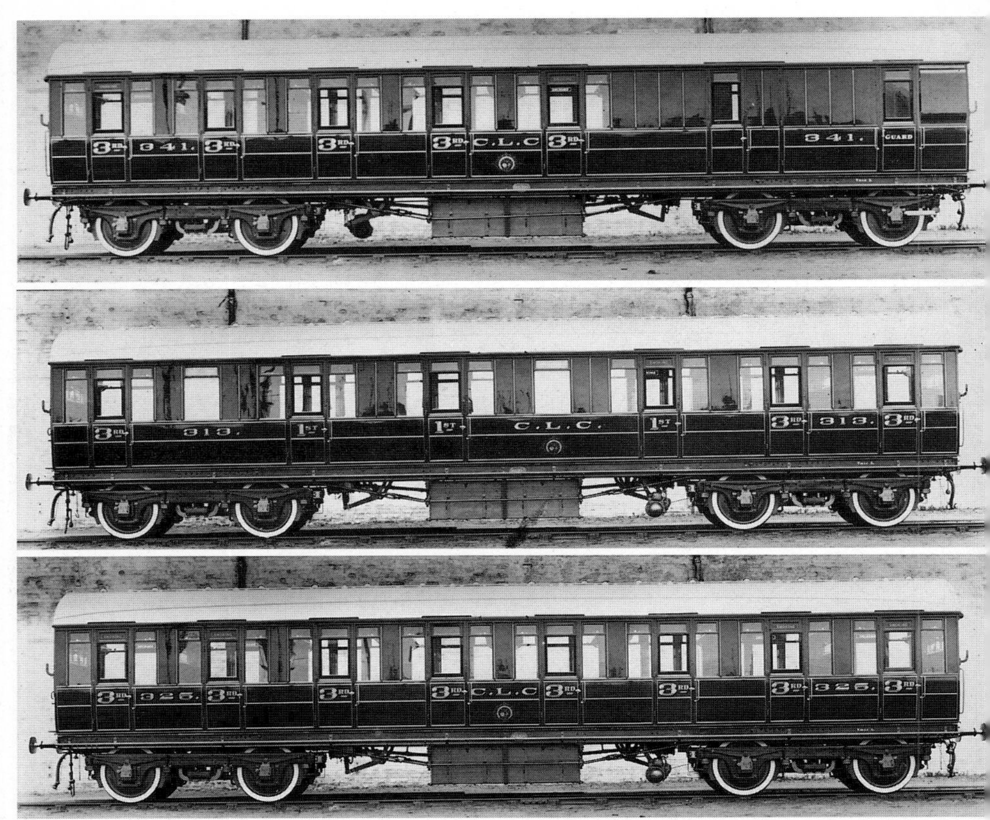

Plates 110/1/2: Examples of the first series of non-vestibuled stock built at Doncaster in 1911 for the Cheshire Lines Committee. All photographs are of the carriages as built and were taken at Doncaster in May 1911. Note the CLC coat of arms which embodied the devices of the Midland, GN and Great Central Railways. Brake third No. 341 (originally CLC Dia. 14). Lavatory composite No. 313 (originally CLC Dia. 15). One third-class (left-hand end) and all three first-class compartments had access to a lavatory. Third No. 325 (originally CLC Dia. 13).

National Railway Museum

Plate 113: CLC Saloon No. 201 does not carry class designations but was described as a first-class saloon when built by the GNR in 1912. This non-vestibuled vehicle is shown with the two saloons at the left-hand end. Just above the battery boxes is the GNR builder's plate, affixed to these, and to the GNR and ECJS vehicles built at Doncaster. Photograph taken March 1912, this being the only one of the CLC carriages built that year at Doncaster to have had an official photograph.

National Railway Museum

Plate 114: Unfortunately, the negative of this photograph has become damaged over the years, but it is valuable in showing the effect of a newly-shopped CLC vehicle in pre-Nationalisation days. The vehicle is CLC No. 324 (originally CLC Dia. 13). Photographed at Grimsby in May 1946. *R.M. Casserley*

Plate 115: For a short time after Nationalisation, the CLC vehicles retained their old numbers, prefixed by 'M', for London Midland Region which now took responsibility for them; the stock remained with 'CLC' lettering. This is M 336 (originally CLC Dia. 19 and one of the 1912-built batch of this type), seen at Manchester Central in April 1951. *R.M. Casserley*

Plate 116: The GNR built three types of composite for the CLC in 1911/2 but this (Dia. 16) had the strangest layout. The left-hand end had one third-class compartment with access to a lavatory, but all the other first- and third-class compartments were denied this facility! CLC No 316 is seen here at Rugby in April 1954, as M 19946 M. *R.M. Casserley*

Plate 117: A down semi-fast at Bell Bar in 1937 hauled by class 'C1' 4-4-2 No. 4400, its train comprising a GNR design articulated twin, most probably to GNR Dia. 218QQ, and a similar LNER twin. The different roof profiles of the two types show clearly. *RAS Marketing*

Plates 118/9: Two views of a GNR-design articulated twin brake composite (GNR Dia. 218QQ, built Doncaster, 1923), seen in BR unlined maroon livery at Mexborough in April 1957. *Above*: The brake third, originally 4031, as E 44031 E. *Below*: The lavatory composite, originally 4032, as E 44032 E. There were lavatories for both first and third-class. *R.M. Casserley*

Plate 120: GNR suburban twin brake second, both bodies numbered 3258. (GNR Dia. 424, built Doncaster, 1912). Photograph dated December 1912. The vehicles are lettered in the style used at Doncaster for all carriages before Gresley's arrival. These were later converted to form part of a quadruplet set. *National Railway Museum*

Plate 121: 'N1' class 0-6-2T No. 4557 at Greenwood in 1935 on a down empty stock train composed of two ex-GNR quadarts. *RAS Marketing*

Plate 122: A third-class compartment in carriage No. 8473, formed in quadruplet comprising 8471 - 4 (GNR Dia. 467A, rebuilt by Cravens in 1921, from suburban twins). Gas lighting is retained. The spartan slatted wooden seating and plain seat backs ensured scant comfort!

National Railway Museum

Plate 123: GNR rail-motor No. 2, built at Doncaster, 1905. The varnishing and lifting dates which represent the completion date for this pioneer read 28th October, 1905. The Gresley high-roofed carriage portions of the rail-motors later became an articulated twin. *Robert Humm Collection*

Plate 124: Brake third No. 8601 (furthest) as BR E 48601 E, and third No. 8602 as BR E 48602 E of an all-third GNR quadruplet, rebuilt from twins by Cravens, 1921 (GNR Dia. 467). The set was photographed at Hull in August 1956, by which time the 20 ex-GNR gas-lit quads had been displaced on the GN inner suburban services. *R.M. Casserley*

Plate 125: The construction of HM the King's saloon, ECJS No. 395, at Doncaster during 1908. Although fitting-out of the body is still in progress and the windows and doors are missing, the lining-out on the varnished panelling is complete. *National Railway Museum*

Plate 126: The interior of No. 395, showing the main saloon as furnished after the alterations had been carried out at Doncaster in 1925. The light fittings and clock are new, the seating has been supplemented and reupholstered, and new curtains and carpeting have been fitted. *Author's Collection*

Plate 127: No. 396, photographed in 1962, by which time it was painted in the royal claret livery. The number appears as '396' on the solebars. *National Railway Museum*

Plate 128: The interior of saloon No. 3099 (GNR Dia. 4, built at Doncaster, 1908). This shows the main saloon, looking from inside the adjacent 8 ft long saloon, alongside which is a side corridor. *National Railway Museum*

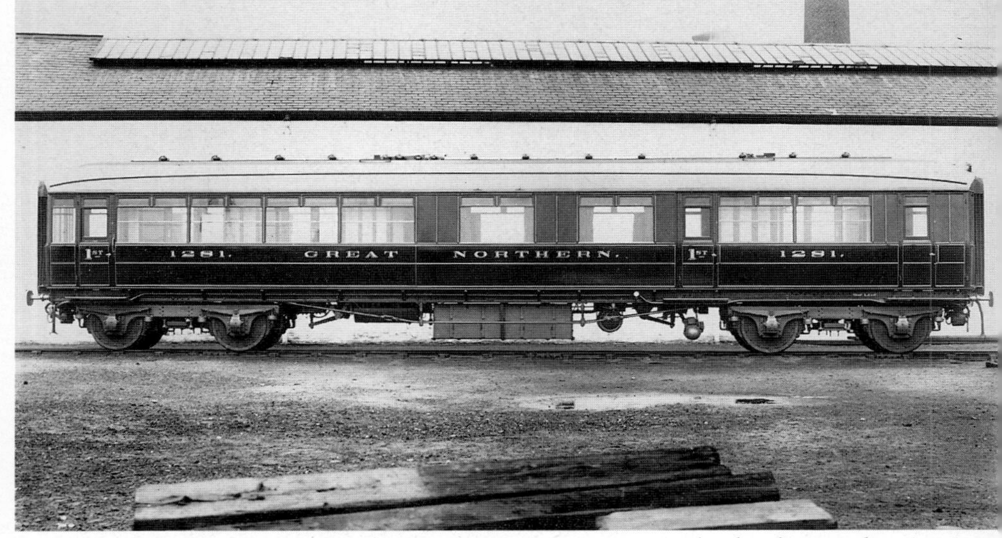

Plate 129: GNR Saloon No. 1281 (GNR Dia. 6, built Doncaster, 1906). The photograph is dated September 1907, at which time this vehicle was still described as a convertible first-class saloon for private parties, 'convertible' because it could be arranged with eight beds for overnight accommodation. These was a gas-heated water supply for a full-size bath. How often, if at all, was it used for overnight trips? *National Railway Museum*

Plate 130: A more ordinary royal train, than that seen in *plate 106*, with 'Royal Claud' class 'D16/2' 4-4-0 No. 8783, near Potters Bar in October 1930 with a Kings Cross - Wolferton working. Two former ECJS vans, probably Nos. 82 and 135, one of the four attendant semi-royal saloons, No. 396 and a couple of less-obvious vehicles. *Ken Nunn Collection/LCGB*

Plate 131: Royalty paid to travel by train and so, if possible, costs were reduced by attaching royal vehicles to service trains. This seems to be the case on 14th August, 1924 when HM Queen Mary was travelling to Goldsborough, Harrogate. The train is the 11.15 am King's Cross - Harrogate Pullman and, bringing its prestigious train around the curve from New Barnet towards Greenwood, is ex-GCR 'B3' class 4-6-0 No. 6168 *Lord Stuart of Wortley*. The first carriage would seem to be GNR brake first No. 3177, by now 3177N, built at Doncaster in 1910; it was shown in the GNR Diagram Book as having the end compartment 'altered . . . to run with the royal train'. Next is one of the two GN Dia. 5 saloons, Nos. 3099/3100, no doubt being used by Queen Mary. One way of confirming its identity is the rather obvious recessed doorway at the leading end.
Rail Archive Stephenson

Plate 132: ECJS bogie brake van No. 126 in original condition (EC Dia. 39, built Doncaster, 1906). Photograph dated March 1906. Of the various features of interest, note the Howlden-style guard's ducket; two pairs of sliding doors and the application of just the ECJS circlet to the lowest panel of the ducket. Not very visible are the four characteristic skylights, to provide interior illumination.
National Railway Museum

Plate 133: GNR bogie brake van No. 1742 (GNR Dia. 308, built Doncaster, 1912). This vehicle later became 432 and it was fitted with heavy-type bogies. The photograph is dated June 1913 after No. 1742 had been in traffic for nearly a year and so provides evidence of the weathering of the finish. The van is gas-lit - as was ECJS No. 126 as built - and conversion to electric lighting increased the tare weight by two tons. Note the wider vertical panelling, as compared to No. 126.
National Railway Museum

Plate 134: GNR bogie brake van No. 1800, as BR No. E 441 E (GNR Dia. 308, built Doncaster, 1914). Electric lighting has been fitted, as have the heavy-type bogies. Seen at Stratford, August 1957.
R.M. Casserley

Plate 135: GNR bogie brake and milk van No. 1405, as LNER No. 404 (GNR Dia. 310, built Doncaster, 1922). This shows the appearance of a freshly shopped teak-panelled vehicle, photographed in 1926. Four pairs of skylights were fitted. *National Railway Museum*

Plate 136: GNR bogie brake and milk van No. 1537, as BR No. E 405 E (GNR Dia. 310, built Doncaster, 1922). Electrically-lit and in BR unlined maroon livery and designated as 'Milk', despite the fact that milk had last been moved in churns by BR in the late 1940s/early 1950s. The van was photographed at Crewe in September 1959 with two years of life ahead of it.

R.M. Casserley

Plate 137: GNR TPO van No. 1858, in original condition (GNR Dia. 313, built Doncaster, 1909). Photograph dated July 1909. Note the two coats-of-arms, also the Late Fee box in the panel above the space between 'G.N.R.' and '1858'. There were two marker lights on the bodyside. At this stage No. 1858 was non-vestibuled. *National Railway Museum*

Plate 138: GNR TPO van No. 1858, as BR No. E 6134 E. Note the sealed door in the body end and removal of net (done in 1924) and traductor arms. No. 1858 had been fitted with electric lighting in 1933. The GNR fitted TPO vans with centrally-positioned gangways but when No. 1858 went to the GE Section as 6134 it had an offset-gangway fitted at one end. Photographed at Edinburgh Waverley in July 1957, its customary working was on the 8.5 pm Edinburgh Waverley - York, returning empty in a parcels train the next day. This van was replaced by a GWR-design van in 1960 and condemned. *R.M. Casserley*

1. Carriages.
2. Passenger brake vans.
3. Non - common user vans.
4. Horseboxes and special cattle vans.
5. Carriage trucks.

The separate series allocated to carriages and to passenger brake vans meant that there was duplication of numbers, as indeed there was with ranges 3 - 5 above!

Vehicles transferred from one Area or section to another were renumbered in the case of almost all standard LNER vehicles and usually - although not always - with pre-Grouping stock. Vehicles transferred from the East Coast stock to Areas or sections were renumbered.

The full range of numbers for carriages and passenger brake vans was as follows:

East Coast stock
Carriages: 10 - 19; 100 - 199; 1000 - 1999. Also 6431 - 3, 6441 - 3, later 16431 - 16533. Vans 10 - 19; 100 - 199; 1000 - 50.

North Eastern Area
Carriages: 20 - 29; 200 - 299; 2000 - 2999; 20000 - 26179. Vans 20 - 29; 200 - 299; 2000 - 2500.

Southern Scottish Area
Carriages 30 - 39; 300 - 399; 3000 - 3999; 30000 - 33000. Vans 30 - 39; 300 - 399; 3000 - 3200.

Southern Area - Great Northern section
Carriages 40 - 49; 400 - 499; 4000 - 4999; 40000 - 49419. Vans 40 - 49; 400 - 499; 4000 - 4375.

Southern Area - Great Central section
Carriages 50 - 59; 500 - 599; 5000 - 5999; 50000 - 59349. Vans 50 - 59; 500 - 599; 5000 - 5482.

Southern Area - Great Eastern section
Carriages 60 - 69; 600 - 699; 6000 - 6999; 60000 - 65369. Vans 60 - 69; 600 - 699; 6000 - 6999; 60000 - 60023.

Northern Scottish Area
Carriages 70 - 79; 700 - 799; 7000 - 7963. Vans 70 - 79; 700 - 799, 7000 - 7159.

Diagram Numbers

GNR

Diagrams were allocated to each new design, commencing at 1. These numbers corresponded to the relevant page in the GNR Carriage Diagram book. The dates of issue of the diagram books are not known but new designs or modifications to existing designs were accommodated by allocating a suffix to an appropriate earlier design. Even so, it is not clear just why some of the numbers were allocated when they were often confusing, e.g., Diagram 164 was a vestibuled composite dating from 1910, 164A was a non-vestibuled composite dating from 1910, as was 164B, but 164F was a vestibuled composite dating from 1911 and 164K, a vestibuled composite dating from 1922. The process became somewhat ridiculous by final pre-Grouping days, viz. the articulated twins referred to as 218QQ, 218RR etc.

The suffix-ed identities were also allocated after 1923 to LNER Gresley standard designs in the stock of the GN Section of the LNER but the standard all-sections Diagram numbers were increasingly used from the late 1920s. Carriage working notices sometimes ignored either identification and referred to a particular type of carriage by the number of the first vehicle in the batch, eg '41596' or '43133'.

Examples of Diagram numbers allocated to LNER Gresley standard designs were:

Diagram No.	*Type*	*LNER Diagram No.*
218Y	Vestibuled brake composite	32
248S	Vestibuled third	23
248T	Vestibuled open third	28
248U	Vestibuled open third	27A
248V	Non-Vestibuled twins	105/106
248W	Vestibuled third	115
248X	Vestibuled open third	150
248Y	Restaurant pantry car	151
248Z	Tourist vestibuled twin open	171
249	Vestibuled open third	186
249A	Vestibuled third	115 (again!)
255	Vestibuled open brake third	191
285E	Vestibuled brake third	40
285F	Vestibuled brake third	39
285H	Vestibuled brake third	37
285J	Vestibuled brake third	114

The blocks of GNR carriage diagram numbers relevant to the post-1905 period are as follows:

1 - 45 saloons; 46 - 85 catering vehicles; 86 - 285 general service stock including: firsts, 86-88, composites, 102 - 218, thirds, 219 - 285; 286 - 335 passenger brake vans, milk vans and TPO vehicles; 337 - 376 calf vans, hound vans, horseboxes, pedigree cattle vans, carriage trucks and covered carriage trucks; 400 - 423 suburban carriages; 424 - 476 articulated suburban carriages, twin-art and quad-art.

The Diagram numbers are prefixed GN in the list of vehicles given in the appendix.

ECJS and GN/NE Joint Stock

As in the case of the GNR, the description of these Diagrams was similarly unnecessarily complicated as far as their numbering was concerned but the general principles were similar to the system adopted by Doncaster.

A Diagram book was introduced in April 1903 with numbers allocated from 1 upwards, each Diagram being allocated a page in the book. Subsequent designs were allocated Diagram numbers with suffixes. A new book of Diagrams was introduced in 1909 with the result that vehicles known by one Diagram number in the 1903 book usually - but not always - had a new one. In this Appendix the 1909 number is the one used. Numbers ranged between 1 and 82 until 1923.

The Diagram numbers are prefixed EC in the list of vehicles that follows.

After Grouping, new standard LNER designs were allocated (usually) suffixed Diagram numbers in the ECJS 1908 book until *c.* 1930, despite being listed under an LNER allocated Diagram in the LNER Diagram book.

Examples of EC Diagram Nos. allocated to LNER Gresley standard designs were:

Diagram No.	*Type*	*LNER Diagram No.*
79D	Restaurant car first-class	10C
79B/79C	Restaurant car triplets	12,13,14 etc
64C	First-class sleeping car	17
68A/68B	Twin first-class sleeping car	18
62	Third-class sleeping car	95
28B	Restaurant pantry car	112
39J	Passenger brake van	113
3	Vestibuled composite	137
64D	First-class sleeping car	138
61A	Vestibuled first-class	139

Diagram No.	*Type*	*LNER Diagram No.*
61B	Vestibuled first-class	147
30A	Restaurant pantry car	151
61C	Vestibuled first-class	156
64E	First-class sleeping car	157

These Diagrams were included in the ECJS Diagram book as tracings drawn separately to the representations appearing in the LNER Diagram book.

GN/NE Joint stock had its own Diagram book, with diagrams 1 - 18. The Diagram numbers are prefixed JS in the list of vehicles that follows as the appendix.

CLC vehicles

The vehicles built by the GNR for CLC stock were allocated Diagram numbers by the GNR in a series shown in the Doncaster archives as Nos 13 - 20. However, these do not correspond with the list of CLC Diagrams, typified by one prepared by J.B. Dawson which included all CLC vehicles added to stock up until 1937. In the appendix lists that follow, the original 'Doncaster' Diagram number is given in brackets and the later CLC Diagram below.

As to the original CLC carriage running numbers, the sequentially allocated series eventually comprised 1 - 724 (the highest known number) and included such items as passenger vans, horseboxes, carriage trucks and the four CLC Sentinel steam railcars.

Introduction to the list of GNR and ECJS carriages built from 1905 - 23

The tables list the following vehicles: 1. All carriages and vans built for the GNR from 1905 until 1923; 2. All carriages and vans built for the East Coast Joint Stock and GN/NE Joint stock 1905 until 1923. 3. Carriages built in 1923/4 to GNR and ECJS designs.

Notes on format, listing and codes used:

Column No.	*Heading in table*	*Notes*
1	None	V - vestibuled design. No code for non-vestibuled.
2	Type	( ) denotes articulated vehicles as twin, quadruplet, quintuplet. Semi-open denotes a vehicle with seating in an open saloon and side-corridor compartments. Unclass denotes vehicle with seating used for first or third-class passengers. Lavatory composite - non-vestibuled vehicle with lavatories adjoining compartments.
3	Dia. No.	Prefixes GN, EC and JS as described above. * following a diagram number indicates that other vehicles were built to this diagram in some other year.
4	Dimensions	All overall dimensions, over body end panels and width over the panels.
5	Compartments/seats	These are shown as 4 : 32 etc where 4 denotes the number of compartments and 32 the number of seats. † as a suffix denotes seating in open saloons, by number of saloons. Composite vehicles are shown as 2/5 : 14/48 where 2 is the number of first-class compartments, 5 the number of third-class. A coupé compartment is shown as ½.
6	Built at	Doncaster DR, York YK or Cowlairs CW.

7/8	Running Numbers	The number first shown in column 7 is that allocated when new. Subsequent numbering is shown by brackets - (1234). Column 8 Number allocated under the 1925 scheme. Pre-Grouping carriages were not (generally) renumbered by the LNER after 1943.
9	Notes	§ Gas-lit as built. ∑ ECJS vehicles remaining dual-fitted - vacuum and air - after 1912 W/O written off as a result of the accident indicated if the location is known. Trans - vehicle transferred from East Coast to Area or section stock, or between Areas and sections. Abbreviations used: NEA - North Eastern Area; SSA - Southern Scottish Area; GN Sec - Southern Area - Western; GC Sec - Southern Area Western; GE Sec - Southern Area - Eastern; NSA - Northern Scottish Area. C/B - Compound bolster, when referring to bogie types. For transfers, the following description is used - 'Trans to NEA, 1936 as (23456)' indicating the actual date of transfer and the new number assumed on transfer to the Area. The transfers were effected under the LNER Carriage Building Programme for a particular year although the transfer often took some time to be completed.

Carriages of pre-Grouping GNR designs completed in 1924 to the LNER Carriage Building Programme for 1923 are shown under a different columnar heading as under:

Type	*LNER Dia. No.*	*LNER CBP*	*Order No. Year*	*Dimensions*	*Comps /Seats*	*Built At*	*Running numbers Original 1925 and 1943*

LNER Dia. No., as in the LNER Carriage Diagram Book introduced by the CME in 1927; LNER CBP Year, the agreed annual carriage programme; Order No., the official LNER order number.

List of GNR, ECJS and GN/NE Joint vehicles built 1905 -1923

Type	*Dia. No.*	*Dimensions*	*Comps/seats*	*Built At*	*Running numbers* *Original*	*post-1925, with subsequent renumbering in brackets*	*Notes*
1905							
V Open third	GN248H	63'6¼" x 8' 6"	3† 47	DR	1762/3, 2548, 2973-6	41762/3, 42548, 42973-6	§ 11'9" bogies 2975 steel u/f
V Brake open third	GN270	50'10½" x 8'0"	2† 37¶	DR	393, 641, 783, 1796/7	4393, 4641, 4783, 41796/7	§ Delivered 1905 ¶ Altered layout at a later date and then seated 35 seats. Classified GN Dia 271
V Composite	GN101	63'6¼" x 8'6"	2/2½:41	DR	2977	42977	§ 11'9"bogies. Originally 45 seats
Composite steam railcar			3† 53¶	DR	1, 2	¶44151/2	¶ After rebuild Dia. GN 217A as twin-art
V Brake Composite	EC45	65'6" x 8'9¾"	2/3:8/18	YK	EC 80/1, 142/3	180/1 (2321/2) 1142/3 (2327/-)	All Trans to NEA 1936 except No 1143, cond 1937, Six -wheeled bogies All Σ
V Semi-open first	EC57	53'6" x 8'9¾"	4: 24/1† 14¶	YK	EC 92/121	192/1121	Both Trans to GN Section 1931 as (4149) and (4150) ¶ Both converted to full first, 1914 - 36 seats
V Composite sleeping car	EC69	55'0"x 8'9¾"	6 berths, 12 3rds¶	YK	EC 90, 106/87	190, 1106/87	190, 1106 Cond Dec '33 1187 Cond Nov 1931. 187 rebuilt as full first class car, 1921 and then Dia. 64A. ¶ with locker
V First-class dining car	JS1	53'6" x 8'9¾"	3† 26§	YK	GN/NE 1/2	1401/2	Both Trans to GC Section 1925 as 2001/2C, then (52001/2) § Later 25 seats
V Third-class dining car with pantry	JS2	53'6" x 8'9¾"	2† 36¶ /48	YK	GN/NE 5/6	1405/6	Both Trans to GC Section 1925 as 2005/6C, then (52005/6) ¶ When used for dining
V Brake third	JS3	53'6" x 7'11¾"	2:12	YK	GN/NE 3/¶4	1403≠/404J¶	≠ Trans to NEA and converted to van as 288, 1937 ¶ Converted to van 1908, became ECJS 151, 1925, Trans to NEA as 289, 1937

Above Diagrams EC 45/57/69 and JS1-3 all NER straight sided stock, with matchboard panelling.

Type	Dia. No.	Dimensions	Comps/seats	Built At	Running numbers: Original	post-1925, with subsequent renumbering in brackets	Notes
1906							
V First saloon	GN6	58′6″ x 9′0″	see text	DR	1281	41281	EC royal train 1908, 8 ft bogies to 8 ft 6 in. C/B
V First saloon	GN6A	58′6″ x 9′0″	see text	DR	1280	41280	EC royal train 1908, 8ft bogies to 8ft 6 in. C/B
V Brake first	GN96	58′6″ x 8′6″	4: 16	DR	3042-4	43042-4	Sheffield stock, 8ft bogies to 8ft 6 in. C/B
V Semi-open third	GN220	58′6″ x 8′6″	2†, 4:48	DR	2364-7/9/71, 2439-42	42364-7/9/71, 42439-42	8ft bogies to 8ft 6in. C/B
V Brake third	GN256	58′6′ x 8′6″	5: 30	DR	3048-50	43048 - 50	Sheffield stock, 8 ft bogies to 8 ft 6 in. C/B
V Semi-open brake third	GN258	58′6″ x 8′6″	1†, 3 :30	DR	372/85, 1798/9, 2372/3	4372/85, 41798/9, 42372/3	8 ft bogies to 8 ft 6 in. C/B 41799 DEA Sheffield, 12/40
V Open third	GN224*	58′6″ x 8′6″	2† 42¶	DR	3045-7	43045-7	Sheffield stock ¶ later 56 seats
V Composite	GN109	58′6″ x 8′6″	3/2+1† :12/27	DR	250, 362, 955, 1009, 1813, 2393	4250, 4362, 4955, 41009, 41813, 42393	8 ft bogies to 8 ft 6 in. C/B, exc 955 which see text
V Brake composite	GN176	58′6″ x 8′6″	3/3: 12/18	DR	38, 316/69/75/8, 1806-12, 2399	438, 4316/69/75/8, 41806-12, 42399	§ 8 ft bogies to 8 ft 6 in. C/B. (4)38 lost its guard's duckets, date unknown
V First dining car	GN46	65′6″ x 9′0″	2† 20	DR	3033-5	43033-5	Six-wheel bogies, 43034/5 rebuilt as cafeteria cars, 1953
V Third dining car	GN68	65′6″ x 9′0″	2† 42¶	DR	3036-8	43036-8	Six-wheel bogies ¶ 3038 three saloons
V Composite dining car	GN60	65′6″ x 9′0″	1†/1†:8/18	DR	3039-41	43039, 3040/1N	Sheffield stock six-wheel bogies 3040/1 Trans to SSA as (32302/3), 1927, then converted as kitchen cars
V Kitchen car		65′6″ x 9′0″	-		-	22262, 2334/5	New identities as kitchen cars. 43039 Trans to NEA as 22262, 1933 and converted to kitchen car, 1936. 32302/3 became 2334/5. See text.

V Third	EC16	53′6″ x 8′6″	7: 42	YK	EC 27/9	127/9	8 ft bogies to 8 ft 6 in. C/B 1926 Trans to NEA, 1929 as (22339/22142)
V Third	EC17	53′6″ x 8′6″	7: 42	DR	EC 30-3	130-3	8 ft bogies to 8 ft 6 in. C/B 1923/4. 130/1/3 Trans to GC Sect, 1929 as (52031/2/3). 132 Trans to SSA, 1929 as (3626). DEA Stratford, 1943.
V Locker third	EC18	53′6″ x 8′6″	6:36	DR	EC 34-7	134-7	8 ft bogies to 8 ft 6in. C/B 1924-7. 134/5 Trans to GE Sect 1934/3 respectively as (61794/8). 61798 badly damaged Sleaford 1937. 136 Trans to GC Sect as (52052), 1934 and 137 to SSA, 1934 as (31051) All ∑
V Third	EC34*	58′6″ x 8′ 6″	8: 48	YK	EC 24, 69-72, 207	124/69-72, 1207	8ft bogies to 8ft 6in C/B 1924-9. 124/69-72 Trans to SSA, 1933 as (31049/52/4/7/61) 1207 Trans to GE Sec 1934 as (61796) 31061 W/O Castlecary, 1937
V Passenger brake van	EC39	56′6″ x 8′0″	-	DR	EC 126/7/8¶/30-2	#110/1/-/112-4	¶ 128 W/O near Finsbury Park, 1920 132 royal train use ∑. 110 - 3 Trans to GN Sec, 1928 as (4037/9/44/75) 114 Trans to GE Sec, 1928 as (6732) # Renumberings applied 1925/6
V Passenger brake van	EC35*	56′6″ x 8′0″	-	CW	EC 19, 133-7	#13-18	13/5/7 Trans to GN Sec, 1928/9 as (4180, 4021/31), 14/6/8 Trans to SSA, 1928 as (311/3/6) # Renumberings applied 1925/6
V First-class sleeping car	EC64*	56′6″ x 9′0″	10:10	YK	EC 165-70	1165-70	Dual-fitted as built, 165 - 8 ∑; vacuum-only after 1924/5. Cond 1931 except 1169, in 1932
V Third	JS4	53′6″ x 8′6¾″	7: 56¶	YK	GN/NE 7/8	1407/8	1407/8 Trans to GC Sec, 1934 as (52057/56) ¶ Later 42 seats
V First brake	JS5¶	53′6″ x 7′11¾″	4: 16, 6: 24¶	YK	GN/NE 9¶/10(13)	1409¶/13	10 reno 13 1922. ¶ No 9 rebuilt as all-first in 1908 on JS15 then became third, 48 seats when Trans to NEA as (2318) in 1936. No 13 altered as brake third, 1934 and Trans to NEA as (2319), 1938

Type	Dia. No.	Dimensions	Comps/seats	Built At	Running numbers: Original	post-1925, with subsequent renumbering in brackets	Notes
1907							
V Brake third	GN257	58'6" x 8'6"	5: 30	DR	3056-61	43056-61	8 ft bogies to 8ft 6 in., C/B
Lav brake third	GN274*	58'1½" x 8'6"	2†: 42	DR	3082-6	43082-6	
V Composite	GN108	58'6" x 8'6"	3/2 + 1†: 27	DR	1006/21, 3078-81	41006/21, 43078-81	8 ft bogies to 8 ft 6 in. C/B
Lav composite	GN121	58'1½" x 8'6"	3/2 + 1†:15/33	DR	3073-7	43073-7	8 ft bogies to 8 ft 6 in. C/B
Lav brake composite	GN183*	58'1½' x 8'6"	2/1 + 1†: 10/24	DR	1000, 1148, 1274, 1434/8, 2635/42, 2953, 3062	41000, 41148, 41274, 41434/8, 42635/42, 42953, 43062	8 ft bogies to 8 ft 6 in. C/B
V PO sorting van	GN313*	56'6" x 8'0"	-	DR	2407 (4202)	4202 §	Trans to GE Sec as (6133), 1933 See text for alterations
V Third	EC22	58'6" x 8'6"	8: 48	DR	EC 73-5, 96, 375-86	173-5, 196, 1375-86	8 ft bogies to 8 ft 6 in. C/B 1923-7
173/4 Trans to SSA, 1933 as (31081/2); 1379-83 to SSA, 1934/5 as (31084/7-90); 175, 1378/84 Trans to GC Sec, 1929 as (52034/7/8); 1375-7 to GC Sec, 1934 as (52053-5); 1386 to GC Sec, 1935 as (52076); 196 Trans to GE Sec, 1933 as (61795), 1385 Trans to NEA, 1934 as (21433); 31090 W/O Castlecary 1937							
V Third	EC34*	58'6" x 8'6"	8: 48	YK	EC 356-74	1356-74	8 ft bogies to 8 ft 6 in. C/B 1924-9 ∑ 356-63
1356 Trans to NSA, 1935 as (752); 1357 Trans to SSA, 1934 as (31083); 1358-61/3 to SSA, 1935 as (3902/10/8/20/3); 1362 Trans to GE Sec, 1934 as (61797);1364-74 Trans to GC Sec, 1935/6 as (52065-75); 31083 W/O Castlecary 1937							
V First-class sleeping car	EC63*	56'6" x 9'0"	10:10	YK	EC 120	1120	Cond Nov 1937
V Composite sleeping car	EC74	56'6" x 9'0"	6 berths, 2 3rd compts:12	YK	EC 231	1231	Cond Dec 1932
V First	JS6	58'6" x 8'6"	7:28	YK	GN/NE 29/30	1429/30	8ft bogies to 8 ft 6 in.; C/B 1925, 1929 C/B 1925, 1929; 1429/30 Trans to NSA, 1936 as thirds (784/6)
V Third	JS7	58'6" x 8'6"	8: 48	YK	GN/NE 16-20	1416-20	1420 - 8 ft bogies to 8 ft 6 in. C/B 1926
		1416-8 Trans to GC Sec 1933/4 as (52058-60), 1419/20 Trans to NEA, 1934 as (21431/4)					
V Brake third	JS8	58'6" x 8'6¾"	2:12	DR	GN/NE 15	1415	8 ft bogies to 8 ft 6 in.; C/B 1927; Trans to GC Sec. 1935 as (52086)

V Open third	JS9	58′6″ x 9′0″	3† 45	DR	GN/NE 21-3	1421-3	8ft bogies to 8 ft 6 in.; C/B 1923/4 Converted to buffet cars and 1421 Trans to GE Sec, 1933 as (61799), later to GN as (43137); 1422/3 Trans to GN Sec as (43133/4). In this form, 43133/4/7 on GN Dia 78V
V Third-class dining car	JS10	65′6″ x 9′0″	1† 24	DR	GN/NE 26/7	1426/7	(1436/7 from July 1944) Six-wheeled bogies
V Open first	JS11	58′6″ x 9′0″	2† 26	DR	GN/NE 31-3	1431-3	Trans to NSA, 1940 as open thirds (7122-4)
V Brake first¶	JS12	58′6″ x 8′6¾″	5: 20¶	DR	GN/NE 34	1434	¶ Conv to full first, 7: 28 seats 1911; Trans to NSA, 1937 as third-class(788)
V Passenger brake van	JS13	56′6″ x 8′0″	-	DR	GN/NE 35 (435J)	150	Trans to GN Sec, 1928, as (4019)
1908							
V HM King's saloon	EC81¶	67′0″ x 9′0″	See text	DR	395	∑ 395J, then 395 ¶ Dia. 81A as rebuilt by the LNER	
V HM Queen's saloon	EC82	67′0″ x 9′ 0″	See text	YK	396	∑ 396J, then 396	
V First saloon	GN4	58′6″ x 9′0″	See text	DR	3099	43099	Royal train; 8 ft bogies to 8 ft 6 in.; C/B
V First saloon	GN5	58′6″ x 9′0″	See text	DR	3100	43100	Royal train; 8 ft bogies to 8 ft 6 in.; C/B
V First saloon	GN9	50′0″ x 9′0″	14/6	DR	3101/2		§ Cond 1939; 8ft bogies to 8 ft 6 in.; C/B
V Semi-open third	GN219	58′6″ x 8′6″	2†/4 :48	DR	51, 1093, 2410, 2700, 3108-13	451, 41093, 42410 42700, 43108-13	8 ft bogies to 8 ft 6 in.; C/B
Third saloon	GN21*	58′1½″ x 8′6″	4: 56	DR	7, 1377, 3118	47, 41377, 43118	8 ft bogies to 8 ft 6 in.; C/B
Lav composite	GN122	58′1½″ x 9′0″	2/3 + 1† :14/44	DR	3105	43105	8 ft bogies to 8 ft 6 in.; C/B
V Brake composite	GN175*	58′6″ x 8′6″	2/4: 8/24	DR	3114/5	43114/5	8 ft bogies to 8 ft 6 in.; C/B
Lav brake composite	GN183*	58′1½″ x 8′6″	2/1 +1† :10/24	DR	3063-72	43063-72	8 ft bogies to 8 ft 6 in.; C/B
Lav brake composite	GN184	58′1½″ x 8′6″	2/1 + 1† :14/26	DR	3103/4	43103/4	8 ft bogies to 8 ft 6 in.; C/B
V Passenger brake van	GN287*	56′6″ x 8′0″	-	DR	961/80, 1013, 1968, 3116/7	421-26	1968 had its duckets removed

Type	Dia. No.	Dimensions	Comps/seats	Built At	Running numbers Original	post-1925, with subsequent renumbering in brackets	Notes
V Passenger brake van	EC35*	56′6″ x 8′0″	-	DR	82	∑ 82J (109)	Royal train
V First	EC58	58′6″ x 8′6″	7:42	DR	EC 122/295	1122/1295	8 ft bogies to 8 ft 6 in.; C/B 1924/5. 1122 Trans to GN Sec, 1935 as (4194), 1295 Trans to NSA, 1936 as third (785)
V Brake third	EC49 EC49A¶	58′6″ x 8′6″	6: 36 3: 18¶	DR	EC 97/8	197/8	∑ until 1914 ¶ (1)97 so converted 1914 and had attendant's compt I/L lav for 'Flying Scotsman' from 1914-28; 197/8 Trans to GC Sec, 1935 as (52092/61)
V Open third	JS9*	58′6″ x 9′0″	3† 45	DR	GN/NE 24/5	1424/5	8 ft bogies to 8 ft 6 in.; C/B 1923/4. Converted to buffet cars and Trans to GN Sec as (43135/6) on GN Dia. 78T
V Third-class dining car	JS10	65′6″ x 9′0″	1† 24	DR	GN/NE 28	1428	(1438 from July 1944) Six-wheeled bogies
V First-class sleeping car	JS16	58′6″ x 9′0″	11: 11	YK	GN/NE 13¶/4	1410/4	¶ Became No 10 1922. 8 ft bogies to 8 ft 6 in.; C/B 1924. Cond Jan 1935, Feb 1936
1909							
V Third	GN228	52′6″ x 8′6″	7:42	DR	3123-7	43123-7	8 ft bogies to 8 ft 6 in.; C/B
V Brake open third	GN264	52′6″ x 8′6″	2† 30	DR	138, 1492, 1955, 2631	4138, 41492, 41955, 42631	8ft bogies to 8 ft 6 in., C/B
V Open third	GN229	52′6″ x 8′6″	3† 42	DR	3128-32	43128-32	8 ft bogies to 8 ft 6 in.; C/B. 43130/1 converted to buffet cars 1932-6
Third saloon	GN21*	58′1½″ x 8′6″	4: 56	DR	3143-5	43143-5	
V Open composite	GN114	52′6′ x 8′6″	2/2† :8/27	DR	3146-9	43146-9	8 ft bogies to 8 ft 6 in.; C/B
V Invalid saloon	GN10A	50′0″ x 9′0″	13	DR	3087	43087	8 ft bogies to 8 ft 6 in.; C/B
V Brake composite	GN171	61′6′ x 9′0″	3/3 :18/24	DR	4, 2637/90, 3150	44, 42637/90, 43150	10 ft bogies
V Brake composite	GN175*	58′6″ x 8′6″	2/4 : 8/24	DR	3119-22	43119-22	8 ft bogies to 8 ft 6 in.; C/B

Passenger brake van	GN293*	51′1½ x 8′3″	-	DR	3155-8	445-448	
Milk brake	GN326	51′1½″ x 8′3″	-	DR	3159-61	4155-7	
(V) PO sorting van	GN313*	56′6″ x 8′0″	-	DR	1858 (4203)	4203	§ See text for alterations. Trans to GE Sec, 1933 as (6134)
V Brake third	EC49 EC49A¶	58′6″ x 8′6″	6: 36 3: 18¶	DR	EC 387-94	1387-94	∑ ¶ (1)388 so converted 1914 and had attendant's compt I/L lav for 'Flying Scotsman' from 1914-28. 1387/9-91 Trans to GC Sec, 1935 as 52087-90; 1388 Trans to GE Sec, 1934 as 62650, 1392/3 to GE Sec, 1935 as 62666/7; 1394 Trans to SSA, 1935 as (3937)
V First-class sleeping car	JS17	58′6″ x 9′0″	11:11	DR	GN/NE 11/2	1411/2	1412 - 8 ft bogies to 8 ft 6 in.; C/B Cond Feb 1936, Jan 1937
1910							
V Brake first	GN97	61′6″ x 9′0″	5: 20	DR	3177/8	43177/8	10 ft bogies
V Third	GN248*	58′6″ x 8′6″	8:48	DR	3179-84	43179-84	8 ft bogies to 8 ft 6 in.; C/B
V Open third	GN224*	58′6″ x 8′6″	2† 42¶	DR	3223	43223	Sheffield stock. ¶ Later 56 seats
V Semi-open brake third	GN284	61′6″ x 8′6″	3/1† :36	DR	3208-13	43208-13	Some 10ft bogies. (4)3209 later had its duckets removed
Brake third	GN274	58′1½″ x 8′6″	2†:42	DR	3219-22	43219-22	
V Semi-open composite	GN164	58′6″ x 8′6″	3 1st, 1†, 2 3rd 12/27	DR	3174-6	43174-6	
V Brake composite	GN216	58′6″ x 8′6″	3/3 :12/18	DR	3204-7	43204 - 7	
Lav composite	GN164A	58′1½″ x 8′6″	3/4 :15/33	DR	3214/5	43214/5	
Lav composite	GN164B	58′1½″ x 9′0″	2/5 :14/44	DR	3218	43218	
Lav brake composite	GN217	58′1½″ x 9′0″	2/1+1 :14/26	DR	3216/7	43216/7	8 ft bogies to 8ft 6 in.; C/B
V Passenger brake van	GN286	56′6″ x 8′0″	-	DR	957, 1016, 3224-6	Renumbered 4xx series, 1016 became 412;	Heavy-type bogies later fitted

Type	Dia. No.	Dimensions	Comps/seats	Built At	Running numbers Original	post-1925, with subsequent renumbering in brackets	Notes
Passenger brake van	GN293*	51′1½″ x 8′3″	-	DR	3168-73	449-54	
V Sleeping composite (First-class sleeping car¶)	EC70A EC63A¶	56′6″ x 9′0″	10:10 6/2: 6/12	YK	146/8/50/1	1146/8/50/1	∑. 1146/8/51 Cond Jan 1935, ¶ As rebuilt as full first-class cars 1150 Cond Feb 1936
V Passenger brake van	EC34A	56′6″ x 8′0″	-	YK	EC 5-7¶	15, 16	¶ 7 - W/O Burntisland,1914. Renumbered (11/12), 1926. Trans to GE Sect, 1928 as (6726/7)
V Passenger brake van	EC39A	56′6″ x 8′0″	-	DR	EC 8-10/26, 129	18, 19, 110/26, 1129	Renumbered (115/¶/7-9), 1926; No 19 Trans to GE Sec, 1928 as (6736); 115/7/8 Trans to GE Sec, 1928/9 as (6733 - 5); 119 Trans to GN Sec, 1929 as (4176); 4176 W/O Westborough 1941 6735 DEA Stratford 1943 ¶ not apparently renumbered.
1911							
V Third	GN248C	52′6″ x 8′6″	7: 42	DR	2443-5/70	42443-5/70	8 ft bogies to C/B 8 ft 6 in.
V Open third	GN248A*	58′6″ x 9′0″	3† 45	DR	1577, 1651, 1709/10	41577/651/709/10	41577/651 converted to buffet cars 1935
V Semi-open third	GN248B	58′6 x 8′6″	2†,4: 48	DR	928, 1292	4928, 41292	§ 8 ft bogies to C/B 8 ft 6 in.
V Semi-open brake third	GN285	61′6″ x 8′6″	1†, 3: 36	DR	411, 689, 1419, 1652	4411, 4689, 41419, 41652	§ 10 ft bogies
V Composite	GN164F	58′6″ x 8′6″	3½ /5: 10/30	DR	3191/2	43191/2	
V Brake composite	GN218A	61′6″ x 8′6″	2½/3½: 12/24	DR	2689, 2702/8/12	42689, 42702/8/12	§ 2702/12
(Second) (Brake second)	GN425	38′1¼″ x 9′0″ 38′1¼″ x 9′0″	7: 84) 5: 60)	DR	3238/9 (4001/2) (?4011/2)	§ London suburban articulated twin. Later reb as quad	
(Third) (Third)	GN440*	43′6″ x 9′0″ 43′6″ x 9′0″	8: 96) 8: 96)	DR	3232/3 (4201/2) (?4211/2)	§ London suburban articulated twin. Later reb as quad	
(Brake third) (Third)	GN452	38′1¼″ x 5′0″ 38′1¼″ x 5′0″	5: 60) 7: 84)	DR	3236/7 (4301/2) (?4311/2)	§ London suburban articulated twin. Later reb as quad	

Type	Dia. No.	Dimensions	Comps/seats	Built At	Original	post-1925	Notes
(Composite¶)	GN468*	43′6″ x 9′0″	3/4: 36/40)	DR	3234/5 (?4101/2) (?4111/2)		§ London suburban articulated twin. Later reb as quad ¶ Third/first, ≠ First/second
(Composite≠)		43′6″ x 9′0″	4/3: 40/36)				
V Passenger brake van	GN286*	56′6″ x 8′0″	--	DR	3227-31	Renumbered 4xx series, 3230 became 417; 3231, 418	Heavy-type bogies later fitted
Passenger brake van	GN307*	51′1½″ x 8′3″	-	DR	1850/3, 2697, 2707	457-60	
V Composite¶	EC2B/2A	58′6″ x 8′6¾″	2½/5: 10/30	DR	EC 1-4	11-14	8 ft bogies to C/B 8 ft 6 in. 1924 ¶ 11 Trans to NEA, 1937 as (2315); 12-14 Trans to SSA, 1936/7 as (31152/3/5) All Trans as eight-compartment thirds
V Brake composite	EC47B	61′6″ x 8′ 3″	2/2: 8/12	DR	EC347		W/O Retford 1923

Type	*Dia No*	*Dimensions*	*Comps/seats*	*Built At*	*Running numbers* *Original*	*Numbers in former LMS coaching stock series allocated from 1950*
Third	(CL13) CLC16	51′1½″ x 8′6″	8: 80	DR	CLC 324-30/47	(M) 14943-8/-/57 (M) 14949 allocated but not applied
Brake third	(CL14) CLC29	51′1½″ x 8′6″	5: 50	DR	CLC 338-45	(M) 22524-30/- 22531 allocated but not applied
Lav composite	(CL15) CLC59	51′1½″ x 8′6″	3/3 : 15/29	DR	CLC 310-3	(M) 19940-3 (M)
Lav composite	(CL16) CLC58	51′1½″ x 8′6″	3/4 :18/39	DR	CLC 314-7	(M) 19944-7 (M)

Type	*Dia. No.*	*Dimensions*	*Comps/seats*	*Built At*	*Running numbers* *Original*	*post-1925, with subsequent renumbering in brackets*	*Notes*
1912							
V First saloon	GN45C	52′6″ x 9′0″	16 + 6	DR	6	46	Originally dual-fitted
V First saloon	GN45D¶	52′6″ x 9′0″	14 + 6	DR	397, 807	4397, 4807	4397 with cocktail bar 1934. Both originally dual-fitted. ¶ No. 397 later Dia. 45K
V First	GN86	61′6″ x 8′6″	7: 28	DR	15/16	415/6	§ 10 ft bogies
V Third	GN248D*	52′6″ x 8′6″	7: 42	DR	1596, 1641, 1708, 2091, 2325, 2733	41596, 41641, 41708 42091, 42325, 42733	§ 8 ft bogies to C/B 8 ft 6 in in 1920/1

Type	*Dia. No.*	*Dimensions*	*Comps/seats*	*Built At*	*Running numbers* *Original*	*post-1925, with subsequent renumbering in brackets*	*Notes*
V Open third	GN248A*	58′6″ x 9′0″	3† 45	DR	2746/8/9, 2950-2	42746/8/9, 42950-2	§
V Open brake third	GN285A	52′6″ x 8′6″	2† 30	DR	1606/37	41606/37	§
V Brake composite	GN218F	61′6″ x 8′6″	3/3 ;12/24†	DR	32, 115, 229/52, 309, 1539/41/55	432, 4115, 4229/52, 4309, 41539/41/55	† Originally 18 seats
Lav brake composite	GN218E	58′1½″ x 8′6″	2/1 + 1 :10/24	DR	44/46	444/6	§ 10 ft bogies
((Second) (Brake second)	GN424*	38′1¼″ x 9′0″ 38′1¼″ x 9′0″	7: 84) 5: 60)	DR	3258/9 (?4021/2) (4031/2)		§ London suburban articulated twin. Later reb as quad
(Third) (Third)	GN440*	43′6″ x 9′0″ 43′6″ x 9′0″	8; 96) 8: 96)	DR	3252/3 (?4221/2) (4231/2)		§ London suburban articulated twin. Later reb as quad
(Brake third) (Third)	GN451*	38′1¼″ x 9′0″ 38′1¼″ x 9′0″	5:60) 7: 84)	DR	3256/7 (?4321/2) (4331/2)		§ London suburban articulated twin. Later rebuilt as quad
(Composite¶) (Composite≠)	GN468*	43′6″ x 9′0″ 43′6″ x 9′0″	3/4: 36/40 4/3: 40/36	DR	3254/5 (?4121/2) (4131/2)		§ London suburban articulated twin. Later reb as quad
V First dining car	GN75	52′6″ x 9′0″	1† 18	DR	3251	43251	8 ft bogies to C/B 8 ft 6 in. Rebuilt as a cafeteria car, 1953
V First dining car	GN76	52′6″ x 9′0″	1† 19	DR	3250	43250	8 ft bogies to C/B 8 ft 6 in., 1924. Rebuilt as a cafeteria car, 1953
Passenger brake van	GN307*	51′1½″ x 8′3″	-	DR	1008, 1566	455/6	
V Passenger brake van	GN308*	56′6″ x 8′0″	-	DR	1739/42	431/2	Heavy-type bogies later fitted
Milk brake	GN325A*	51′1½″ x 8′3″	-	DR	3013/4	4151/2	
V Passenger brake van	JS18*	56′6″ x 8′0″	-	DR	GN/NE 36	152	Trans to GN Sec, 1929 as (4191)

Type	*Dia. No.*	*Dimensions*	*Comps/seats*	*Built At*	*Running numbers* *Original*	*Numbers in former LMS coaching stock series allocated from 1950*
Saloon	(CL17) CLC1	51′1½″ x 8′6″	14 + 6	DR	CLC 201	(M) 997 (M)
Brake third	(CL18) CLC 29	51′1½″ x 8′6″	5: 50	DR	CLC 346/8/9	(M) 22532-4 (M)
Third	(CL19) CLC 16	51′1½″ x 8′6″	8: 80	DR	CLC 331-7	(M) 14950-6 (M)
Composite	(CL20) CLC 48	51′1½″ x 8′6″	4/3: 24/30	DR	CLC 318-23	(M)16860-5 (M)

Type	*Dia No*	*Dimensions*	*Comps/seats*	*Built At*	*Running numbers* *Original*	*post-1925, with subsequent renumbering in brackets*	*Notes*
1913							
V Brake first	GN 98*	61′6″ x 8′6″	5: 20	DR	1	41	10 ft bogies
V Third	GN248D*	52′6″ x 8′6″	7: 42	DR	343, 555, 745, 834	4343, 4555, 4745, 4834	§ 8ft bogies to C/B 8 ft 6 in. 1920/1
V Open third	GN248E*	58′6″ x 9′0″	3†: 45	DR	1442/88, 1552	41442/88, 41552	§ 41442/88 to GC Section, then converted to buffet cars 52062/3 in 1933, GN Dia. 78T. 41552 converted to buffet car 1933, GN Dia. 78T
V Brake composite	GN218G*	61′6″ x 8′6″	3/3:12/18	DR	45, 90, 293	445, 490, 4293	§
(Second) (Brake second)	GN424*	38′1¼″ x 9′0″ 38′1¼″ x 9′0″	7: 84) 5: 60)	DR	3266/7, 3268/9, 3270/1, 3354 (spare) (4041/2, ?4051/2, ?4061/2, 4071/2, ?4081/2, 4091/2, 3354)		§ London suburban articulated twin. Later reb as quad
(Third) (Third)	GN440*	43′6″ x 9′0″ 43′6″ x 9′0″	8: 96) 8: 96)	DR	3272/3, 3274/5, 3276/7, 3356 (spare) (4241/2, ?4251/2, ?4261/2, ?4271/2, ?4281/2, 4291/2, 3356)		§ London suburban articulated twin. Later reb as quad
(Brake third) (Third)	GN451*	38′1¼″ x 9′0″ 38′1¼″ x 9′0″	5: 60) 7: 84)	DR	3278/9, 3280/1, 3282/3, 3357 (spare) (4341/2, ?4351/2, ?4361/2, 4371/2, ?4381/2, ?4391/2, 3357)		§ London suburban articulated twin. Later reb as quad

Type	*Dia. No.*	*Dimensions*	*Comps/seats*	*Built At*	*Running numbers* *Original*	*post-1925, with subsequent renumbering in brackets*	*Notes*
(Composite¶)	GN468*	43′6″ x 9′ 0″	3/4: 36/40)	DR	3260/1, 3262/3, 3264/5, 3355 (spare) (4141/2, ?4151/2, ?4161/2, ?4171/2, ?4181/2, ?4191/2, 3355)		§ London suburban articulated twin. ¶ Third/first, ≠ First/ second
(Composite≠)		43′ 6″ X 9′ 0″	4/3: 40/36)				Later reb as quad
V Passenger brake van	GN308*	56′6″ X 8′ 0″	-	DR	978, 1282/94	433-5	Heavy-type bogies later fitted
V TPO sorting van	GN312	56′6″ x 8′0″	-	DR	1969	4201	§
Milk brake	GN325A*	51′1½″ x 8′3″	-	DR	3009, 3188	4153/4	
1914							
V Third	GN248*	58′6″ x 8′6″	8: 48	DR	409, 728	4409, 4728	
V Brake third	GN285B	58′6″ x 8′6″	5: 30¶	DR	704	4704	¶ Later 40 seats. 8 ft bogies to C/B 8 ft 6 in.
V Open third	GN248E*	58′6′ x 9′0″	3†: 45	DR	56, 256/68	456, 4256/68	
V Brake Composite	GN218G*	61′6″ x 8′6″	3/3 :12/18	DR	748, 1601	4748, 41601	§ 748. 10 ft bogies
V First dining car	GN 78C¶	52′6″ x 9′0″	1† 18¶	DR	1697, 1707	41697, 41707	¶ Originally on Dia. 78C when there were 12 seats. Altered to 18 seats. Both converted to cafeteria cars, 1953.
Passenger brake van	GN307*	51′1½″ x 8′3″	-	DR	379, 542, 708/37, 1208, 1283	461-6	
V Passenger brake van	GN308*	56′6″ x 8′0″	-	DR	697, 832, 941, 1096, 1755/800	436-41	Heavy-type bogies later fitted 440 badly damaged Doncaster 1934
V Locker composite	EC2B	61′6″ x 8′6¾″	2½, 4: 10/24¶	DR	EC 76/7	176/7	1914 'Flying Scotsman' 10 ft bogies. 176, 177 Trans to SSA and GN Sec respectively, 1935/6 as seven-compt¶ thirds (3367, 42515) with the locker converted as compt
V Composite	EC3A	58′6″ x 9′0″	4½, 2½ :10/27¶	YK	EC 78/9	178/9	1914 'Flying Scotsman'. 8ft bogies changed to C/B 8 ft 6 in. 1925 178, 179 Trans to NSA, 1936 as seven-compt¶ thirds (7819/20)

V First dining car	EC75A	58′6″ x 9′0″	2† 28	DR	EC 190/1	1190/1	1914 'Flying Scotsman' 1190 Trans to GC as open first (52103), 1936. 1191 became open first, 1943
V Third dining car	EC29A	58′6″ x 9′0″	2† 48	DR	EC 192/3	1192/3	1914 'Flying Scotsman'. 1192/3 Trans to SSA, 1935 as open thirds (3925/7)
V Kitchen car	EC80A	53′6″ x 9′0″	-	YK	EC 211-3	1211-3	1914 'Flying Scotsrnan' 1212/3 Trans to GN Sec 1929, as (42182/3). 1211 Trans to GC Sec 1930, as (52039)
V Passenger brake van	EC39B*	56′6″ x 8′0″	-	DR	EC 152-7	1152-7	# 122-7. 123/4 Trans to GC Sec, 1935 as (5251/2). 122/5/6 to GC Sec, 1936 as (5250/3/4) and 127 in 1937 as (5261)
				YK	EC 44, 158/60 161/4/75	144, 1158/60, 1161/4/75	#121/8-32 121 Trans to SSA in 1936 as (310). 132 Trans to GC Sec in 1936 as (5266). 128-31 to GC Sec, 1937 as (5262-5). # Renumbered 1925-7
1915							
V Third	GN248D*	52′6″ x 8′6″	7 :42	DR	71, 132, 283	471, 4132, 4283	
V Brake composite	GN2188BB*	61′6″ x 8′6″	2½, 3½: 10/21	DR	223/58, 367	4223/58, 4367	
V (Brake open third) V (Composite)	GN218CC	49′3″ x 8′6″ 49′3″ x 8′6″	2† 30 2½/3 :10/18	DR DR	4861/71/81/91 4862/72/82/92	44861/71/81/91 44862/72/82/92	Articulated twins
V Passenger brake van	GN308*	56′6″ x 8′0″	-	DR	950, 1004/5	442-4	Heavy-type bogies later fitted
1916							
V Passenger brake van	EC39B*	56′6″ x 8′0″	-	YK	EC 7	17	Renumbered (120), 1925 Trans to GE Sec, 1928 as (6728)
1917							
V (Brake first) V (First)	GN218J¶	49′3″ x 8′6″ 49′3″ x 8′6″	2: 8 6: 23	DR DR	4921, 4931 4922, 4932	44921, 44931 44922, 44932	Articulated twins 8 ft bogies to 8 ft 6 in. C/B. ¶ Also shown as GN9
1918	No vehicles added to stock						
1919							
V (Brake open pantry third) V (Composite)	GN218DD	49′3″ x 8′6″ 49′3″ x 8′6″	2: 16 2½/3 : 10/30	DR DR	4901, 4911 4902, 4912 Lettered 'Restaurant Car' Feb 1924-August 1925	44901, 44911 44902, 44912	Articulated twins. Heavy-type 8′6″ bogies later fitted

Type	*Dia. No.*	*Dimensions*	*Comps/seats*	*Built At*	*Running numbers* *Original*	*post-1925, with subsequent renumbering in brackets*	*Notes*
1920							
V Third	GN248D*	52'6" x 8'6"	7: 42	DR	553, 743/61, 1583, 2450	4553, 4743/61, 41583, 42450	
V Brake composite	GN218BB*	61'6" x 8'6"	2½, 3½: 10/21	DR	278, 1369, 1614, 2093, 2307†/12†	4278, 41369, 41614, 42093, 42307/12	† 10 ft bogies, rest 8 ft bogies to 8 ft 6 in. C/B
Passenger brake	GN309	51'1½" x 8'3"	-	DR	952/4, 1514, 2763	467-70	
V Brake third	EC49A	58'6" x 9'0"	3: 18	DR	EC 41	141	Attendant's compt I/L lavatory W/O Welwyn June 1935
1921							
V First	GN87	61'6" x 8'6"	7: 42	DR	290/2/5	4290/2/5	
V Third	GN248D*	52'6" x 8'6"	7: 42	DR	2727/32	42727/32	
V(Brake first)	GN78F	55'2¼" x 9'6"	3: 18	DR	9011	49011	Leeds quintuplet set
V (First diner)		45'11" x 9'6"	2† 30¶		9012	49012	¶ Originally a single saloon
V (Kitchen car)		37'6" x 9'6"	-		9013	49013	
V (Third diner)		45'11" x 9'6"	2† 48¶		9014	49014	¶ Originally a single saloon
V (Brake third)		55'2¼" x 9' 6"	4: 32		9015	49015	
Brake third	GN467	38'1¼" x 8' 6"	5: 60	CR	8451/81, 8551/81, 8601	48451/81, 48551/81, 48601 etc	
Third		38'1¼" x 8' 6"	7: 84	CR	8452/82, 8552/82, 8602		
Third		43'6" x 8'6"	8: 96	CR	8453/83, 8553/83, 8603		
Third		43'6" x 8' 6"	8: 96	CR	8454/84, 8554/84, 8604		
Above are London suburban quadruplets, gas-lit and utilising suburban twins from 1911-3							
Brake third	GN467	38'1¼" x 8'6"	5: 60	CR	8621/41/61/81, 8701	48621/41/61/81, 48701 etc	
Third		38'1¼" x 8' 6"	7: 84	CR	8622/42/62/82, 8702		
Third		43'6" x 8'6"	8: 96	CR	8623/43/63/83, 8703		
Third		43'6" x 8'6"	8: 96	CR	8624/44/64/84, 8704		
Above are London suburban quadruplets, gas-lit and all new construction							
Brake third	GN467A	38'1¼" x 8' 6"	5: 60	CR	8461/71, 8561/71/91	48461/71, 48561/71/91 etc	
Third		38'1¼" x 8' 6"	7: 84	CR	8462/72, 8562/72/92		
Third		43'6" x 8'6"	8: 96	CR	8463/73, 8563/73/93		
Third		43'6" x 8'6"	8: 96	CR	8464/74, 8564/74/94		
Above are London suburban quadruplets, gas-lit and utilising suburban twins from 1911-3							

Brake third	GN467A	38'1¼" x 8'6"	5:60	CR	8611/31/51/71	48611/31/51/71 etc	
Third		38'1¼" x 8' 6"	7: 84	CR	8612/32/52/72		
Third		43'6" x 8'6"	8: 96	CR	8613/33/53/73		
Third		43'6" x 8'6"	8: 96	CR	8614/34/54/74		
Above are London suburban quadruplets, gas-lit and all new construction							
Composite (1st/3rd)	GN475	43'6" x 8'6"	3 3rd/4 1st 36/40	CR	8414/44/94, 8524/44	48414/44/94, 48524/44 etc	
Composite (1st/3rd)		43'6" x 8'6"	4 1st/3 3rd 40/36	CR	8413/43/93, 8523/43		
Second		38'1¼" x 8'6"	7: 84	CR	8412/42/92, 8522/42		
Brake second		38'1¼" x 8'6"	5: 60	CR	8411/41/91, 8521/41		
Above are London suburban quadruplets, gas-lit and utilising suburban twins from 1911-3							
Composite (1st/3rd)	GN475	43'6" x 8'6"	3 3rd/4 1st 36/40	CR	8724/44/64/84, 8804	48724/44/64/84, 48804 etc	
Composite (1st/3rd)		43'6" x 8' 6"	41st/ 3 3rd 40/36	CR	8723/43/63/83, 8803		
Second		38'1¼" x 8'6"	7: 84	CR	8722/42/62/82, 8802		
Brake second		38'1¼" x 8'6"	5: 60	CR	8721/41/61/81, 8801		
Above are London suburban quadruplets, gas-lit and all new construction							
Composite (1st/3rd)	GN476	43'6" x 8'6"	3 3rd/4 1st 36/40	CR	8424/34, 8504/14/34	48424/34, 48504/14/34 etc	
Composite (1st/3rd		43'6" x 8'6"	4 1st/3 3rd 40/36	CR	8423/33, 8503/13/33		
Second		38'1¼" x 8'6"	7: 84	CR	8422/32, 8502/12/32		
Brake second		38'1¼" X 8'6"	5: 60	CR	8421/31, 8501/11/31		
Above are London suburban quadruplets, gas-lit and utilising suburban twins from 1911-3							
Composite (1st/3rd)	GN476	43'6" x 8'6"	3 3rd/4 1st 36/40	CR	8714/34/54/74/94	48714/34/54/74/94 etc	
Composite (1st/3rd)		43'6" x 8'6"	4 1 st/3 3rd 40/36	CR	8713/33/53/73/93		
Second		38'1¼" x 8'6"	7: 84	CR	8712/32/52/72/92		
Brake second		38'1¼" x 8'6"	5: 60	CR	8711/31/51/71/91		
Above are London suburban quadruplets, gas-lit and all new construction							
Milk brake	GN310*	51'1½" x 8'3"	-	DR	963/8, 1030/4/60/70, 1074, 1732, 2391, 2508	41-9, 400	dual-fitted as built
V Third	EC31A	58'6" x 9'0"	8:48	YK	EC 163/71/7/8/80, 206	1163/71/7/8/80, 1206	8 ft bogies to 8 ft 6 in. C/B 1924/5. All Trans to GC Sec: 1163/71/8, 1206 in 1935 as 52077/8/80/2, 1177/80 in 1936 as 52079/81
V Passenger brake van	EC39C*	56'6" x 8'0"	-	YK	EC 214/8/9/60	1214/8/9/60	Renumbered 136-9, 1926. 136 Trans to GN Sec, 1931 as(4018). 137 Trans to GC Sec, 1931 as (5215). 138 to GC Sec, 1938 as (5268), 139 to GC Sec as (5269)

Type	*Dia. No.*	*Dimensions*	*Comps/seats*	*Built At*	*Running numbers*		*Notes*
					Original	*post-1925, with subsequent renumbering in brackets*	
1922							
V Brake first	GN98*	61'6" x 8'6"	5: 20	DR	148/88	4148/88	
V Composite	GN164K	61'6" x 9'0"	3½, 4: 21/32	DR	47/69, 308, 2701/4/5/9-11, 2997	447/69, 4308, 42701 42704/5/9-11, 42997	2705 ran with PLM bogies, 1922/3
Milk brake	GN310*	51'1½" X 8'3"	-	DR	1296, 1301/76, 1405 1537/58, 1931/50, 2309/18	401-10	
V First	EC59	61'6" x 8'9"	7: 42	DR	49/60/87, 123/96, 353	149/60/87, 1123/96, 1353	149 8 ft bogies 1930. 149 Trans to GC Sec, 1933 as 52049; 160 to GC Sec, 1934 as 52050. 187 Trans to SSA, 1935 as 31936. 1123 Trans to GN Sec, 1937 as 4145. 1196 Trans to GC Sec, 1937 as 52102. 1353 Trans to SSA, 1937 as 31925
V (First sleeper) (First sleeper)	EC68*	56'2½" x 9'0" 56'2½" x 9'0"	10: 10 10: 10	DR	181/181A	(1181/2)	Twin articulated sleeping car
V Passenger brake van	EC39C*	56'6" x 8'0"	-	DR	EC 128/44/5	1128/44/5	Renumbered 133-5, 1926. 133 Trans to GC Sec, 1937 as 5267. 134 remained in EC stock. For 135, see below
V Passenger brake van	EC39E	56'6" x 8'0"	-	DR		EC 135	To royal train - remained as 135

Carriages of pre-Grouping GNR and ECJS designs completed in 1923 to the LNER Carriage Building Programme for 1923 and to GNR and ECJS programmes.

Type	Dia. No.	CBP Year	Dimensions	Seats	Built At	Running numbers Original	1925	Braking	Notes
V First sleeping car	EC64B	1923	61′6″ x 9′0″	10: 10	YK	159J/62J, 172-4/6J	1159/62/72-4/6	V	
V (First sleeper)	EC68*	1923	56′2½″ x 9′0″	10: 10	DR	198J/200J	1198/1200	V	Twin articulated
(First sleeper)			56′2½″ x 9′0″	10: 10		199J/201J	1199/1201	V	sleeping cars
(Brake third)	GN218QQ	1922	55′6¼″ x 8′6″	5: 50	DR	4001/11/21/31	44001/11 etc	V	Twin articulated
(Composite)			55′6¼″ x 8′6″	3/4 :22/38	DR	4002/12/22/32	44002/12 etc	V	Twin articulated. 44011/2 + 44002 damaged at Shepreth 1928
(Brake third)	GN218RR	1922	55′6¼″ x 8′6″	5: 50	DR	4041/51/61/71/81/91	44041/51 etc	V	Twin articulated
(Composite)			55′6¼″ x 8′6″	2/5: 14/48	DR	4042/52/62/72/82/92	44042/52 etc	V	Twin articulated
Brake third	GN467A/	1922	38′1¼″ x 8′6″	5: 60	DR	8691 8121¶	48691-4	V	
Third	GN467B¶		38′1¼″ x 8′6″	7: 84	DR	8692 8122¶	48121-4		
Third			43′6″ x 8′6″	8: 96	DR	8693 8123¶			
Third			43′6″ x 8′6″	8: 96	DR	8694 8124¶			

Above are London suburban quadruplets Dia 467A GN type vehicles, Dia 467B LNER type vehicles

Type	Dia. No.	CBP Year	Dimensions	Seats	Built At	Running numbers Original	1925	Braking	*Numbers after 1943*
Composite (1st/3rd)	GN478	1922	43′6″ x 9′0″	3 3rd/4 1st	DR	8144/54	48144/54	V	86247/51
Composite (1st/3rd)			43′6″ x 9′0″	4 1st/3 3rd :40/36	DR	8143/53	48143/53		86246/50
Second			38′1¼′ x 9′0″	7: 84	DR	8142/52	48142/52		86245/9
Brake second			38′1¼″ x 9′0″	5: 60	DR	8141/51	48141/51		86244/8

Above are London suburban quadruplets 8141-4 had 8 ft bogies and 8151-4, 8 ft 6 in. bogies

Carriages of pre- Grouping GNR designs completed in 1924 to the LNER Carriage Building Programme for 1923

Type	LNER Dia. No.	LNER CBP Year	Order No.	Dimensions	Comps /Seats	Built At	Running numbers Original	1925 and 1943
Brake third	72B*	1923	-	38′1¼″ x 8′6″	5: 60	DR	8131, 8811/21/31/41/51/61/71	1925 Nos 48131-4, 48811-4 etc
Third	73*			38′1¼″ x 8′6″	7: 84	DR	8132, 8812/22/32/42/52/62/72	1943 Nos
Third	74*			43′6″ x 8′6″	8: 96	DR	8133, 8813/23/33/43/53/63/73	86360-3, 86364-7, 86368-71, 86372-5
Third	75*			43′6″ x 8′6″	8:96	DR	8134, 8814/24/34/44/54/64/74	86376-9, 86380-3, 86384-7, 86388-91

Above are London GN section suburban quadruplets Diagrams 72B, 73-75 also referred to as GN Dia. 467B

Type	LNER Dia. No.	LNER CBP Year	Order No.	Dimensions	Comps /Seats	Built At	Running numbers Original	1925 and 1943
Composite (1st/3rd)	71*	1923	-	43′6″ x 9′0″	3 3rd/4 1st	DR	8894/904/14/24/34/44/54/64	1925 Nos 48894-1, 48904 - 1 etc
Composite (1st/3rd)	70*			43′ 6″ X 9′ 0″	4 1st/3 3rd :40/36	DR	8893/903/13/23/33/43/53/63	1943 Nos 86255-2, 86259-56 , 86263-60
Second	69*			38′1¼″ x 9′0″	7: 84	DR	8892/902/12/22/32/42/52/62	86267-4, 86271 -68, 86275-2, 86279-6,
Brake second	68B*			38′1¼″ x 9′0″	5: 60	DR	8891/901/11/21/31/41/51/61	86283-80

Above are London GN section suburban quadruplets Diagrams 68B - 71 also referred to as GN Dia. 478

Acknowledgements

This book contains material that first appeared in the author's *Gresley's Coaches*, published in 1973. However, as compared to the 1960s when research was carried out for that title, more archives are more readily accessible. I am most grateful to everyone who provided me - then and now - with facilities, information and photographs.

The custodians of the major archives relating to GNR and ECJS carriages are the Public Record Office, Kew and the National Railway Museum. The staff at Kew were always ready to provide the material requested and it was a pleasure to work there. Similarly, too, at the National Railway Museum where I would like to thank Andrew Dow, in his time as Head of Museum, for the facilities made available and also his colleagues, in particular, Phil Atkins, the Librarian, Mike Blakemore and Mike Rutherford.

In the case of the PRO, the principal records studied in the RAIL series were:

110 - 18, minutes of the meetings of the CLC from 1910-13; 110-175, regarding CLC rolling stock; 172-10 *et seq.*, regarding the East Coast Conference, the EC Directors' Committee and the minutes of meetings of the EC superintendents; 227, regarding ECJS stock transferred to the GE Section; 236-676/7, for papers relating to GNR rolling stock and the GNR's involvement with the ECJS; 390-58 *et seq.*, the LNER Traffic Committee minutes; 390-236 *et seq.*, for the minutes of the superintendents and passenger managers' committee from 1921 onwards; 390-282, extracts from the LNER Traffic Committee minutes relating to sleeping cars built in 1923; 390-464, memo from R.L. Wedgwood to the LNER Traffic and Locomotive Committees; 390-997, regarding the conversion of GNR vehicles as buffet cars by the LNER; 394-184, for former ECJS vehicles transferred to LNER Areas; 396-8, for correspondence dealing with the preparation of vehicles for the LNER royal train; 527-1541, regarding ECJS stock built and maintained by the NER; 527-1606, the inventory of East Coast stock; 527-1621, plans of NER and ECJS train formations; 527-1817, for correspondence relating to vehicles built for the ECJS by the NER; 527-1820, which deals with the test runs of elliptical-roofed stock over the East Coast route in 1905; 527-1823, for correspondence relating to the royal train saloons, from 1905; 1135-12/13, the through carriage and loading instructions for East Coast Railways, dated 1914/5; AN 109-780, for information relating to ex-GNR catering vehicles rebuilt as cafeteria cars; AN 109-961 and 962, specifically dealing with the cafeteria cars.

I would like to thank Wilf Wells, Secretary of the LNER Study Group, who was invaluable in affording me access to the records of the late Stephen Gradidge.

I would like to thank Peter Trewin, Secretary to the British Railways Board, for giving permission for me to examine records held at the Public Record Office but not normally available for inspection.

Richard Casserley has not only most kindly made available his photographs, and those taken by his father, but also provided a useful list of the renumbering of CLC stock after 1950.

Andrew Dow has most generously loaned photographs of ECJS and GNR armorial devices from the George Dow Collection.

Of other well-wishers and providers of greatly appreciated information and photographs, my thanks go to Michael Brooks, John Dawson, Robert Humm (for his kindness in loaning me archive illustrative material), John Lloyd, David Lowther, the late John Parke, Graham Stacey and to RAS Marketing, Brian Stephenson, Ron White and Peter Winding, to Peter in particular for his drawings reproduced in this book. I am grateful to H.S. Wilson for information relating to the GNR TPO vehicles, in particular their employment during World War I.

In the preparation of *Gresley's Coaches*, I recorded my thanks to the then Chief Mechanical Engineer of British Railways Eastern Region for permission to visit Doncaster Works to examine the records held there prior to 1968. At Doncaster, Messrs D. Haines of Doncaster paintshop and Boyd of the drawing office were extremely helpful in answering numerous enquiries.

Chris Bishop has most helpfully read the proofs of this book and made a number of valuable suggestions.

Not least, I would like to thank my family, Carol, Edmund and Georgia, for their patience in putting up with my long absences, researching or glued to the indispensable Mac, and for their many helpful suggestions and unstinting interest. At least they are able to find some use for ECJS artefacts - a first-class rug and silver plate from restaurant car stock!

References

The History of the Great Northern Railway by Charles H. Grinling (1903 edition) which is of particular interest for its informed view from within the GNR of matters relating to that company and to the formation of the ECJS.

Hamilton Ellis's *Four Main Lines* which conjures up the atmosphere of the East Coast route and its trains and stock in an incomparable way. So does E.L. Ahrons' *Locomotive and Train Working in the Latter Part of the Nineteenth Century*.

Due note was taken of the late K. Hoole's *The Illustrated History of East Coast Joint Stock* and an attempt has been made to illustrate the present book with as many alternative photographs and drawings as possible.

Of value was the unpublished manuscript, *A History of the Doncaster Plant Works* by J.E. Day, kindly made available by the Borough Librarian of Doncaster. The Post Office allowed me access to information relating to TPO vehicles operating on the GNR and the LNER.

Bradshaw's *Railway Guides* of April 1910 and July 1922 have been most useful.

Much recommended is Eric Neve's *East Coast from Kings Cross* which makes use of material from that doyen of East Coast observers, R.A.H. Weight whose posthumous article, 'By the Great Northern lineside', is similarly valuable as a source - it appeared in the 1981 *Railway World Annual*.

Finally, many useful references have come from study of the following journals: *The Engineer*, *The LNER Magazine*, *The Locomotive Magazine*, *The Railway Engineer*, *The Railway Gazette*, *The Railway Magazine*, *The Railway Observer*, *Railway World* and *Trains Illustrated*.

Index

Index to Drawings

East Coast Joint Stock

Great Northern & North Eastern Joint Stock

Great Northern Railway

Other Drawings

Other Reproductions

Index to Photographs

East Coast Joint Stock

Great Northern & North Eastern Joint Stock

Great Northern Railway